M000288865

The World Market and Interreligious Dialogue

Interreligious Dialogue Series

Catherine Cornille, Series Editor

VOLUMES IN THE SERIES:

1 *Criteria of Discernment in Interreligious Dialogue* (2009)

2 *Interreligious Hermeneutics* (2010)

3 *The World Market and Interreligious Dialogue (2011)*

4 *Interreligious Dialogue and the Cultural Shaping of Religions* (forthcoming)

5 *Interreligious Dialogue and Utopia* (forthcoming)

The World Market and Interreligious Dialogue

edited by
CATHERINE CORNILLE
& GLENN WILLIS

CASCADE *Books* • Eugene, Oregon

THE WORLD MARKET AND INTERRELIGIOUS DIALOGUE

Interreligious Dialogue Series 3

Cascade Books
An Imprint of Wipf and Stock Publishers
199 W. 8th Ave., Suite 3
Eugene, OR 97401

ISBN 13: 978-1-61097-500-1

Cataloging-in-Publication data:

The world market and interreligious dialogue / edited by Catherine Cornille and Glenn Willis.

Interreligious Dialogue Series 3

xxii + 294 p. ; 23 cm.

ISBN 13: 978-1-61097-500-1

1. Economics—Religious aspects. 2. Religion—Relations. 3. Religious pluralism. 4. Dialogue—Religious aspects. I. Cornille, C. (Catherine). II. Willis, Glenn. III. Title. IV. Series.

BL41 W63 2011

Manufactured in the U.S.A.

Contents

Acknowledgements vii

Introduction: On Economic Development and Interreligious Dialogue ix
CATHERINE CORNILLE

Part I: Religious Perspectives

1 Prophets and Profits: Interreligious Dialogue and Economic Development 3
PAUL F. KNITTER

2 Judaism, Economic Life, and Business 28
ELLIOT N. DORFF

3 Islamic Law, Sharīʿah-based Finance, and Economics 52
CANER K. DAGLI

4 Linking Ethics and Economics for Integral Development: The Need for a New Economic Paradigm and the Three Dimensions of Islam 70
WALEED EL-ANSARY

5 The Poverty of Economic Development 91
DAVID R. LOY

6 Liberation from Economic Dukkha: A Buddhist Critique of the Gospels of Growth and Globalization in Dialogue with John Cobb 107
CHRISTOPHER IVES

7 Buddhist Economics and Thailand's Sufficiency Economy 128
DONALD K. SWEARER

8 Rethinking Hinduism for Socioeconomic Empowerment and Ecological Engagement 147
SIDDHARTHA

9 African Indigenous Spirituality, Ecology, and the Human Right to Integral Development 164
LAURENTI MAGESA

10 Journey towards Faith Development Partnerships: The Challenge and the Potential 190
KATHERINE MARSHALL

11 The Next Horizon in Interreligious Dialogue: Engaging the Economists 211
JAMES BUCHANAN

Part II: Economists' Responses

12 Charity and the Technical Economist: A Response to Paul Knitter 237
JOSEPH KABOSKI

13 Theology, Economics, and Economic Development 250
PETER N. IRELAND

14 Different Views of the World: Economists and Theologians 263
WALTER NONNEMAN

15 Economics and Religion: A Theoretical Problem 278
FRANCIS McLAUGHLIN

List of Contributors 289

Acknowledgements

The topic of this volume has required the collaboration of scholars not only from different religions, but also from such different fields as theology/religious studies and economics. In an academic atmosphere which praises hyper-specialization, it is indeed uncommon to find scholars willing to reflect on topics and engage insights from beyond their own disciplinary field and from outside of their religious framework. We wish to thank all those who have contributed to this volume and to the 2010 Boston College symposium on Interreligious Dialogue. Professors John Makransky, Ruth Langer, and James Morris played an indispensible role in the organization of the symposium. Thanks in particular go to Professor Peter Ireland from the Economics department at Boston College for his help in envisioning and planning the symposium, and to the economists involved in the project: Francis McLaughlin (BC), Joseph Quinn (BC), Drew Beauchamps (BC), Jenny Aker (Tufts University), Joseph Kaboski (University of Notre Dame), and Walter Nonneman (University of Antwerp). All provided invaluable critical and constructive contributions to the discussions.

Our continuing gratitude goes to Brien O'Brien and Mary Hasten, whose support has made these symposia possible, and whose own formation in both economics and theology bears witness to the importance and fruitfulness of combining insights from the two fields.

—Catherine Cornille and Glenn Willis
March 2011

Introduction: On Economic Development and Interreligious Dialogue

Catherine Cornille

Among the many social issues which may engage religious traditions in dialogue, that of economic development presents both real promise and a considerable challenge. It is first of all a topic which confronts all religious traditions alike. Even though certain religions may be more dominant in particular economically developed regions, there is no obvious correlation between religious affiliation and economic status, at least on a global scale. All religions are equally challenged by questions of how to alleviate poverty and hunger and combat the growing disparity between the rich and the poor, environmental degradation, and the unequal access to education and opportunities for the development of one's capabilities.[1] Though not strictly speaking religious or spiritual topics, most religious traditions have something to say about these issues, either directly or indirectly. They touch upon central religious beliefs about human nature and the common good, and upon fundamental religious concerns with suffering and justice. Ideals about the proper distribution of wealth, ethical business practices and the relationship between worldly and ultimate pursuits are all part of an integral approach to life.

However, while religions are equally faced with the challenges of economic development, they may approach these challenges from very different perspectives and with differing sets of solutions. Some

1. Amartya Sen, *Commodities and Capabilities* (Amsterdam: Elsevier, 1985) and *Development as Freedom* (Oxford: Oxford University Press, 1999).

may emphasize issues of social justice and basic human rights while others focus their attention on the deeper causes of greed, consumerism and economic inequality. Some religions may be more attuned to the problems of ecological degradation, which accompanies unbridled economic growth, while others may call attention to the social, racial and gender issues involved. Some may focus on structural solutions to the problems of economic development, while others may offer more personal and spiritual solutions. These differences may become the occasion for genuine mutual enrichment and learning, but also at times for disagreement.

Beyond the sphere of mutual edification, dialogue between religions on questions of economic development may also create a forum for common action. It has become clear that the challenges of economic development far exceed the competency and control of any single religion. Some religions may be more directly implicated than others in the successes and failures of economic life. But all religions are equally affected by economic policies determined largely irrespective of any particular religious perspective. Moreover, with the ascendency of free market economics as the sole dominating economic system in the world, it becomes increasingly difficult for any religious or ideological system to resist the market's overwhelming impact upon cultures and societies. It is thus only by means of collaboration that religions may hope to contribute to a wider discussion on economic development. In this process, religions may also come to agreement on a set of common goals which become the basis for a continuing dialogue, and on measures for the success of such dialogue.

One of the critiques often leveled against traditional forms of dialogue is that they are dominated by particular religions which set the agenda, shape the discussions and determine the outcome. In focusing on a common challenge such as economic development and setting a common goal, religions may become more equal participants. Whereas dialogue on more doctrinal or ritual issues often leads to impasses and to a sharper awareness of irreconcilable differences, ethical questions often generate greater mutual understanding and agreement. Even though religions may disagree on the exact meaning of justice or on the best way to combat poverty and inequality, they tend to agree on the importance of establishing greater justice and distribution of wealth. Finally, commitment to common social causes fosters a sense of solidarity and friendship between members of different religious traditions, which is the basis and the minimal goal of all interreligious dialogue.

While economic development thus forms an opportunity, it also represents a real challenge for interreligious dialogue and collaboration. Whereas religious thinkers may exchange critical and constructive ideas among themselves, it is questionable whether their voices would be heard and heeded in circles of economists and economic policy-makers. The economic and financial world has become a fully autonomous and self-regulating mechanism, driven by the ultimate (and often only) goal of efficiency, and thus relatively impervious to external critiques or proposals. Economists may be interested in religion in so far as some religious teachings and practices may affect thrift or charitable giving. But the ethical and normative teachings of religions are not seen to affect economic systems, at least not in any necessary or integral way. On the other hand, economic theory has become so complex that few religious thinkers have the tools to critically and effectively engage economists in their own discourse. This has created a deep alienation and an atmosphere of mutual suspicion between economists and religious thinkers. While economists tend to approach religion at best as a purely private matter, religious thinkers tend to identify economists with economic policies or with a consumer culture which they abhor. As such, dialogue between religious thinkers and economists is as urgent (at least from the perspective of religious thinkers) as it is difficult.

However, one notable and hopeful recent change has been the greater interest, at least by some economists, in ethical, ecological, and broadly spiritual values and ideals. A series of books written in the past few years by economists focus on critical questions regarding not only the environmental sustainability of current models of economic growth, but also their human and spiritual impact.[2] This opens the door to a dialogue between economists and religious thinkers in which the latter may be consulted not only to console and provide for those

2. To name just a few notable examples: Catherine Cowley, *The Value of Money: Morality and the World of Finance* (Edinburgh: T. & T. Clark, 2006); Tim Jackson, *Prosperity without Growth: Economics for a Finite Planet* (London: Earthscan, 2009); Nicholas Stern, *The Economics of Climate Change* (Cambridge: Cambridge University Press, 2007); Avner Offer, *The Challenge of Affluence* (Oxford: Oxford University Press, 2006).

left behind by economic development, but to address more fundamental questions.

In this volume, we have brought together religious thinkers and economists to reflect on various aspects of economic development, and to respond to one another. The religious thinkers approach the topic from their particular religious perspective: Judaism, Christianity, Islam, Hinduism, Buddhism, and African Religions. Though approaching the topic from a particular religious tradition, the papers in this volume touch upon certain common themes: conceptions of human nature underlying a religious approach to economic development, the place of economic development among other human and spiritual goals, the role of religions in fostering or impeding economic development, and the need for a dialogue between religious thinkers and economists. Each of these topics may become the occasion for a fruitful dialogue between religions. At the end of the volume, economists offer feedback and reflections on particular papers or on the general topic, with a particular focus on the challenges of dialogue between economists and religious thinkers.

Human Nature and Economic Development

Religious views of economics and economic development are of course closely related to their conceptions of human nature and the goal of human life and community. It is clear that most religions recognize the pursuit of worldly goods and material gain not only as a necessity, but also as a good. Meaningful work contributes to human flourishing and to advancing the common good. Elliot Dorff points out that Judaism has a positive approach to business since it involves cultivating and using the earth which was created for the benefit of human beings. The Jewish concept of *tikkun 'olam*, or fixing the world, also implies responsibility for those in need, which requires a certain degree of wealth. Since economic growth also implies competition and self-interest, Judaism does not condemn *a priori* the self-centered drives to self-preservation and personal advancement which lie at the basis of economic development. However, these drives must be kept in check. This is why two tractates of the Torah are devoted to business law. Since human beings are created with equal inclinations to good and to evil, rules are necessary to regulate business practices. Dorff discusses various rules which have been developed in Jewish Scriptures to ensure honest business practices. Many of these rules have to do with fair pricing and sincere business intentions. While these laws were established in times when economic exchanges were much less complex, he believes (against more conservative Jewish thinkers) that they can and must be adapted to modern economic systems.

Like Judaism, Islam focuses on the regulation of proper business practices through religious law. Caner Dagli discusses the nature and working of Islamic law, distinguishing the purpose of the law, the nature of the law and the law itself. He focuses on two important Islamic notions which inform Islamic approaches to economic development: *riba* and *gharar*, the former referring to a prohibition against usury and the latter to a prohibition against trading in risk or uncertainty. Dagli argues that the loss of attention to such principles may be attributed to modern anthropology which is largely based on a Darwinist view of human nature. Here, base human impulses for survival and self-preservation are regarded as not only a reality but the norm. And this is fundamentally at odds with an Islamic anthropology which regards humans as capable of overcoming self-interest and called to the pursuit of higher values and goals.

Within the Christian tradition, the focus of attention in reflection on economic matters has been less the individual or human nature per se, but the idea of the common good. This is of course based on a conception of the human person as a fundamentally social or communal being. This tendency within Christianity is reinforced and in fact intensified in Laurenti Magesa's article, which brings Christian thought into dialogue with African religious anthropology. He points out that the African approach to work and wealth is essentially communal, done for the greater good of the community and distributed among all. Here, the human person is regarded not as an individual, but as a network of relationships. And it is in light of these relationships that one's value and merit are measured. As such, African anthropology may be seen to offset the tendency to focus only on economic indices as criteria for human development. But it also supplies one of the strongest bases for emphasizing the interconnection between human beings, past, present and future.

Rather than dictating rules for proper economic behavior, or projecting ideals for the equitable distribution of wealth and the just management of goods, Buddhism focuses its attention on understanding the origins of distorted economic attitudes and relationships in the human mind. As David Loy points out, whereas the Semitic religions respond to the challenges of economic development on the basis of justice, Buddhism locates the ultimate problem in ignorance. Going right to the heart of a Buddhist analysis, he links the cause of poverty directly with the delusion of the wealthy. It is the illusory attempt to construct a stable sense of self based on worldly possessions and the resulting esteem from others which feeds into insatiable greed and the endless pursuit of wealth, at the expense of the poor and the powerless. Continuing in the same line of Buddhist thought, Chris Ives refers to consumerism as a salve for fear of impermanence and as hopeless clinging to signs of human flourishing. Though Buddhism does not reject wealth as such, it is the obsession with economic development and growth which is in conflict with the Dharma. This is expressed in the title of Loy's paper, "The Poverty of Economic Development," as well as in Ives' alternative understanding of development as the reduction of human desires. For Buddhism, true development can only be based on a proper realization of the human person as empty of an enduring or substantial self (*anatta*), and an understanding of all of reality as interconnected. While the former leads to a greater detachment from material pursuits and the exorbitant accumulation of wealth, the latter incites compassion for the material (and other) suffering of others.

The religions are largely in agreement that the problem with the prevalent conceptions of economic development lies in the fact that they take human selfishness and individualism as a fact, rather than as a problem to be overcome. The difference between economic and religious approaches to human nature are sketched in Walter Nonneman's discussion of Thomas Sowell's distinction between the tragic worldview of economists and the "vision of the anointed" typical of religious thinkers and intellectuals in general. Whereas the former attempt to offer concrete proposals based on an acceptance of the limitations of human nature, the reality of fate and a scarcity of resources, the latter tend to propose general theories based on a belief in the possibility of reforming human nature, regulating human behavior and solving social problems. From Sowell's point of view, it is the religious thinkers who fail the test of relevancy. In contrast with this, economist Francis McLaughlin laments the fact that modern economics seems to be based on a very particular, Hobbesian view of human nature as essentially solitary and ruled by passions, rather than by reason. This is at variance with a classical Aristotelian view of human nature which may be seen as oriented to the common good. For McLaughlin, the "tragic worldview" of economists is not in fact a purely descriptive account of human nature. Its emphasis on subjective utility maximization is on the contrary itself a moral choice. There are thus fundamental differences of opinion on human nature, not only among religious thinkers, but also among economists.

While religious traditions tend to agree on the need to overcome human selfishness in the pursuit of a more integral economic development, they may differ in terms of their understanding of the cause of such selfishness and the cure for it. Whereas these different approaches may be regarded as mutually exclusive, they may also at times be seen as complementary and as mutually enriching. Paul Knitter suggests that each set of traditions has something particular to offer to a prophetic critique of neoliberal approaches to economic development: the Semitic religions emphasizing justice, the eastern religions inner peace, the East Asian religions harmony between peace and justice and the native religions a greater attention to nature and creation. Beyond this, religions may also be inspired by particular teachings of other religions. Chris Ives, for example, while acknowledging the way in which Buddhism has learned from a Christian attention to the broader social and political dimensions of economic development and deprivation, also points to the ways in which Buddhist analysis may offer a deeper understanding of the personal and psychological causes of distorted economic relationships. In combining the monotheistic notion of justice and the Buddhist understanding of interdependence, he advances the notion of participatory justice, which involves an ability to participate in society in relation with others and for the greater good of the whole. Conversely, many thinkers within the monotheistic traditions have been fascinated with the Buddhist analysis and critique of consumerism and greed.

The most quoted author within this volume is E. F. Schumacher, whose book *Small Is Beautiful* (1973) offers an alternative to dominant economic systems based on a Buddhist worldview. As Waleed El-Ansary points out, Schumacher was a Christian who was strongly influenced not only by Buddhism, but also by Islamic thought. While economists may view this work as marginal (cf. Nonneman), it continues to unite religious thinkers from various traditions around an ideal which sheds a critical light on neoliberal economic policies and decisions.

Besides complementing one another in the analysis of derailed economic systems and behaviors, diverse religious thinkers may largely agree in their accounts of an alternative model of human flourishing which, rather than measuring such flourishing in terms of economic indices, GDP and personal wealth, understands social and personal wellbeing in terms of peace, solidarity, community, contentment, compassion, wisdom, etc. These are values and virtues which play a central role in all religions. They are based on a communal understanding of the human person which forms an important critical counterweight to the individualism which informs most modern economic systems.

Economic Development and Other Human and Religious Goals

Most of the articles in this volume do not take issue with the reality and importance of economic development, but rather with its elevation as the highest or the ultimate human goal. The obsessive pursuit of material possessions and increase of wealth tends to stifle other dimensions of human flourishing and spiritual nourishment. Contemporary models of economic development are based on a never-ending manipulation of human desire and on a disregard for the difference between wants and needs. This forms the starting point for Waleed El-Ansary's Islamic critique of neoliberal economics. He points out that current economic models not only conflate wants and needs, but that they do not assign a distinct category to the latter. In contrast with this, Islam distinguishes different types of needs: fundamental needs, complementary needs and supplementary benefits, attributing a clear hierarchy to them. Rather than ignoring the differences between wants and needs, El-Ansary, himself a trained economist, calls for a "multiple utility approach" to economics which would differentiate between the relative utility of particular goods, and regulate production according to this approach. Since economics qua economics cannot attend to these issues, it requires greater collaboration between economics as a science and the fields of ethics and spirituality. Such collaboration would also shed light on the often dehumanizing approaches to work characteristic of purely secular approaches to economic development. He argues that it is only through dialogue between economists and religious and ethical thinkers that renewed attention may be drawn to the integrity and the spiritual nourishment of particular kinds of work.

One area of human flourishing which seems to be sacrificed at the altar of economic development is that of a healthy environment. Several contributions refer to the ecological havoc wrought by the rapid economic development of the past century. This is of course not news to economists, and numerous measures have been taken by governments and corporations to address this problem. Joseph Kaboski and Peter Ireland also point out that the more developed a particular economy, the more it is able to contain pollution. While ecological concerns are certainly not the prerogative of religions, religious traditions are united in their preoccupation with ecological degradation. Paul Knitter discusses ecology as one area in which religions may sound a prophetic warning and call for a steady-state economy rather than a growth-based economy. And Siddhartha offers an example of the ways in which religious dialogue and collaboration may actually change ritual practices which themselves are harmful to the environment. Widespread Indian devotion to Ganesha is expressed in famous festivals where painted statues of the god with the elephant head are immersed in rivers and lakes, releasing paint toxins into the water. As a result of raising awareness of this fact in his interreligious ashram, villagers have actually come to adjust their ritual behavior. Siddhartha warns that this is only one small change in what he considers to be an impending ecological disaster in the Indian subcontinent, leading to millions of ecological refugees.

Religion as Means or Obstacle to Economic Development

Most of the contributions to this volume start from the presupposition that the religions have something significant to contribute, both in theory and in practice, to the question of economic development. They point not only to the important critical and corrective function of religions, but also to their ability to propose constructive alternatives to present economic systems and practices, and to marshal the energy of religions to collaborate in addressing the problems and helping the victims of economic development. Siddhartha offers examples of ways in which interreligious collaboration and the reinterpretation of resources within the Hindu tradition may lead to a new political and economic consciousness among rural women in India and mobilize communities to resist exploitation.

In his discussion of the Sufficiency Economy of Thailand, Donald Swearer points to traditional Theravada Buddhist values of moderation and generosity and to the influence of "development monks" in conceiving of and disseminating an alternative model of economic development. However, he also points to the role of the political establishment, particularly King Bhumibol Adulyadej, in making its nationwide implementation possible. While such political support of religious values and principles plays an important role in effecting widespread social and economic change, mobilization to change economic behavior is by no means dependent upon political intervention. Swearer as well as Ives point to the person of Ariyaratne and the Sarvodaya movement in Sri Lanka as an example of an effective movement to eradicate poverty based on Buddhist spiritual principles. Such examples may of course be multiplied on smaller or larger scales throughout the world. In reflecting on the difference religions and interreligious dialogue can make, Knitter calls for the establishment of "Grassroots Multi-religious Communities for economic and environmental wellbeing" which would raise broader awareness about the interconnection between religious and economic principles, and which would form a significant forum for engaging economic and political actors.

Having worked for many years on the crossroads between governmental development activities and interfaith cooperation through the World Faiths Development Dialogue, Katherine Marshall reflects on the importance and challenges of such initiatives. She indicates, on the one hand, increasing levels of attention to issues of economic development and the alleviation of poverty on the part of interfaith organizations, as well as a greater interest in partnerships with religious organizations on the part of development institutions. She also points out, on the other hand, that an important challenge in bringing about sustained interreligious collaboration in development programs is the absence of established structures or formal institutional bases for such activities. This is where the World Faiths Development Dialogue could fulfill an important function. The institution was created in the late 1990s as a function of the World Bank in order to engage religious groups more effectively in the process of development work. This has led to some notable successes, such as the effort to eradicate malaria in Nigeria and the collaboration in efforts to rebuild in Indonesia following the 2004 tsunami. However, support for the organization is tenuous, as some governments do not see the importance of focusing on religious organizations for development purposes, and some religions are wary of collaborating with governmental organizations. Such mutual suspicion cannot but impede effective development.

In addition to resisting collaboration with other religions and with government initiatives for advancing economic development, religions may at times also be the cause, directly or indirectly, of economic stagnation and of poverty and injustice. This is the case not only because of the occasional religious justification of social and economic inequalities, but also because of the complicity of religions in social and ethnic conflicts. Joseph Kaboski points out that civil war and ethnic conflicts represent some of the main impediments for economic development and growth. In so far as religions are often implicated in such conflicts (as was abundantly clear in Ireland or in the Balkans), they may be regarded as a hindrance to a healthy and just form of economic development. This reinforces the importance and urgency of peace and dialogue between religions.

Dialogue between Religious Thinkers and Economists

While religious thinkers may have much to say and to learn from one another on the question of economic development, it is clear that constructive reflection on the topic requires an expansion of the dialogue to include economists and their expertise in the actual functioning of markets and the concrete challenges of attaining particular economic goals. But whereas the dialogue between different religions may not always be easy, dialogue between religious thinkers and economists seems yet more strenuous. This may have to do with the different worldviews operative in the two disciplinary areas, as Nonneman points out, or with fundamentally different methodological approaches to the questions involved, leading to a degree of mutual ignorance and suspicion. James Buchanan thus suggests that many of the hermeneutical tools which apply to the dialogue between religions[3] may also be applied to the dialogue between religious thinkers and economists.

One of the highly contested issues in this volume is the status of economics as a religion. Both Paul Knitter and David Loy argue that free market economics has come to assume the status of a religion. Knitter argues that, like religions, it is based on claims to ultimate and exclusive truth, while David Loy points to the ways in which consumerism and the accumulation of material wealth have come to function as the ultimate concern, and as fulfilling the promise of absolute happiness. Joseph Kaboski and Peter Ireland, on the other hand, strongly reject any likening of economics with religion. They point out that economics has become a highly mathematical field and compare their work with that of technicians who "spend most of their time under the hood, trying to figure out what makes things work, and what seems to be broken" (Kaboski). The difference between the two views on the status of economics, or at least of neoclassical economics as a religion may be largely a semantic one. While the religious thinkers (Knitter and Loy) tend to approach religion from a more functionalist perspective (in terms of what functions as the ultimate concern from the perspective of subjects), the economists assume a more essentialist understanding of religion (as relating to absolute and transcendent realities). Regardless of whether or not neoliberal economics falls within the category of religion, it is clear that economic actors (both economists and economic policymakers) need to be part of the broader dialogue between religions on economic development.

Suspicious of the probability and success of a direct dialogue between economists and religious thinkers, James Buchanan in fact suggests that politics might be the arena in which religious thinkers may encounter economists in a joint attempt to set policies which might serve the common good. This does not circumvent the need for a deeper understanding of the discipline and discourse of the other. Buchanan calls in particular on religious thinkers to familiarize themselves with economic theories. And because it is ultimately in the arena of politics that economic policies are determined, this is where religious thinkers and economists should meet to exchange views and to attempt to affect policies which more efficiently serve the common good.

3. See volume 2 in this series on *Interreligious Hermeneutics* (2010).

In their responses to the contributions of religious thinkers, the economists in this volume attempt to clarify and correct some of the common religious conceptions and misconceptions about economics. Religious thinkers tend to harbor deep suspicions about economic development. The category is usually associated with crude capitalism, multinational expansionism, profit-driven exploitation of nonrenewable resources, the abuse of vulnerable workers, and the globalization of social injustice. While all agree that these are genuine dangers to be addressed, both Kaboski and Ireland also remind us that the economic growth which has taken place in many parts of the world has also led to higher life expectancy, better education, less child mortality, and in time ecological improvements as well. Kaboski points out that, largely due to free market economy, poverty rates in China have been reduced by about 60 percent in the past thirty years. Walter Nonneman calls upon religious thinkers to pay attention to some of the more solid scholarly analyses of economic development and the lack thereof, such as Paul Collier's book *The Bottom Billion*, which identifies civil war, a lack of natural resources, bad governance, and being landlocked with bad neighbors as primary causes of stunted development. All of this should help nuance and advance the religious understanding of economic development.

While economists and religious thinkers may approach the challenges of economic development from different perspectives and with differing sets of tools, Peter Ireland argues that economists and theologians in fact agree on much more than they think. They first of all agree that there is too large a gap between what is and what should be. As an expert in Federal Reserve policies, he discusses the redistribution of wealth after the financial crisis of 2008 as an instance of perversion about which economists and religious thinkers (or at least some of both) can agree. He also acknowledges that both economists and religious thinkers are acutely aware that free markets tend to lead to ecological disaster. However, he also points out that the regulation of emissions lies not so much with economists, but with economic policy-makers, a distinction which he believes is not always appreciated by religious thinkers. This reinforces Buchanan's insistence on the need to also include economic policy-makers in the dialogue on economic development.

While no single dialogue between religions, between religious thinkers and economists, or between religious thinkers, economists and policy-makers will likely be able to address all of the complex issues involved in the challenges of economic development, it is clear that integral development requires involvement of all those who have a stake in the decisions, as well as the combination of their expertise and vision. This volume points to the challenges and to the opportunities of such dialogue. Rather than being a source of tension and conflict, the differences between religions, and between religions and economics, may serve as an occasion for mutual edification and growth. The goal of interreligious dialogue on economic development is not the development of a unified religious stance on the question or the problems, even less the proposal of a religious vision to which all religions must surrender their own distinctive views. It is an opportunity for each religion to deepen its understanding of the obstacles to integral development and to learn from the proposals offered by other religions and by professional economists. Each of the papers in this volume offers a valuable contribution to the ongoing discussion on economic development. But it is the aggregate of critical and constructive ideas and suggestions, and the authors' combined commitment to justice and a better world, which forms grounds for genuine hope.

Part I

Religious Perspectives

1

Prophets and Profits: Interreligious Dialogue and Economic Development

Paul F. Knitter

If a modern-day Tertullian were asked to write on economic issues, he probably would revise his famous "*Quid ergo Athenis et Hierosolymis*"[1]—"What has Athens to do with Jerusalem"—and would quip: "What has New York (Wall Street) to do with Jerusalem (the religious main street)?" What have economics and economic development to do with religion and interreligious dialogue?

My title, "Prophets and Profits," is meant to convey a clear answer to Tertullian: A lot! Jerusalem and New York (or London, or Beijing) have much to say to each other. In what follows, I argue that in their present nature and state the global economic system, and the world's religious communities, need to, and are very able to, engage each other in dialogue. In other words, those who qualify as religious prophets (i.e., those who speak from convictions about their religious vision and values) and those who are responsible for market profits (i.e. those who are committed to the values and goals of the marketplace) need to start talking to each other.

I'd like to lay out my case in four pieces: 1) For the sake of analysis, we can consider the Free Market Economy as a religion among religions. 2) Even more than other religions, the Free Market Economy

1. Tertullian, *De Praescriptione Haereticorum*, ch. 7, 9.

is in need of dialogue with its faith-based counterparts. 3) In their engagement with the market, the religions share a common prophetic message; yet each also delivers its own particular challenge for any economic system. 4) Because this dialogue between religious prophets and market profits is presently more an urgent possibility than a widespread actuality, I end with some practical proposals for interreligious action toward economic change.

The Free Market Economy: A Religion among Religions

Today no one would dare to speak about "*the* global religion," and yet there is much talk about "*the* global economy." With many religions populating our planet, no one religion holds sway over all the others (though some of them might want to). But while there have been, and still are, a variety of ways to organize economic life, one economic system, especially since the collapse of the Soviet Union, has come to dominate. There is today, for all practical purposes and sundry outcomes, one global economic system.

As powerful and dominant as it is, this system is a slippery beast that has been referred to by a variety of names, both nice and nasty: "new classical economics," "neoliberal economics," "the rational and efficient market," and "general equilibrium theory." More judgmental descriptives include: "market fundamentalism," "economism," "utopian economics," or the disdainful "casino capitalism."

The name I will be using throughout this chapter will be the "Free Market Economy." With it, I refer broadly—I hope not too broadly—to the understanding of the market that has been taught in American universities and followed in the global market since the late 1970s. Essentially, it asserts that the market can best function when it is given "free range," when it is left to itself and to its own inner dynamic with a minimum of outside, especially governmental, interference. Clearly, after the financial chaos that has descended on Wall Street and the world as of 2008, this "minimal interference" is being questioned. But not, so it seems, in a way that questions the fundamental capitalist structures and the necessary free processes of the market.[2]

2. For a critical description of the economic system since the "fall," see John Cassidy, *How Markets Fail: The Logic of Economic Calamities* (New York: Farrar, Straus & Giroux, 2010); Paul Krugman, "How Did the Economists Get It So Wrong?"

In his classic 1997 essay, David Loy made an observation that many have since recognized: "Religion is notoriously difficult to define. If, however, we adopt a functionalist view and understand religion as what grounds us by teaching us what the world is, and what our role in the world is, then . . . our present economic system should also be understood as our religion, because it has come to fulfil a religious function for us."[3]

John Cassidy agrees: "The free market . . . goes beyond a scientific doctrine: it is a political philosophy, a secular faith."[4] Joerg Rieger concludes: the "invisible hand of the market" is a "quasi-theological concept which symbolizes the force that guarantees economic prosperity and success . . . This belief in the self-regulating power of the free markets rests squarely on the assumption of a transcendent factor."[5]

This points us to another characteristic of the Free Market Economy that it shares with most of the religions of the world. This trait is embodied in the traditional claim of the Roman Catholic religion (a claim qualified but not renounced in Vatican II): *Extra ecclesiam nulla salus*—Outside the church, there is no salvation. For all kinds of reasons, most religions have an inner propensity to exclude or subordinate all other religions. Each believes that it has the only, or the final, or the normative truth that will lead people of all other religions to the fullness of well-being and happiness. The neoliberal Free Market Economy has this same kind of exclusive Good News. Not only does it make the claim that it is the best and the final way for human beings to organize their economic lives, it argues that this claim has recently been proven to be true. With the fall of Soviet Communism in the West and the melting away of socialist economies in Latin America and Asia, the Free Market, so it seems, has attained what it has always proclaimed.

Rieger makes a sobering observation: "we do not even need to be told anymore that there is no alternative to capitalism [as we did dur-

---

New York Times Sunday Magazine (Sept. 6, 2009); and Joseph Stiglitz, *Freefall: America, Free Markets, and the Sinking of the World Economy* (New York: Norton, 2010).

3. Loy, "The Religion of the Market," http://www.religiousconsultation.org/loy.htm.

4. Cassidy, *How Markets Fail*, 32–33.

5. Joerg Rieger, *No Rising Tide: Theology, Economics, and the Future* (Minneapolis: Fortress, 2009) 65; see also notes 8 and 20.

ing the Reagan/Thatcher years of the '80s]. We simply believe it, unaware of the transcendent status that this particular form of economics has assumed." Even more soberingly, he adds: "At present, most people in the United States appear to find it easier to imagine the end of the world than the end of capitalism."[6] So the Free Market religion ups the ante for the Catholic Church: Outside the market, no salvation!

Admittedly, many, perhaps most, economists will recoil at seeing their discipline described as a religion, pointing out that their trade is not an "ideology" or a personal commitment but a falsifiable attempt to achieve an objective understanding of how an economic system works. Still, in an effort to carry on an interdisciplinary conversation, I request that they bear with, and keep talking with, philosophers and theologians who offer their reasons why the Free Market and the phenomenon called religion do bear striking "family resemblances."[7] Carrying on my side of the conversation, I would now like to make the case that the Free Market Economy, like all its religious family members, is in need—in dire need I would add—of dialogue with other religions.

The Free Market Economy: A Religion in Need of Dialogue

The Free Market needs dialogue with the religious communities of the world for the simple and disquieting reason that the market isn't working. In its present state, both nationally here in the United States and globally throughout the world, the Free Market Economy is a religion that is not achieving its intended end, its stated goals.

At this point, I'm clearly stepping beyond my professional competence. I'm going to offer a general assessment of the "state of the economy," and I do so as a layperson, a non-economist. So I am exposing myself to the criticism that we theologians often hear: "You religious types don't know what you're talking about in your proclamations about the economy." I'm sure that is very often the case, but it

6. Ibid., 71–72.

7. See for instance: Loy, "The Religion of the Market." Robert H. Nelson, *Economics as Religion: From Samuelson to Chicago and Beyond* (University Park: Pennsylvania State University Press, 2001). Harvey Cox, "The Market as God: Living in the New Dispensation," *Atlantic Monthly* (Mar. 1999), online: http://bit.ly/eQvDlT. Dirk Baecker, ed., *Kapitalismus als Religion* (Berlin: Kulturverlag Kadmos, 2003).

doesn't have to be. Analyses and criticisms of the economy cannot be reserved to economists and business leaders. That would be like claiming that you have to be a pope or bishop to know what the Catholic Church really believes.

My description of "the state of the economy" consists of what I think are three undeniables: the suffering billions, the endangered planet, and the handicapped invisible hand.

The Suffering Billions

If one of the central purposes of any market system is to organize and facilitate the production and exchange of goods and services so that the basic human needs of all can be met and general well-being fostered, then it is quite evident, I trust, that our present Free Market Economy isn't measuring up to its self-assigned task. We can advance this assertion under two different, but very related, rubrics: *justice* is not being served, or *suffering* is not being addressed. I prefer the latter. It's a lot more difficult to argue about justice than it is about suffering. While the question, "whose justice?" may perplex and lead to extended scholarly discussion, the question, "whose suffering?" is stirred by simply looking around. And while justice may call for deliberation, suffering calls for response.

So I want to start my commentary on the state of the economy with the reality of human suffering—the kind of suffering that human beings feel when they cannot provide shelter, food, medicine or education for their children—the kind of suffering that prevents living and fosters dying. I'm speaking of the kind of suffering that evokes in any empathetic human being what Edward Schillebeeckx calls "a negative experience of contrast." Something which, when we see, hear or understand it, immediately arouses a negative emotion: this should not be![8]

Yet, to adequately understand and feel such suffering, I don't want to isolate it. I want to focus on the simple reality that, as Jeffrey Sachs starkly states, "Currently, more than eight million people around the world die each year because they are too poor to stay alive,"[9] or as Frei

8. Edward Schillebeeckx, *The Church: The Human Story of God* (New York: Crossroad, 2000) 5.

9. Jeffrey D. Sachs, *The End of Poverty* (New York: Penguin, 2006) 1; see also 20–25.

Betto reminds us, "more than three billion people—almost half the world's population—live below the poverty line [and] 1.3 billion [of these] live below the total despair line."[10] I also want us to face and feel the fact that these billions of human beings suffer from this dehumanizing need alongside others who have much more than they need. The starved live and die alongside the stuffed. Islands of opulence exist in oceans of poverty.

While we may argue whether the global Free Market has increased or diminished global poverty,[11] or whether the tide that has raised the yachts of the wealthy will eventually raise or capsize the boats of the poor, no one can deny that over the past forty years the distance between lavish wealth and grinding poverty has broadened. After World War II and into the early '70s, most developed countries were intolerant of excessive economic inequality. But as Tony Judt observes:

> Over the past 30 years, we have thrown all of this away . . . All around us, even in a recession, we see a level of individual wealth unequaled since the early years of the twentieth century . . . The wealthy, like the poor, have always been with us. But relative to everyone else, they are today wealthier and more conspicuous than at any time in living memory.[12]

Thus the BBC could report in 2008 that the top two hundred wealthiest people in the world control more wealth than the bottom billion. Today, the United States is the most economically stratified society in the Western world. As reported by the Bill Moyers Journal, a recent study in the *Wall Street Journal* found that the top 1 percent, or 14,000 American families, holds 22.2 percent of wealth, while the bottom 90 percent, or over 133 million families, can claim only 4 percent of America's wealth.[13]

10. Frei Betto, "Values in the Post-Crisis Economy," in *Faith and the Global Agenda: Values for the Post-Crisis Economy* (Geneva: World Economic Forum, 2010) 21.

11. Peter Singer, *One World: The Ethics of Globalization* (New Haven: Yale University Press, 2002) 51–106; and Jagdish Bhagwati, *In Defense of Globalization: With a New Afterword* (New York: Oxford University Press, 2007) 51–67.

12. Tony Judt, "Ill Fares the Land," *New York Review of Books* (Apr. 29, 2010) 18.

13. Bill Moyers Journal (June 13, 2008); see http://www.pbs.org/moyers/journal/blog/ (accessed July 22, 2010). See also Robert Reich, "Inequality in America and What to Do about It," *The Nation* (July 16/26, 2010) 13–15.

Certainly such glaring disparity in the sharing of the goods of this earth will stir up cries of injustice. I join those cries. But I want to keep the focus on suffering, on "the pathologies of inequality." The greater a nation's discrepancies in wealth, the higher its rates of physical and mental illness and crime will be, and the lower its social mobility and life expectancy. In many metrics, the United States registers the most extreme scores on both inequality and pathology values.[14] Tony Judt draws the evident but generally ignored conclusion: "Inequality, then, is not just unattractive in itself; it clearly corresponds to pathological social problems . . . What matters is not how affluent a country is but how unequal it is."[15]

So the pathologies of economic inequality eat away at the very roots of democracy. As Robert Reich, who had an insider's view as Labor Secretary under Clinton, warns: "If nothing more is done, America's three-decade-long lurch toward widening inequality is an open invitation to a future demagogue who misconnects the dots, blaming immigrants, the poor, government, foreign nations, 'socialists' or 'intellectual elites' for the growing frustrations of the middle class."[16] I give you the Tea Party—and the architects of recent legislation in Arizona.

I do not believe that Judt is in any way exaggerating when he admonishes: "Of all the competing and only partially reconcilable ends that we might seek, the reduction of inequality must come first. Under conditions of endemic inequality, all other desirable goals become hard to achieve . . . [U]nequal access to resources of every sort—from rights to water—is the starting point of any truly progressive critique of the world."[17]

But can the Free Market Economy, by itself, reduce inequality? It will probably need help, maybe lots of it, from unexpected sources.

14. Tony Judt, *Ill Fares the Land* (New York: Penguin, 2010) 15–20.

15. Judt, "Ill Fares the Land," *New York Review of Books*, 19. This case is made even more elaborately by Richard Wilkinson, *The Impact of Inequality: How to Make Sick Societies Healthier* (New York: New Press, 2005).

16. Reich, "Inequality," 15. See also Judt, *Ill Fares the Land*, 220.

17. Judt, *Ill Fares the Land*, 184–85.

The Endangered Planet

Hoping that we have substantial agreement about the first "undeniable" indication that the religion of the Free Market is not working—the billions suffering because of economic disparity—I turn to my second undeniable, which I believe is even more blatantly evident than the first: the *Endangered Planet.*

Bill McKibben uses a simple image that captures the present relationship between economy and ecology:

> For most of human history, the two birds *More* and *Better* roosted on the same branch. You could toss one stone and hope to hit them both. That's why the centuries since Adam Smith have been devoted to the dogged pursuit of maximum economic production . . . But the distinguishing feature of our moment is this: *Better* has flown a few trees over to make her nest. That changes everything. Now, if you've got the stone of your own life, or your own society, gripped in your hand, you have to choose between them. It's More *or* Better.[18]

This is our plight: like Dr. Frankenstein we have created a system intended for good, but which now menaces us. As the Millennium Ecosystem Assessment report, fashioned by some 1,300 scientists gathered at the UN, puts it forthrightly: "Human actions are depleting the Earth's natural capital, putting such strain on the environment that the ability of the planet's ecosystems to sustain future generations can no longer be taken for granted."[19] Or, with the stark realism of economic analysis, Kenneth Arrow asks and answers a sobering question: "Is our use of the earth's resources endangering the economic possibilities open to our descendants? . . . We find reason to be concerned that consumption is excessive."[20]

There we are. Like an alcoholic who finally realizes that his consumption of alcohol is ruining his life and that of his family, we have to sober up. We have to stop consuming the earth's resources the way we have. That means we have to stop producing the way we have. The reason is stark and simple: We're running out of planet. And when

18. Bill McKibben, *Deep Economy: The Wealth of Communities and the Durable Future* (New York: Holt, 2007) 1.

19. Ibid., 18.

20. Ibid., 26, quoting from Arrow's article "Are We Consuming Too Much?" *Journal of Economic Perspectives* 17 (2003) 147–72.

that happens, we not only endanger "economic possibilities," as Arrow fears. We endanger possibilities of breathing or feeding or maintaining borders between land and sea.

But can we do it? Can we limit growth? That is, first of all, a *systemic* question. Does the economic system of capitalism allow for limited growth, limited production, limited consumption? Most people, I suspect, would say it doesn't. To ask the capitalist machine to limit growth would be like asking a merry-go-round to limit turning. When it stops, it's no longer a merry-go-round. And yet, if our free market system cannot stop without denying itself, it can, because it must, slow down. The reason for this is also systemic. To continue producing and consuming as we are (the "we" here are those of us in industrialized countries) is to destroy the possibility of future producing and consuming.

If we choose "More," we will certainly lose "Better," for we will destroy the whole forest that sustains them both. Thus the religion of the Free Market is being called upon to reassess and to reinterpret its traditional doctrines and norms. As a solution, Herman Daly suggests what we theologians would call a capitalist "doctrinal development." Can a growth-based economy become a *steady-state economy*?

> The closer the economy approaches the scale of the whole Earth the more it will have to conform to the physical behavior mode of the Earth. That behavior mode is a steady state—a system that permits qualitative *development* but not aggregate quantitative *growth*. Growth is more of the same stuff; development is the same amount of better stuff (or at least different stuff) . . . Clearly the economy must conform to the rules of a steady state—seek qualitative development, but stop aggregate quantitative growth.[21]

Such proposals on how to limit growth are complex. My point for the moment is that a dialogue on how to develop an economic system that limits growth—or better, that distributes and balances growth amid the economic disparity between nations—is absolutely essential. Such a dialogue, of course, must be open to all voices.

21. Herman E. Daly, "A Steady-State Economy," lecture delivered to the Sustainable Development Commission in the UK (Apr. 24, 2008) 2–3.

The Handicapped Invisible Hand

My final "undeniable" indication that our Free Market Economy is not doing the job it wants to do may have been contested just three or four years ago. But since the chaos and crisis that exploded on Wall Street in 2008 and flowed into the highways and byways of the global economy, there is abundant empirical evidence for the claim I place on our conversation table. Putting it somewhat tritely: the invisible hand that the neoliberal economic doctrine has invoked and trusted, explicitly or implicitly, over the past forty years has proven itself to be handicapped.

Perhaps the most sweeping and stinging censure of the "neoclassical economics" of the Chicago school is that it was not classical at all!

- John Cassidy's comment does indeed sting: "The notion of financial markets as rational and self-correcting mechanisms is an invention of the last forty years."[22]
- Even more stinging is the Stiglitz Commission Report, commissioned and received by the UN General Assembly: "The crisis is not just a once in a century accident, something that just happened to the economy, something that could not be anticipated, let alone avoided. We believe that, to the contrary, the crisis is manmade: It was the result of mistakes by the private sector and misguided and failed policies of the public."[23]
- Arguments abound about whether we could have and should have seen, or actually did see and then ignored, the economic tsunami that first started to sweep the Wall Street shores in 2007. But looking back at what did happen, we can clearly draw the conclusion that the Free Market Economy, as it was theorized and as it was practiced, broke down catastrophically. Frei Betto's comment is extreme but not inaccurate: "The *invisible hand* was amputated by the financial crisis."[24] Joseph Stiglitz is perhaps even more caustic with his announcement that the financial collapse we have expe-

22. Cassidy, *How Markets Fail,* 36.

23. *Report of the Commission of Experts of the President of the United Nations General Assembly on Reforms of the International Monetary and Financial System* (Sept. 21, 2009) 7-8; http://scr.bi/gT9XK5.

24. Betto, 21.

rienced has "made hash" of the economic theories and policies of Friedman and Greenspan.[25]

Economia Semper Reformanda

However we assess the degree to which our present Free Market Economy has broken down—whether we believe that the invisible hand has been amputated and must be replaced, or broken and can be fixed, or handicapped and in need of external help—I trust that we can all agree that our present economic system, within this country and around the globe, is in clear and profound need of reform. If you allow me, what has been said of the Christian church applies just as much to the economy: *Economia semper reformanda.*

The economy, like the church, is in constant need of reformation—at particular points in history more than at others. And like the Catholic Church in the fifteenth century, the beliefs and structures and practices of our global economic system are not working properly. They're not working because, like the church of that time, they are being exploited, or because they have not kept up with the times, or because they have lost touch with the very purpose for which they were fashioned. The particular reasons for the collapse will have to be determined in the process of reform. And whether this reform will lead, as it led Luther and Calvin, to a brand-new system (which, however, still called itself Christian) or whether it will lead to a repair and renewal of the old system (as Catholic leaders tried to do in Trent, then again in Vatican II), will also have to be determined in the process of reform.

But reform we must. Paul Volker writes that, as we stand in the midst of the debris left by the recent financial collapse,

> We are left with some very large questions, questions of understanding what happened, questions of what to do about it, and ultimately, questions of political possibilities. The way those questions are answered will determine whether, in the end, the financial crisis has, in fact, forced the changes in thinking and in policies needed to restore a well-functioning financial system, and better-balanced growing economies . . . The na-

25. See Jeff Madrick's review of Stieglitz's *Free Fall:* "Can They Stop the Great Recession?" *New York Review of Books* (Aug. 8, 2010) 54–58.

ture and depth of the financial crisis is forcing us to reconsider some of the basic tenets of financial theory.[26]

What Religious Prophets Have to Say to Market Profits

In this reformation of the economic system, I am claiming that the religious communities have an important, if not essential, contribution to make. Prophets and profits have to engage each other in dialogue. I suspect, however, that in such a dialogue, religious believers and scholars will feel a lot more comfortable, perhaps even eager, than economists and businesspersons.

So may I remind my economist colleagues that this was not always the case. Benjamin Friedman describes how theology and theologians were part of the broad conversation of literati out of which Adam Smith and the first economists shaped their theories and proposals. "[T]here is reason to think that the influence of religious thinking was essential to the creation of economics as we know it as an intellectual discipline, in the eighteenth century. Adam Smith and his contemporaries lived in a time when religion was both more pervasive and more central than anything we know in today's Western world."[27] For Smith, and dare I say for the majority of his economist progeny through the next two centuries, an "efficient market" presupposed a moral context. Trust was the primary virtue, but Smith recognized that the virtue of trustworthiness must be fed and sustained by a menu of other moral qualities, which he lists as "humanity, justice, generosity, and public spirit."[28] But to talk of ethics is to talk, or to invite the talk, of the religious and philosophical foundations that sustain one's moral convictions and commitments.

Adam Smith offers us further reasons why the denizens of Wall Street and board rooms should welcome—maybe even solicit—con-

26. "The Time We Have Is Growing Short," *New York Review of Books* (June 24, 2010) 12.

27. Benjamin M. Friedman, "Economic Origins and Aims: A Role for Religious Thinking?" in *Money and Morals after the Crash: Reflections* (Yale Divinity School, Spring 2010) 6.

28. Amartya Sen, "Capitalism Beyond the Crisis," *New York Review of Books* (March 26, 2009) 28 [27–30]. See Adam Smith, *An Inquiry into the Nature and Causes of the Wealth of Nations*, ed. R. H. Campbell and A. S. Skinner (Oxford: Clarendon, 1976) I,I,viii.26 (p. 91). See also Judt, *Ill Fares the Land*, 38.

versations with religious believers and scholars. He points out, gently but resolutely, that in all our efforts to assess reality and determine how we want to conduct ourselves in it, we need the perspectives of—and that means the conversation with—"impartial spectators." Without such spectators who become partners in conversation we run the risk, as Amartya Sen interprets Smith, of becoming caught in the confines of "vested interests," or "local parochialisms," or "entrenched tradition and custom."[29] Inviting impartial spectators to our meetings and boardrooms can provide what Sen quaintly terms "liberation from positional sequestering."[30] Kathryn Turner contextualizes such suggestions: "The discipline of theology in a time of economic dead ends can work to open up the economic imagination."[31]

So, how might the theologians and specialists "open up the economic imagination"?

Other essays in this volume explore that question from their particular religious perspectives. I want to suggest some common cues. In an effort to stimulate our conversation, let me throw postmodern caution to the wind and offer three prophetic proclamations which I believe can claim the endorsement of all (or at least most) religious traditions.

Homo Economicus vs. *Homo Empatheticus*

I don't want to make a straw man out of the oft-targeted *homo economicus*, but he does seem to be the singular incarnation of the capitalist "logos." The product and the patron of the free market system is the human being understood as genetically disposed, or determined, to seek and satisfy his or her own self-interest and to do that before all other interests. Amartya Sen is more concise: "The assumption of the completely egoistic human being has come to dominate much of the mainstream economic theory."[32]

29. Sen, *The Idea of Justice* (Cambridge: Harvard University Press, 2009) 45.

30. Ibid., 155. See Adam Smith, *The Theory of Moral Sentiments*, III.3.38 and III.1,2, cited in Sen, *The Idea of Justice*, 125.

31. Tanner, *Economies of Grace* (Minneapolis: Fortress, 2005) 33.

32. Sen, *The Idea of Justice*, 184. A classical exposition and broadly influential argument for *homo economicus* was made by Gary Becker, a protégé of Milton Friedman, in his 1976 opus *The Economic Approach to Human Behavior* (Chicago: University of Chicago Press).

How, then, does this anthropology of the Free Market line up with that of the other religions? The two are diametrically—or at least broadly—opposed. Although each religion will make the point differently, and all of them with qualifications that vary in quantity and kind, religions teach that *self*-interest must be brought into relation with, and be balanced or expanded by, *other*-interest. *Religious ethics are always paradoxical.* In a variety of symbols and with different emphases, all the religious traditions tell humanity that paradoxically but promisingly, *self-interest equals other-interest.* In the ideals of their teachings, though often not in the reality of their actions, the wisdom traditions of humankind call humans to realize a life-giving, peace-giving co-inherence of self-interest and other-interest. We receive our being from "the other," and we can maintain our being only in, as it were, giving it back to "the other."

As John Hick puts it (with David Tracy agreeing), religious experience includes, in some form or fashion, a shift or an expansion *from self-centeredness to other-centeredness.* This "other" is always distinguishable from, or more than, oneself, both Other with a capital *O* (the Source or Inner Life of all) or other with a lowercase *o* (one's neighbor). So Jesus tells us that we can truly love ourselves only when we love our neighbor. For Buddha, to experience enlightenment is to feel compassion for all sentient beings. In Confucian ethics: "In order to establish ourselves, we must help others to establish themselves; in order to enlarge ourselves, we have to help others to enlarge themselves."[33] Thus, we can say: *homo religiosus* is *homo empatheticus* rather than *homo economicus.* To be who we really are, we must be more than what we think we are.

So to the capitalist axiom (as currently understood) "If we seek our own interest we will also promote that of others," the religious communities respond, "But if you are not also seeking the interests of others, you won't succeed in achieving your own." The religious prophets, I suggest, are telling the seekers of market profits that there cannot be any prioritizing. Paradoxically, both come first, self-interest and other-interest. To put one first, as contemporary capitalism seems to do, is to court catastrophe—or a breakdown of the entire system.

33. *The Analects*, 6:30.

The *Free* Market Must Be the *Moral* Market

If there is broad agreement among religious believers that human beings are better understood primarily as *empathetic* (or social) beings rather than as *economic* (or individual) beings, then the religions will also be unanimous in their insistence that if an economic system must be *free* in order to work, it will also have to be *moral* in order to work well. Unless we build a consensus of moral values (values that call us to care for others in order to care for ourselves) into the principles, guidelines, and yes, laws of an economic system, the system is destined to self-destruct. Morality cannot be an externality.

If ever the community of nations and economies is going to arrive at a working, international agreement on what Hans Küng calls a "Global Ethic," and what I would prefer, more modestly, to term an "ongoing ethical conversation," the religious communities will need to be part of that conversation. This is so not only because, as stated, the religions are ancient, still vibrant repositories of humanity's moral values and ideals. They are also the generators of the spiritual energies needed not just to affirm but to personally and existentially live those ideals. The moral market requires moral marketers. The ethical must be the personal. The religions are not the only forces that can transform the heart, certainly not, but they are among the most widespread, available forces.

The Religions Vote for a Democratic Economy

With my final common religious challenge to the Free Market, I show even greater disregard for postmodern correctness. If we could imagine an interreligious political party, and if that party were to elaborate an interreligious platform for economic policy, I suggest that such a policy would be much more *democratic* than anything we can presently find in the Republican or the Democratic parties. It would be an economic vision that injects into every aspect of economic theory and practice a pervasive concern for *demo-cratia*—for "people power" (*demou kratos*), or, in a less confrontational and more accurate free translation, for "shared power."

If the anthropology found in most religions leans toward what we called *homo empatheticus*—if, in other words, religions in various manners affirm both the sanctity of the individual and the dangers of the individual, both the necessity of affirming the rights of individuals within the community as well as the necessity of limiting the power of individuals over the community—then the religions are implicitly but emphatically endorsing an economic system that can best be described as democratic. It will be a system that, in order to promote the economic well-being of all, will solicitously guard against the concentration of economic power in the hands of a few. Or more positively, an economy inspired by the religious values of mutuality and compassion will share not just love but power, not just charity but opportunity.

What I've said so far bears the haze of generality. To give it more body and feel, let me propose that what I am calling "democratic economy" would be fittingly embodied in what is being proposed from various quarters as *economic democracy.* Such proposals are coming from different quarters and in a variety of shapes and structures. All of them intend a reappraisal and a restructuring of the divisions between the owners of the means of production and the producers or workers themselves. I mark two different but complementary ways of achieving this reappraising and restructuring. One seeks a *blending* of owners and workers; the other strives for a more collaborative *interaction* between the two. Both, I believe, are movements toward forms of democratized ownership that contribute to an economic democracy in which the religions' *homo empatheticus* is able to breathe, explore, and create.

Efforts toward economic democracy that stress the *blending of owners and workers* focus on worker ownership; one of their most lauded, though not uncontroversial, embodiments is in the Mondragon Cooperative Corporation in the Basque Country of Spain. My colleague at Union Theological Seminary, Gary Dorrien, predicts that though such efforts of workers to take on the ownership *and* management of the means of production are still experimental, their prospects are positive.

> Experiments with various kinds of worker ownership increased dramatically in the 1990s, aided by a growing network of policy experts, and some unions began to bargain for worker ownership, worker control over pension funds, and worker management rights. These developments have the potential to become the building blocks of a serious movement for eco-

> nomic democracy . . . Today there are approximately 12,000 worker-owned firms in the United States.[34]

Figures are even more promising in Europe. Worker-owned companies such as Mondragon in Spain, Italy's supermarket chain Coop Italia, Poland's housing coop TUW, and England's consumer-owned Co-operative Group produce an estimated 12 percent of the European Union's GDP and directly or indirectly engage at least 60 percent of the population.[35]

While such cooperative efforts seek a *union* or blending of workers/owners, other explorations into the new terrain of economic democracy strive for a *unity* or *interaction between owners and workers.* Steven Hill, in recent publications, describes such ventures as "social capitalism," and he finds them well established in Europe.[36] They are proofs of the possibility of "co-determination" between management/owners and workers/consumers.[37]

34. "A Case for Economic Democracy," *Tikkun* (May/June 2009), online: http://bit.ly/eFLoB1. See also Gary Dorrien, *Economy, Difference, Empire: Social Ethics for Social Justice* (New York: Columbia University Press, 2010) 168–84. Dorrien presciently notes that for ownership to be effectively democratized it must also extend to "democratic capital formation" in the form of public banks and mutual funded holding companies. Such worker-owner enterprises are not only growing but taking on a green coloring in poverty-wracked Cleveland. See Gar Alperovitz, Thad Williamson, and Ted Howard, "The Cleveland Model," *The Nation* (March 1, 2010). See also the more elaborated proposal of David Schweickart in *After Capitalism* (New York: Rowman & Littlefield, 2002) 50–56.

35. Hill, "Europe's Answer to Wall Street," *The Nation* (May 10, 2010) 23 [23–26].

36. Hill, *Europe's Promise: Why the European Way Is the Best Hope in an Insecure Age (*Berkeley: University of California Press, 2010).

37. This co-determining, Hills points out, is carried out and managed mainly in two structural forms: 1) On *Supervisory Boards* workers, elected by and representing their peers, sit alongside stockholders in collaborating in the management of the company. In Germany, fully half of supervisory boards of the main corporations (Siemens, BMW, Daimler, Deutsche Telekom) are elected by workers; in Sweden, one-third. 2) *Works Councils* are elected councils of workers that have input in evaluating and determining working conditions, including veto power over certain management decisions regarding how workers are treated. Their powers include "co-decision rights" to meet with management to discuss the company's finances, work schedules, vacation assignments. "In 1994 the EU issued a pioneering directive on works councils, stipulating that every multinational with at least 1000 workers, and at least 150 workers in two or more EU nations, must negotiate agreements with works councils" (Hill, "Europe's Answer," 24). These democratic forms of interaction or "co-determination" between owners and workers—supervisory boards and works councils—have become "a core element of the European economy." Clearly,

While I strongly believe that religious prophets, in their dialogue with market profits, will all favor what has been called an economic democracy, the forms that such a "power to the people" economy will assume are very much an open question, a question that the wisdom traditions by themselves do not have enough wisdom to answer. This is the work of the ongoing, never-ending dialogue and collaboration between economists, politicians, entrepreneurs, workers and religious prophets. But what has become clear, I trust, is that the dialogue cannot be reduced to a simplistic choice between "isms" such as capitalism or socialism.

Individual Voices in the Polyphonic Multireligious Choir

This claim that prophets and believers from multiple religious communities would—or better, *could*—sing in unison around the themes of *homo empatheticus*, the "moral market," and "economic democracy," does not intend to muffle their distinctive voices. All too briefly and schematically, let me try to identify what I think are these distinctive but complementary religious voices.[38] Note that what I will be describing represents the affirmed ideal, not necessarily the actual practice, of each tradition.

The Monotheistic Abrahamic Traditions: There will be no economic flourishing without justice for all.

For the religious offspring of Abraham—Jews, Christians, Muslims—"to know God is to do justice" (Jer 22:13–16). Jahweh, Theos, Allah is a reality that seeks not only to transform the human heart but also human society. To experience this God, and to experience the urge to do something about the pain of poverty, are really one experience in its reciprocal expressions. The voice of God is heard in the voices of

they have not stood in the way of—indeed they may have been a stimulus for—this economy.

38. In trying to identify the *distinctive* voice or ingredient in each religion, I am not after what is *unique*—that is, what one religion has and no others have. Rather, I'm seeking to locate those elements of belief and conviction that occupy a central, defining place within the identity of each religion—elements without which, religious members of that tradition would not recognize themselves.

those who are poor, or more demandingly, of those who have been impoverished. What Christians call a "preferential concern for the poor" identifies a common ingredient in the morality and spirituality of all three of these monotheistic religions. Monotheism, so it seems, is the belief not only that God is one, but that God is just.

All three of these religions, therefore, in varying degrees and forms, have grave reservations about a too neat or too absolute separation between church and state, or between religion and politics. The justice called for by God's prophets—Moses, Jesus, Mohammed—must be embodied in the structures, laws, and practices of the state and the marketplace. For the children of Abraham, living one's faith will often be a messy affair, leading to conflicts with city hall or boardrooms. All of these traditions would agree, therefore, with the dictum "If you want peace, work for justice."

The Indic Traditions: There will be no economic flourishing without inner peace and compassion.

To achieve a society in which there will be widespread economic flourishing—that is, a society in which basic needs will be met and differences balanced—the religious traditions that were born in India and that color the cultures of Asia generally prioritize the need for a transformation of human consciousness. Recognizing that I am painting on a vast canvas and using broad brush strokes that can conceal as much as they reveal, I still believe that whether it be the motionless yogi in meditation, or the dancing devotee of Krishna; the empty awareness of the Zen meditator, or the Pure Land practitioner basking in the love of Amida; all of these practices aim at a transformation of consciousness, without which nothing else will really work.

Through an expanding or a losing of the individual self, the practitioner experiences an inner peace or centeredness which, because it is based on a transcending of limited self-identity, will spontaneously and necessarily lead to a sense of connectedness with, and therefore compassion for, others. Unless one is engaging others and society from the place where one has overcome (or better, is in the process of overcoming) ego-needs, and where one acts out of a genuine compassion for others, one will really not be able to make much of a difference in transforming society. In the provocative but encouraging phrase of Thich Nhat Hahn, "In order to make peace, one must be peace."[39] Therefore, to the clarion call of the monotheistic faiths, "If you want peace, work for justice," the Indic traditions complete the circle and respond, "If you want justice, work for peace (in yourself and with others)."

The Sinitic Traditions: There will be no economic flourishing without a constant balancing of difference.

For the religions that were conceived and nourished in China, Taoism and Confucianism, a society and economy will do well only if they recognize incorrigible differences, and then seek to keep those differences in a balancing relationship. These Sinitic understandings of the way the world works hold up what no one can succeed in keeping down—the way in which plurality, real head-butting differences, are built into the fabric of reality, and thank God, Heaven, or the Tao for it! For every yin, there will always be a yang. For every assertion that is pushed toward certainty, there will arise, naturally and unavoidably, a qualification or an opposing claim that will temper that assertion and so keep it alive. The Chinese spiritualities and ontologies, therefore, celebrate differences but only on the condition that the differences are brought into a dynamic, balancing, and life-giving relationship.

So if the Abrahamic vision leans toward a priority of justice over peace, and the Indic traditions prefer to place peace before justice, the Chinese, especially the Taoists, would suggest that neither peace nor justice can come first. In the economy, as in society, as in reality, there are no absolute "firsts"—only a constant, life-giving and sustaining interaction in which the first shall be last and the last shall be first.

The Indigenous traditions: There will be no economic flourishing without the flourishing of the earth and all its creatures.

The distinctive contribution of the indigenous traditions, which all too often are left out of the equation of the "world religions," is perhaps the most relevant and urgent. Simply and to the point: there will be no human flourishing unless it is part of earth flourishing. Among the oldest of humankind's spiritualities, they are sustained by, and

39. *Being Peace* (Berkeley: Parallax, 1996).

continue to sustain what Thomas Berry would call the original and most fundamental revelatory book—the earth and all its creatures. This is the *Ur-offenbarung*, the primal and therefore primary revelation, which precedes and must always provide context and criteria for the written revelations of the so-called world religions. These indigenous traditions, in all their tremendous variety, insist that we build this primacy and integrity of the earth into every economic system, no matter what its name. If, as I have suggested, all religions lean toward some form of democratic economy, the indigenous or primal religions will add the crucial reminder that the *demos* (people) who have *kratos* (power) within the economy must include the creatures of the earth community.

The indigenous spiritualities therefore would admonish us all that the requisite component of a successful, flourishing economy must not only be "peace" and "justice" but also the "integrity of creation." Justice must always be eco-human justice. Peace must be rooted and nurtured in both the human heart and the earth's heart.

Moving from Religious Ideals to Interreligious Action for Economic Change

So we've reviewed the need and possibility for, and some of the promising ingredients within, any dialogue between "prophets and profit"—between religious practitioners and experts on the one hand and market practitioners and experts on the other. But it would be disingenuous to stop there. We must also speak about the *actuality* of such a dialogue, even though, sadly but realistically, there isn't much of such dialogue going on. To conclude, I want to ask why that is the case, and what we might do about it.

I'm suggesting that to launch our envisioned dialogue between religion and economics, we first work on gathering the multireligious conversation partners who, animating and challenging each other, will reach out to invite dialogue partners (or Adam Smith's "spectators") from the world of business, economics and social activism. Somehow, I suspect that beginning with religious believers who then invite economists to their deliberations has greater promise than first gathering the economists in the hope that they will invite theologians to their ranks.

Efforts to gather these multireligious prophetic voices will have to take place, I suggest, "from the top down" as well as "from the bottom up." Let me conclude with some suggestions as to how this might be done.

Gather Multifaith Prophetic Voices from "the Top Down"

We need more of what stands behind this book: conferences, gatherings, programs, workshops in which recognized "experts" from both the world of religion and the world of economics will come together. I understand the word *expert* broadly to include academics, practitioners and leaders as well as engaged laypersons, theoreticians and activists. As I just suggested, we have greater hope for instigating and eventually normalizing such dialogues of experts and recognized spokespersons if we place the ball first in the court of religious leaders.

There are difficulties here, not only financial but also political, and sometimes theological. If we can't expect too much from official church bodies and prelates who have to be careful about what they say and do, we can turn to religiously based private universities. Therefore I can only rejoice over and commend what Boston College has done in making this particular conference possible. I hope that what we have done together will become an example for many other universities.

Another university here in the Boston area has recently provided an even more far-reaching example. I'm referring to what Mary Evelyn Tucker and John Grim did in their "Harvard Series on Religion and Ecology." In a string of ten well-planned and well-financed conferences between 1996 and 1998, they gathered broadly recognized scholars from most of the world's faiths to explore how the wisdom of their traditions can help all of us understand and respond to our environmental crises. All the papers in the series were subsequently published in a string of volumes that are being used in university courses around the world.

My urgent recommendation is that some university with a vision of social justice find some wealthy benefactors who are also committed to social justice and institute a similar series of discussions on "The Religions and the Economy." Such a series would be a logical and a necessary complement to the Harvard series, for if the environmental crisis poses a much greater threat to the planet's well-being than any financial catastrophe, it can also be argued that resolving the root causes of our financial mess would be a giant step toward resolving our environmental mess.

Gather Multifaith Prophetic Voices from "the Bottom Up"

If these "high level" dialogues of experts are vital, even more vital and more promising, I believe, are the dialogues on the "ground level." Here I am rehearsing and updating, in summary form, the case I tried to make back in 1995 in *One Earth Many Religions: Multifaith Dialogue and Global Responsibility*.[40]

I suggest that one of the most effective ways of gathering religious prophets who will act together and in turn invite social activists and engaged economists to join their dialogue will be to form what can be called "*Grassroots Multireligious Communities*" for economic and environmental well-being. Modeled after the "grassroots Christian communities" (*Communidades cristianas de base*) of the Latin American churches, these would be neighborhood associations that would require two things of their members: 1) that they be committed followers of a religious tradition or community, and 2) that, on the basis of their religious beliefs, they want to do something about their neighborhood's (or city's or nation's or world's) economic problems—drug dealing, poor schools, gang activity, or racial tensions threatening all members.

Certainly religious leaders—ministers, priests, imams, rabbis, elders—would generally play an important role in calling forth and coordinating such Grassroots Multireligious Communities, but the source and the energy of these movements would be ordinary people who live and work and maybe have fun together, but who go to different religious sites on Fridays, Saturdays, or Sundays. As these communities bring people together in order to work and struggle in confronting their neighborhood problems, they would produce at least two results: 1) They would raise the awareness among ordinary people that their religious beliefs can and must relate to the economic realities of their lives, thus diluting the *privatization* of religion that leads to religions

40. In making this case, I was standing on the shoulders and recasting the ideas of Asian theological giants such as Aloysius Pieris, Michael Amaladoss, and Samuel Ryan.

being co-opted into sacred canopies; and 2) They would promote the kind of dialogue between religion and market actors that we've been talking about insofar as these communities would soon realize that in order to achieve their ends, they will have to engage, and perhaps bring into their midst, social activists, community organizers, business leaders and even economists.

Are such communities a pipe dream, the musings of idealistic academics? I think not, for they are already taking shape. A recently minted PhD from Union Theological Seminary, Dr. Matthew Weiner, has produced a splendid dissertation, presently in the process of publication, which is an ethnographic study of multiple examples of interfaith collaboration, spurred by shared community problems, throughout the five boroughs of New York.[41] Lucidly and inspiringly, he shows how grassroots multifaith collaboration around social, economic, or environmental problems that affect a neighborhood can bring together people of even so-called conservative or exclusivist religious viewpoints. Dr. Weiner makes it clear, to the discomfort of pluralist theologians like myself, that solidarity can trump theology. Economic realities can join together what theology tends to keep asunder!

Such multireligious communities are taking shape not just in neighborhoods but nationally. One prominent example is the White House Office of Faith-Based and Neighborhood Partnerships. Established by an executive order of President Obama on February 5, 2009, this is a White House offer to help, and a request to be helped by, neighborhood and multifaith groups and movements that are addressing local problems. According to the official press release announcing this Office, the White House hopes that these interfaith partnerships will make "economic recovery" a top priority, so that "poverty [will be] a burden fewer have to bear."[42] While religions in general need to be wary about offers of help from governments, the establishment of a twenty-five-member "Advisory Council" of multireligious leaders who will give regular advice to the Office, as well as ongoing efforts to seek guidance from religious experts and organizers,[43] suggests that this is

41. Matthew Weiner, "Interfaith in the City: Religious Pluralism and Civil Society in New York," PhD diss., Union Theological Seminary, 2008.

42. http://bit.ly/cpvBVU.

43. I was part of one such White House summoned gathering of university and

a genuine and hope-filled attempt to form Grassroots Multireligious Communities.

Let me state clearly my conclusion and conviction: the captains of economic profit, whether working or teaching in New York, London, Tokyo, or Seoul, and the prophets of religion, whether in Jerusalem or Rome or Jakarta or New Delhi, do have much to say to each other. But such a conversation among so-called professionals will succeed only if it is prompted and sustained on the grassroots level by ordinary people who struggle to make vital connections between their efforts to believe and their efforts to feed their children. Such dialogues between prophets and profits, between religious beliefs and economic policies, can make an important, perhaps necessary, contribution, both in theory and practice, to the well-being of all.

---

seminary personnel who were asked to help the President's program to extend the neighborhoods of interfaith collaboration into university campuses. Over one hundred university leaders gathered at the White House on June 7, 2010.

2

Judaism, Economic Life, and Business

Elliot N. Dorff

The "lig" in the word *religion* comes from the same Latin root from which we get the English word *ligament*; the root means to tie or bind. Religions describe our linkages to each other, to the environment, and to the transcendent, just as our ligaments tie the various elements of our body to each other.

One's religion is therefore important in a discussion of economics and business because religions help us to put all our activities *in context*. In describing its particular picture of reality and of the ideal person and society, each religion defines the role of business within that picture. This helps to determine the goals of business and the values and rules by which it must operate in order to achieve these goals. Religion thus helps make business not just a source of livelihood, but part of a meaningful life.

Fundamental Concepts in a Jewish Approach to Economic Life and Business

1. *God as the owner of all creation.* "Mark, the heavens to their uttermost reaches belong to the Lord your God, the earth and all that is on it" (Deut 10:14). "To the Lord belong the earth and all that it holds, the world and all those who inhabit it" (Ps 24:1). These verses bespeak the underlying assumption of all Jewish assessments of busi-

ness. Ultimately, God owns the world. We enjoy the right to use it and to make our living on it only at God's behest, and only when we abide by the rules God has set for such activity.

In the Torah (the Five Books of Moses), these rules have an immediate effect on the profits we may make through the use of God's property. Chapter 25 of Leviticus, the third book of the Torah, delineates a number of ways in which landowners must provide for the poor. This includes not only outright gifts, but also loans so that the poor can ultimately free themselves of their need for support. In specifying these rules, the Torah explains why we must obey them: ". . . for the land is Mine; you are but strangers resident with Me" (Lev 25:23). We are, after all, tenants on God's land, and we therefore may use it only under the conditions that the Owner has set.[1]

God, however, is depicted in Judaism not as disparaging human economic activity, but as encouraging it. In direct contrast to the Prometheus myth, which depicts men as stealing fire from the gods, the Rabbis say that when Adam and Eve were expelled from the Garden of Eden, they were cold and afraid when night fell. God gave them two sticks and showed them how to make fire,[2] such that the very symbol of human hubris in the Greek tradition, is instead, in the Jewish tradition, a gift of God to show mankind how to reshape the world for our own benefit.

Even though ultimately God owns the whole world, individuals can own property vis-a-vis other individuals, and a significant portion of Jewish law addresses how both real estate and movable property are acquired, divested, and used. Similar to American law, private ownership in Jewish law is subject to communal regulations. The communal court can even appropriate private property through rules of eminent domain (*hefker bet din hefker*, "Property declared ownerless by the

1. For more on Judaism's view of, and provisions for, the poor, see Elliot N. Dorff, *To Do the Right and the Good: A Jewish Approach to Modern Social Ethics* (Philadelphia: Jewish Publication Socieity, 2002) chapter 6.

2. B. *Pesahim* 54a; *Genesis Rabbah* 11.
In this and all of the following notes, these abbreviations are used:
M. = Mishnah (edited 200 C.E.).
B. = Babylonian Talmud (edited 500 C.E.).
M.T. = Maimonides' code, the Mishneh Torah (completed 1177).
S.A. = Joseph Caro's code, the Shulhan Arukh (completed 1565).

court is ownerless"[3]), and, as described below, the community can set zoning requirements for private businesses.

2. *Individuals with rights vs. members of a community with duties.* The contemporary Western world is largely the product of the Enlightenment, with its fundamental doctrine that we are all created as individuals "with certain unalienable rights," as the United States' Declaration of Independence asserts. If one begins with this assumption, the burden of proof is always on the one who maintains that I do *not* have the right to do *x*. Western societies certainly impose such limitations on each person's rights through law, but in each case the restriction is constantly subject to challenge on the grounds that it is an unnecessary and unjustified intrusion into an area that belongs to an individual's private judgment. The United States in particular is characterized by a feisty individualism.[4]

This American individualism has some critically important advantages. It affords Americans a degree of freedom unknown in any other time or place. In doing so, it enables people of all religions and ethnic origins to live together in peace and mutual fructification; indeed, the United States is the most pluralistic country that has ever existed on the face of the earth. Moreover, it has given people the free rein to be creative in virtually every area of human endeavor, making the United States the leader, or at least one of the leaders, in science, medicine, technology, the arts, the social sciences, the humanities, and business.

Individualism, however, can mean loneliness, and it can mean lack of care for others. This translates into, for example, the difficulty that Americans have had in creating a health care system that cares for us all and a thin social service network that leaves all too many people homeless and hungry. It also has meant that Americans have had

3. B. *Yevamot 89b;* B. *Nedarim* 45a; B. *Gittin 36b;* M.T. *Laws of Courts (Sanhedrin)* 24:6.

4. This individualism extends even to membership in the society itself: any American who has not committed a felony can renounce his or her citizenship at will. See http://travel.state.gov/law/citizenship/citizenship_776.html, the State Department website that describes the right to renounce one's U.S. citizenship as provided for in Section 349(a)(5) of the Immigration and Naturalization Act and the ways in which it must be done—specifically, by (1) appearing in person before a U.S. consular or diplomatic officer, (2) in a foreign country (normally at a U.S. Embassy or Consulate), and (3) signing an oath of renunciation.

difficulty creating a public school system that works well. American pragmatism, another source of American creativity, has also helped to spawn American materialism, with continual necessity for government to regulate the greed of banks and businesses and to insure employee safety and rights.

Judaism begins with radically different assumptions about who we are—assumptions that bring their own burdens and benefits. The People Israel left Egypt not as individuals but as a group. Every Jew since then must, as the *haggadah* for the Passover Seder asserts, "see himself as if he himself left Egypt" and as if he were part of that band that received God's revelation of the Torah at Sinai and then trekked to the promised land. Moses similarly asserts to the second generation, to those who had not in fact been at Sinai, that they are nevertheless to see themselves as if they had been there: "It is not only with our ancestors that the Lord made this Covenant, but with us, the living, every one of us who is here today."[5] Moreover, this Covenant is for future generations as well:

> I make this covenant, with its sanctions, not with you alone, but both with those who are standing here with us this day before the Lord our God and with those who are not with us here this day . . . Take to heart all the words with that I have warned you this day. Enjoin them upon your children that they may observe faithfully all the terms of this Teaching. For this is not a trifling thing for you: it is your very life . . .[6]

We begin, then, not as individuals with rights, but as members of a community with duties.

This communal identity is not voluntary; it is organic. In the traditional, Jewish way of seeing things, those born Jewish (that is, according to traditional Jewish law, born to a Jewish woman) are part of the community for life, whether they like it or not. Adults who convert to Judaism do so, of course, of their own free will. The very rites of conversion, though, symbolize their rebirth into the Jewish community, and so once converted they too lose all rights to leave the fold. Even those Jews who during their lives convert to another faith become, in Jewish religious law, not members of another community, but apostate Jews. Such people lose the benefits of their Jewish identity (e.g., to be

5. Deut 5:3.

6. Deut 29:13–14; 32:46–47.

married or buried as a Jew, to count in a prayer quorum, etc.), but retain all the obligations![7]

If you are a member of a tightly knitted community, however, privacy can be hard to come by, for your business is everyone else's, and *vice versa*. Moreover, communities can stifle individualism, freedom, and creativity.

On the other hand, there are real benefits in seeing oneself through a communitarian lens. As the first-century sage Hillel said, "If I am here, everyone is here,"[8] a graphic expression of the tenet that, in the Jewish view of the world, the entire Jewish community, past, present, and future, here and abroad, is part of you even when you are physically isolated. You are, therefore, never alone; you are part of an extended family and community throughout time and the world over. The Talmud insists, moreover, that "all Israelites are responsible for each other,"[9] and this attitude prompts Jews to provide a strong safety net for the vulnerable within—and, as we shall see—outside the community. This gives one a mission in life—to fix the world (*tikkun olam*).

These differences in attitude toward the community and individual should not be exaggerated. As President Obama has elegantly articulated, American individualism is accompanied by strong ties to one's family, community, and nation.[10] Conversely, the Torah's doctrine that each human being is created in the image of God has meant that Jewish law also takes great pains to protect the interests of individuals. Furthermore, Jews love to assert their own opinions in arguments—following in the footsteps of Abraham, Moses, Isaiah, and Job, all of whom argued with God, as well as the classical Rabbis, who argue with each other on virtually every page of the Talmud. Even with these important caveats, however, it is nevertheless true that Americans generally begin from a foundation of individual rights, and Jews think of themselves first and foremost as members of a community with duties.

7. Thus the Israeli Supreme Court ruled that Oswald Rufeisen, who was born Jewish, could nevertheless not claim automatic Israeli citizenship as a Jew under the Law of Return because he had converted to Catholicism (and became a monk). See *Rufeisen v Minister of the Interior* (1962) 16 PD (2428). He later became an Israeli citizen through the naturalization process for non-Jews.

8. B. *Sukkah* 53a.

9. B. *Shevu'ot* 39a.

10. Barack Obama, *The Audacity of Hope: Thoughts on Reclaiming the American Dream* (New York: Crown, 2006) 55.

This difference has major implications for economic activity. For example, although Jewish law, like American law, needed to spell out the respective duties of employers and employees, recognizing that their interests conflict in certain respects, it was not until the early twentieth century that Congress and state legislatures enacted laws protecting the safety and rights of employees. Until then employers had full power to decide everything about the working conditions and compensation of their employees. From its earliest stages, Jewish law, by contrast, presumes that employers have duties to those who work within their community, Jewish or not. So, for example, the Torah says this:

> You shall not abuse a needy and destitute laborer, whether a fellow countryman or a stranger in one of the communities of your land. You must pay him his wages on the same day, before the sun sets, for he is needy and urgently depends on it; else he will cry to the Lord against you, and you will incur guilt.[11]

Later Jewish law—but centuries before the founding of the United States and even longer before such provisions were part of American law—stipulates that employers must, for example, permit unions; supply lunch and snacks for employees where that is the custom; and ensure workers' safety.[12]

3. *Expectations of others in one's community.* One's view of the nature of communal ties has direct implications for the expectations that each of us can legitimately have of ourselves and of each other. In Enlightenment social contract thought, I can expect you to fulfill the obligations that have been legislated or that we have mutually agreed upon, but only those. Anything you do beyond what is required of you by law is an act of charity.

In the Jewish view of community, by contrast, we are all members of a people with mutual obligations. This is the default status of each one of us. Therefore, I can expect you not only to fulfill the requirements of Jewish law, which demands considerably more than

11. Deut 24:14–15.

12. A good summary of these provisions is Jill Jacobs, *There Shall Be No Needy: Pursuing Social Justice through Jewish Law and Tradition* (Woodstock, VT: Jewish Lights, 2009) chapter 5.

American law does in caring for the other, but, indeed, to go beyond the law.[13]

In English, when I extend myself to help others, I am doing an act of "charity," from the Latin *caritas*, meaning caring. This often connotes that I am an especially good person. The Hebrew word for these exact same acts is *tzedakah*, from the Hebrew root *tzedek*, meaning justice. In other words, when I go out of my way to help others, from a Jewish perspective I am simply doing what is expected of me in fulfilling the demands of justice.

One example will make this distinction clear. If I see a person drowning or accosted by robbers, in all American states except two I have no obligation to try to save him or her. On the contrary, if I try to do that and in the process unintentionally cause the drowning or robbed person harm, until recently, when most states passed "Good Samaritan" laws, I could actually be sued for negligence or even assault.[14] In Jewish law I have a positive duty to save the drowning person or the one being robbed, assuming that I can do so without putting my own life in danger. Thus, even if I am not a certified life saver, I must at least find and throw out a lifeline and/or find others who are trained to help the drowning person. If I am badly outnumbered or lack proper weapons to save the person being robbed, I must distract the thieves, if I can do that without too much danger to myself, and I must try to enlist the help of the police to stop the robbery or at least catch the

13. This concept, *lifnim m'shurat ha'din*, going beyond the letter of the law, along with other moral duties that complement the duties embedded in Jewish law, are explained and explored in my article "The Interaction of Jewish Law with Morality," *Judaism* 26 (1977) 455–66.

14. See, for example, Samuel Freeman, "Criminal Liability and the Duty to Aid the Distressed," *University of Pennsylvania Law Review* 142:5 (1994) 1455–92; and Mitchell McInnes, "Protecting the Good Samaritan: Defences for the Rescuer in Anglo-Canadian Criminal Law," *Criminal Law Quarterly* 36:3 (1994) 331–71.

Only Vermont and Wisconsin have created a legal requirement to save those in dire straits: Wisconsin Criminal Statutes 940.34, and Vermont Statutes, Title 12, par. 519. Even in those two states, though, violation is a misdemeanor, punishable by a small fine, and the duty is justified as a protection against an abuse of the rights of the person in distress (since s/he has a right to life), not a moral duty of the potential rescuer that is now made a legal obligation. See Lon T. McClintock, "Duty to Aid the Endangered Act: The Impact and Potential of the Vermont Approach," *Vermont Law Review* 7:1 (1982) 143–83.

thieves later on. The Talmud bases this obligation on the Torah's demand, "Do not stand idly by the blood of your brother" (Lev 19:16).[15]

Later Jewish sources take this to mean that God demands of us that we care for each other not only in life-threatening situations, but also in the context of business, where it is used to prohibit knowingly advising others to make a bad business deal.[16] The Rabbis also use another verse—the ban on placing an obstacle before a blind person (Leviticus 19:14)—to prohibit giving bad business advice, extending the verse to cover not only the physically blind, but also those blind to the economic implications or risks of what they are thinking of doing. The Rabbis recognize that someone might claim that they were in fact offering what they took to be good advice, and honest mistakes can surely happen; but they point out that the verse ends with "I am the Lord," indicating that God will know whether the advisor acted in good faith or not.[17]

Another important example of this communitarian ethic is how Jewish law frames our duty to help the poor. Based on earlier sources, Maimonides describes a ladder of philanthropy, from the most desirable to the least. Top on his list is teaching a person a skill to earn a living or giving him or her a loan to begin a business.[18] Given that *tzedakah* (charity) is a duty prescribed by Jewish law and not just the actions of especially nice people, one can see in this graphic evidence

15. *Sifra*, Kedoshim 4:8 (on Lev 19:16): "How do you know that if you see someone in danger of drowning or being attacked by robbers or by a wild beast, you are obligated to rescue that person? Because the Torah says, 'Do not stand idly by when your neighbor's blood is shed.'" See also Targum Pseudo-Jonathan on that verse and B. *Sanhedrin* 73a. On this duty of rescue in Jewish law generally, together with some comparisons to Western law, see Anne Cucchiara Besser and Kalman J. Kaplan, "The Good Samaritan: Jewish and American Legal Perspectives," *The Journal of Law and Religion* 10:1 (1994), 193–219; Ben Zion Eliash, "To Leave or Not to Leave: The Good Samaritan in Jewish Law," *Saint Louis University Law Journal* 38:3 (1994) 619–28; and Aaron Kirschenbaum, "The Bystander's Duty to Rescue in Jewish Law," *Journal of Religious Ethics* 8 (1980) 204–26. I would like to thank Professors Martin Golding and Arthur Rosett for the journal references in this note and n. 11.

16. The Hafez Hayyim (Rabbi Israel Meir Ha-Kohen, Poland, 1838–1933), for example, extends the duty to rescue to include a duty to warn someone if one knows that a business deal that he or she is about to enter is likely to be a bad one; see Zelig Pliskin, *Guard Your Tongue* (based on the Hafez Hayyim) (Jerusalem: Aish Ha-Torah, 1975) 164.

17. *Sifra* on Lev 19:14; B. *Bava Metzia* 75b.

18. M.T. *Laws of Gifts to the Poor* 10:7.

of how the theological and communitarian basis of Jewish law leads Jews to expect quite a lot from each other in economic areas of life as well as many others.

4. *Relationships to those outside one's community.* How does the Jewish tradition understand the status of non-Jews? The chauvinism that might emerge from communitarian doctrines such as those described above is, in Judaism, counteracted by a number of features of Jewish theology and law. For example, the Torah's theological doctrine that every person is created in the image of God attributes divine status to non-Jews no less than to Jews.[19] One implication of this is that every person, according to Jewish tradition, is bound by God to the Covenant God made with all descendants of Noah. That "Noahide Covenant" consists of seven laws: prohibitions of murder, incest/adultery, idolatry, tearing a limb from a living animal, blasphemy, and theft, and the positive obligation to establish a system of justice.[20] In a typically Jewish way, people are honored and loved by being subject to rules![21]

Conversely, although the full gamut of protections within Jewish law applies only to Jews, who are obligated to take on the reciprocal duties,[22] many of the most important duties to others apply to the

19. Gen 1:27; 5:1. The meaning of that doctrine in the Torah apparently refers to the fact that human beings are like God in being able to know the difference between right and wrong and to choose between them (see Gen 3:22). It may also, though, refer to human beings' ability to speak and name things (Gen 2:20), like God (Genesis 1:3, 5, etc.), although not with the same creative force; or, as Maimonides claimed, to the human ability to think (see his *Guide for the Perplexed*, Part I, Chapter 1).

20. Tosefta, *Avodah Zarah* 8:4; B. *Sanhedrin* 56a–56b; *Genesis Rabbah* 16:6; 34:8; *Canticles Rabbah* 1:16; *Pesiqta d'Rav Kahana*, "Bahodesh," pars. 202–3. For more on this doctrine, see David Novak, *The Image of the Non-Jew in Judaism* (Lewiston, NY: Mellen, 1983).

21. Probably the most poignant expression of this is in the prayers said morning and evening just before reciting the *Shema*. The evening version, the shorter one, says this: "With constancy You have loved Your people Israel, teaching us Torah [instruction] and mitzvot [commandments], statutes and laws. Therefore, Lord our God, when we lie down to sleep and when we rise, we shall think of Your laws and speak of them, rejoicing in Your Torah and commandments always. For they are our life and the length of our days; we will meditate on them day and night. Never take away Your love from us. Praised are You, Lord, who loves His people Israel."

22. For a description of at least some of the positions within Jewish sources about exactly who is included in the Jewish duties to "your neighbor"—i.e., to fellow Jews—see Ernst Simon, "The Neighbor (*Re'a*) Whom We Shall Love," in *Modern Jewish Ethics*, Marvin Fox, ed. (Columbus: Ohio State University Press, 1975) 29–56,

relationships between Jews and non-Jews as well. For example, according to the Talmud and later Jewish law, a Jew is duty-bound to save the lives of non-Jews and to care for their poor and their sick and bury their dead if non-Jews need assistance in carrying out these tasks.[23] Given that non-Jews at the time of the Talmud and in almost all times and places since then were not concerned to help Jews in these circumstances—indeed, Muslims and, especially, Christians, Nazis, and Communists were generally discriminating against Jews, if not maiming, expelling, or killing them—it is nothing less than amazing that Jewish law for the last 1800 years has required Jews to care for non-Jews.

Ultimately, the Rabbis assert that the righteous of the non-Jewish world merit a place in the World to Come, for they have done all that God expects of them.[24] And although conversion to Judaism is of course possible, rabbis have historically discouraged conversion, which necessarily imposes all of the Torah's 613 commandments on such people rather than just the seven of the Noahide Covenant, while also subjecting converts to anti-Semitism and potential persecution.[25]

This has immediate implications for business. First, by the Talmud's count, the Torah insists a full thirty-six times that Jews must not only treat non-Jews within their midst fairly, but that they should actually love the stranger, "for you were strangers in the land of Egypt."[26] As a

---

and the response of Harold Fisch, ibid., 57–61.

23. B. *Gittin* 61a. The later codes articulate in law the requirements to sustain non-Jewish poor (M.T. *Laws of Gifts to the Poor* 7:7; M.T. *Laws of Idolatry* 10:5; M.T. *Laws of Kings* 10:12; S.A. *Yoreh De'ah* 151:12), to visit non-Jewish sick people (M.T. *Laws of Kings* 10:12; M.T. *Laws of Mourning* 14:12; S.A. *Yoreh De'ah* 335:9), and to bury the non-Jewish dead (M.T. *Laws of Kings* 10:12; M.T. *Laws of Mourning* 14:12; S.A. *Yoreh De'ah* 367:1).

24. *Sifra* on Lev 19:18.

25. The traditional stance of discouraging conversion to Judaism: B. *Yevamot* 47a: "In our days, when a proselyte comes to be converted, we say to him: 'What is your objective? Is it not known to you that today the people of Israel are wretched, driven about, exiled, and in constant suffering?'" Despite such warnings, in some periods, proselytes were accepted easily, while in other times and places it was all but impossible to convert to Judaism. See "Proselytes," *Encyclopedia Judaica* 13:1182–93. For more general Jewish reflections on the relationship of Judaism to Christianity, see Rabbi Leon Klenicki, ed., *Toward a Theological Encounter: Jewish Understandings of Christianity* (New York: Paulist, 1991).

26. For example, Exod 22:20; 23:9; Lev 19:34. The count of thirty-six times in the Torah prohibiting oppression of the stranger ("and some say forty-six"!): B. *Bava Mezia* 59b.

result, despite the harsh treatment to which Jews were often subjected by non-Jews, Jewish law forbids Jews from cheating non-Jews in any way.[27] Furthermore, in part for practical reasons, no doubt, but also in recognition that Jews would do business with non-Jews, the Rabbinic sage Samuel decrees in the early third century that in business matters "the law of the land is the law" (*dina d'malkhuta dina*)[28]—a precedent that continues ever after to be the stance of Jewish law.

5. *Our relationship with the environment.* In the opening chapters of Genesis, God tells Adam and Eve that they were put into the Garden of Eden "to work it and to preserve it" (Gen 2:15). In other words, we have not only a right, but also a duty, to use the land to support ourselves and to enhance human life, but we concurrently have the duty to preserve the environment as we do so, for we have only one habitable planet and cannot replace it. The Rabbis thus put these words in the mouth of God:

> Look at My works! How beautiful and praiseworthy they are! And everything I made, I created it for you. Be careful, [though,] that you do not spoil or destroy My world, because if you spoil it, there is nobody after you to fix it.[29]

This sets the stage for later Jewish laws that demand preventive and curative measures to be taken against air, noise, and water pollution.[30] Traditional Jewish sources deal, of course, only with the environmental threats that they knew; they did not know, for example, about global warming or petrochemicals in the air and oceans. Still, their recognition that some kinds of shops produce noise that prevent

27. B. *Bava Kamma* 113a–b; B. *Bava Metzia* 87b; M.T. *Laws of Robbery and Loss* (*Hilkhot Gezeilah v'Aveidah*) 1:2; M.T. *Laws of Burglary* (*Hilkhot Geneivah*) 1:1; S.A. *Hoshen Mishpat* 348:2, 359:1.

28. B. *Nedarim* 28a; B. *Gittin* 10b; B. *Bava Kamma* 113a; B. *Bava Batra* 54b–55a. For a discussion of the use and limits of this principle, see Elliot N. Dorff and Arthur Rosett, *A Living Tree: The Roots and Growth of Jewish Law* (Albany: State University of New York Press, 1988), 515–23.

29. *Kohelet Rabbah* 7:13.

30. For summaries of Jewish environmental beliefs and laws, see, in chronological order of publication, Ellen Bernstein, *Ecology and the Jewish Spirit* (Woodstock, VT: Jewish Lights, 1998); Arthur Waskow, ed., *Torah of the Earth: Exploring 4,000 Years of Ecology in Jewish Thought* (Woodstock, VT: Jewish Lights, 2000), 2 vols.; and Jeremy Bernstein, *The Way into Judaism and the Environment* (Woodstock, VT: Jewish Lights, 2006).

sleep, that threshing floors produce air pollution in the form of chaff, and that tanneries produce odious stench—and the zoning restrictions they therefore imposed on such enterprises[31]—are clear indications that they knew about ecological concerns caused by business and took them seriously.

They even had a sense of protecting the public domain:

> Rabban Shimon Ben Gamliel said: Anyone who causes any sort of damage or harm in the public domain, [his damaging goods] are permitted for all to take, on account of [his] robbery [of the public asset] . . .Whoever robs the public must make restitution to the public. Robbing the public is a graver offense than robbing an individual, for one who robs an individual can appease that person and return what he stole, but one who robs the public cannot appease the public and return to all of them what was stolen from them.[32]

Maimonides suggests a way of measuring such damage through a system of the polluter paying for an individual or the public to waive their right to avoid such pollution,[33] not unlike the proposal made by some in recent years of violation points and payments to regulate and reduce pollution.

Still, polluting the public domain even under such a cap-and-trade policy was seen as a compromise of the general principle that people do not have an inherent right to pollute the public domain—and need to understand that they harm themselves if they do so. Thus the Rabbis tell the story of a farmer who was clearing stones from his field and throwing them onto a public thoroughfare. In the course of time, the farmer had to sell his field, and as he was walking on the public road, he fell on those same stones that he had thoughtlessly deposited there.[34] Businesses must limit pollution not only out of respect for God's earth and for the public, but also for their own good.

6. Jewish anthropology. Our duty to preserve the environment, however, is balanced with our duty "to work it." This derives not only from

31. M. *Bava Batra* 2:3, 8, 9. See also M.T. *Laws of Neighbors* 11:4.
32. Tosefta, *Bava Kamma* 2:6; 10:8.
33 M.T. *Laws of Neighbors* 11:4.
34 Tosefta, *Bava Kamma* 10:2; see B. *Bava Kamma* 50b.

God's command to Adam and Eve, but from Judaism's underlying concept of the human being.

The Torah asserts that "the inclination of man is evil from his youth" (Gen 8:21). In Christianity, this and other sources led to the doctrine of Original Sin, from which only a supernatural intercessor, Jesus, can redeem us. The Rabbis, however, maintained that human beings are born with two inclinations, one to do evil (*yetzer ha-ra*) and one to do good (*yetzer ha-tov*). Although that term *yetzer ha-ra* is correctly translated as "the evil inclination," it is not always morally evil. It is the self-centered inclination, which is the source of our drive toward ego enhancement, greed, and selfishness, and it can lead a person to idolatry and to acting immorally toward others—and hence its name "the evil inclination." It is also, however, the source of some very important activities in life, as the following Rabbinic statement makes clear: "The evil inclination is sometimes called very good. How can this be? Were it not for the evil impulse, a man would not build a house, marry a wife, beget children, or conduct business affairs."[35] During the first thirteen years of life, the Rabbis say, the self-centered inclination is dominant (think of how infants care only for themselves), and that is how the Rabbis understand the verse from Genesis cited above. Gradually, though, children learn to care about others as well; they build their superego, Freud would say, and integrate it into their ego. When a girl reaches the age of twelve and a boy thirteen, the two inclinations are equally powerful.[36] The child is then legally responsible for her or his actions, for Judaism presumes that at that time the child both knows right from wrong and has the power to act on that knowledge. For the rest of one's life, one must balance the *yetzer ha-ra* and the *yetzer ha-tov*, blending self-regarding activities with other-regarding ones. This is the nature of human moral struggles, and all of us who are not psychopaths are fully capable—and therefore fully responsible—to carry on that struggle throughout our lives. We will get it wrong sometimes—in theological terms, we will sin, sometimes intentionally and sometimes not—and hence Jewish liturgy has us ask for God's forgiveness three times each day. But we do not need a supernatural intercessor to carry on this struggle: God has given us the

35. *Genesis Rabbah* 9:7.

36. *Ecclesiastes Rabbah* on Eccl 4:13; *Avot D'Rabbi Natan* 16.

faculty to discern what is right and the power to do it, and God has given us the ability to atone for what we have done wrong.

This means that the self-promotion and competition inherent in business are not necessarily bad. Whether those urges are bad or good depends completely on how they are expressed and used. Inevitably, one person's success in business will sometimes harm competitors or customers, and law is therefore needed to regulate business to avoid these effects as much as possible. If people follow the rules laid down by Jewish and secular law, however, their efforts may benefit not only the people in the business and their shareholders, if any, but society as a whole.

This is what God created us to do, to "work the land." "Six days shall you work" is just as much of a commandment as the end of that verse, "and on the seventh day you shall desist" (Exod 23:12). Thus work is very much valued in the Jewish tradition, and not only because it fulfills God's commandment but also because of the importance of work to one's psychological and moral health. According to Rabbi Eliezer in the Mishnah, even if a woman is so wealthy that she brings into her marriage a hundred bondwomen to do her work, she must at least work in wool "because idleness leads to lewdness." Along the same lines, Rabban Simeon ben Gamaliel says that if a man refuses to let his wife do any manner of work, he must give her a writ of divorce and its accompanying marriage settlement, "for idleness leads to lightmindedness."[37] Jewish law stipulates that one of a father's duties is to teach his son a trade, and Rabbi Judah maintains that a father who fails to do this teaches him to steal.[38] Similarly, the Talmud maintains that labor brings one honor[39] and that one may not rely on God alone to provide for one's needs:

> A person should not say, "I will eat and drink and see prosperity without troubling myself since Heaven will have compassion upon me." To teach this Scripture says, "You have blessed the work of his hands" (Job 1:10), demonstrating that a man should toil with both his hands and then the Holy One, blessed be God, will grant divine blessing.[40]

37. M. *Ketubbot* 5:5.
38. B. *Kiddushin* 29a.
39. B. *Nedarim* 49b.
40. *Tanhuma*, "Vayetze," Section 13.

Although the rabbis emphasized the importance of studying the Torah, even placing that on a par with fulfilling all of the rest of the commandments,[41] they nonetheless believed that the life of the soul or mind by itself is not good, that it can, indeed, be the source of sin: "An excellent thing is the study of Torah combined with some worldly occupation, for the labor demanded by both of them causes sinful inclinations to be forgotten. All study of Torah without work must, in the end, be futile and become the cause of sin."[42] Thus, while the rabbis considered it a privilege to be able to study Torah, they themselves—or at least most of them—earned their livelihood through bodily work, and they also valued the hard labor of the field-worker who spends little time in the study of Torah:

> A favorite saying of the rabbis of Yavneh was: I am God's creature, and my fellow [who works in the field and is not a student] is God's creature. My work is in the town, and his work is in the country. I rise early for my work, and he rises early for his work. Just as he does not presume to do my work, so I do not presume to do his work. Will you say, I do much [in the study of Torah] and he does little? We have learned: One may do much or one may do little; it is all one, provided that the person directs his heart to Heaven.[43]

On the other hand, if we use these entrepreneurial urges to help ourselves but harm others, then we have engaged in business badly. This is why Jewish law spells out in great detail laws that govern business. Two complete tractates of the Mishnah and Talmud—*Bava Metzia* and *Bava Batra*—are devoted to business law, and one-fourth of the authoritative sixteenth-century code, the *Shulhan Arukh*—namely, its section titled *Hoshen Mishpat*—is devoted primarily to business regulations.

This also means that Judaism does not presume socialism or communism. In line with its conception of a closely knit community, it bids us create a thick safety net for the poor and vulnerable; but Jewish

41. M. *Pe'ah* 1:1; B. *Kiddushin* 40b.

42. M. *Avot* 2:1. See B. *Berakhot* 35b, especially the comment of Abayae there in responding to the earlier theories about this issue of Rabbi Ishmael and Rabbi Simeon bar Yohai.

43 B. *Berakhot* 17a. The last line refers to B. *Menahot* 110a.

law presumes private property and free enterprise, albeit with substantial provisions to uphold the downtrodden and to prevent fraud.

These fundamental Jewish concepts that delineate our relationship to God, to other humans, and to the environment, and that also describe Judaism's view of who we are as human beings and the role of work in God's plan for us, serve as the grounds for a Jewish view of business. They provide the broad picture of the role of business in life, as Judaism understands it, and they explain and motivate the specific norms that Judaism asserts for business through its laws and ethics.

Formulating Jewish Legal and Moral Norms for Business

Precisely because the economic drive that satisfies our needs and some of our desires and that pushes us to carry out God's mandate to work in the world and improve it as we preserve it stems from the self-absorbed part of our nature, rules are necessary to make sure that people do not get badly hurt when they and others engage in business. In Judaism, these rules are both legal and moral. Indeed, in my view of Jewish law, its legal and moral components continually interact, just as the various systems of the human body do.[44]

Furthermore, the principles and the specific legal and moral norms announced in the Torah concerning business have been refined and applied to new contexts as business conditions changed. Some of the Torah's statutes concerning business have been amended over the ages or totally replaced to accommodate new contexts and forms of business, and some of these new business practices gradually became official Jewish commercial customs when they found their way into rabbinic rulings.

So, for example, while a handshake had no legal power whatsoever to seal a deal in the Torah or Talmud, by the Middle Ages it was recognized as legally binding.[45] This is an example of additions coming into Jewish law through commercial practice. Conversely, while the

44. Elliot N. Dorff, *For the Love of God and People: A Philosophy of Jewish Law* (Philadelphia: Jewish Publication Society, 2007), especially chapters 2, 3, and 6.

45. *Piskei ha-Rosh, Bava Mezia*, Ch. 5, #72; S.A. *Hoshen Mishpat* 207:19. On this topic generally, see Menachem Elon, *Jewish Law: History, Sources, Principles*, trans. Bernard Auerbach and Melvin J. Sykes (Philadelphia: Jewish Publication Society, 1994) 2:916n71, and, generally, 913–20.

Torah forbids charging interest on loans to fellow Jews,[46] during the Middle Ages, when the economy had become much more thoroughly monetary, the rabbis issued "permission to do business" (*heter iska*), which effectively circumvented that Torah rule by theoretically making every lender a partner in the business that was the beneficiary of the loan.[47]

Similarly, in our day, we cannot apply Jewish texts mechanically from previous time periods to ours. We must instead take into account the ways in which contemporary business is done and then seek to apply the principles that emerge from Jewish law to contemporary business conditions. Instant, worldwide communications, fast shipping, mechanized manufacture, and stock markets open to everyone with a telephone, television, or computer are just some of the new realities that traditional Jewish sources could not have contemplated. A pluralistic market, in which it is often not clear who is Jewish and who not, is another important change. To apply Jewish law intelligently to contemporary issues, then, one must use heavy doses of judgment, experience, and wisdom.

In the end, though, neither the Jewish tradition nor the Torah at its base is satisfied with announcing general principles alone. The Torah certainly proclaims such precepts; famous examples include "Justice, justice shall you pursue" (Deut 16:20) and "Love your neighbor as yourself" (Lev 19:18), but equally important are tenets such as these that require fairness, equal treatment, and honesty:

> You shall not render an unfair decision; do not favor the poor or show deference to the rich; judge your kinsman fairly. (Lev 19:15)

> When a stranger resides with you in your land, you shall not wrong him. The stranger who resides with you shall be to you as one of your citizens; you shall love him as yourself, for you were strangers in the land of Egypt: I the Lord am your God. (Lev 19:33–34)

> You shall not falsify measures of length, weight, or capacity. You shall have an honest balance, honest weights, an honest

46. Exod 22:24; Lev 25:35–38; Deut 23:20–21.

47. "Moneylending," in *Encyclopedia Judaica*, 12:255; "Partnership," ibid., 13:153–54; "Usury," ibid., 16:32; and "Economic History," ibid., 16:1282–83.

> *ephah* [=dry measure], and an honest *hin* [=liquid measure]. (Lev 19:35–36)

The Torah and the Jewish tradition thereafter, though, do not content themselves with such general principles but rather delineate particular rules. Jewish sources thereby indicate their conviction that general principles are not enough to create the moral human being or society. Those principles must be spelled out in concrete terms if people are to know what is expected of them and what they can expect of others. Only then do the general principles have even a chance of going beyond people's pious affirmations to become part of their actual practice.

The methodology I have described in the last few paragraphs is that which Jews have used over the centuries and which, from my perspective, Jews need to use now. I recognize, however, that, despite precedents like the ones I cited and despite the many changes that have occurred since times past in the ways in which business is now conducted, Orthodox Jews would be much more reticent than I to deviate from the specific legal rules about business embedded in Jewish legal precedents and codes. They would, in other words, want to use a much larger dose of text and a much smaller dose of judgment in announcing Jewish norms that should govern business today.

Conversely, Reform Jews deny the legal authority of traditional Jewish texts altogether. They would consult those texts only for general guidance, but ultimately it is the individual Reform Jew who must and should make a decision on these and all other matters. Their ideology and methodology would be much closer to the Enlightenment views I described earlier than to the communitarian beliefs inherent in traditional Judaism.

The method I have described above, then, is most clearly identified with the Conservative Movement in contemporary American Judaism. It seeks to preserve the historically authentic ways in which Jewish decisions have been reached in times past (hence the name "Conservative") by balancing a commitment to the legal authority of traditional Jewish texts (Bible, Mishnah, Talmud, Midrash, responsa, and codes) and long-standing customs, on one hand, with the need to use judgment (including attention to current economic and social conditions and contemporary moral sensitivities) in applying those texts to present circumstances, on the other. Moreover, like the tradition for at least the last two thousand years, Conservative Judaism entrusts Jewish legal and moral decisions to rabbis as the designees of the community rather than to each individual Jew, for rabbis, either individually or collectively (as in the Conservative movement's Committee on Jewish Law and Standards), have knowledge of both the tradition and, often with consultation, current conditions. They thus can legitimately speak for the tradition in the modern world.[48]

Finally, from the time that Abraham bought the cave of Makhpelah from the Hittites to bury his wife, Sarah (Gen 23), Jews have been involved in business deals with non-Jews. In trades that involved Jews heavily, such as international shipping during the Middle Ages, Jews took an active role in setting the international rules regulating such transactions, but even in those businesses international law as determined by governments and commercial custom governed these transactions. As noted earlier, already in the early third century the talmudic sage Samuel rules that "the law of the land is the law" (*dina d'malkhuta dina*) with regard to commercial matters.[49] Much later this was one of the issues that Napoleon asked the French Sanhedrin, a group of leaders of the French Jewish community in 1807–1808, to determine whether French Jews would be treated as full citizens under the new Enlightenment regime, or at best as a tolerated minority; they affirmed without problem that they would abide by French commercial law,[50] and the same is true for all Jews today.

48. For more on the varying legal methodologies of the movements, and the differing theories of revelation and theories of law on which they are based, see my books, *Conservative Judaism: Our Ancestors to Our Descendants* (New York: United Synagogue of America, 1996) 96–150; and *The Unfolding Tradition: Jewish Law after Sinai* (New York: Aviv Press [Rabbinical Assembly], 2005). For a series of essays on how contemporary Jews propose to draw moral guidance (if not moral governance) from the tradition, see the essays in Part I of Elliot N. Dorff and Louis E. Newman, *Contemporary Jewish Ethics and Morality: A Reader* (New York: Oxford University Press, 1995).

49 See note 29 above.

50 For a description of this episode, see Gil Graff, *Separation of Church and State: Dina D'malkhuta Dina in Jewish Law, 1750–1848* (Tuscaloosa: University of Alabama Press, 1985).

A Few Examples of Jewish Business Laws and Morals

To illustrate some specific provisions of Jewish law and the easy switching from legal to moral norms and back again in Jewish law, I have chosen a few passages of the Mishnah in *Bava Metzia*, Chapter Four, each of which I shall first cite and then explain.

> Mishnah 3:
>
> Fraud (*ona'ah*, oppression, as forbidden in Leviticus 25:14) is constituted by an overcharge of four pieces of silver in the twenty-four pieces of a *sela*, that is, one-sixth of the purchase price. Until what time is [one suffering from being defrauded] permitted to retract [on the business deal]? Until he can show [the item for an opinion as to its value] to a merchant [who specializes in such items] or to his relative [who has similar expertise] . . .

We usually think of fraud as representing something as other than it is. The Mishnah knows about that kind of fraud also, and we will see what it says about it when we study Mishnah 12 of this chapter below. Here, though, the Mishnah describes what it considers to be another kind of fraud—namely, where an object is bought or sold for considerably more or less than the market price. The Mishnah presumes a relatively stable market in which the price for a common commodity can be easily determined but inexperienced buyers or sellers may not know how—or have time—to check. The Mishnah is clearly not talking about a one-of-a-kind thing, such as a painting, but rather something where many are being sold and therefore a market price exists. Unlike the Roman law of the same period, where the principle was *caveat emptor* ("let the buyer beware"), the Mishnah seeks to protect inexperienced buyers and sellers, at least to some extent. Notice that it does not just say that fraud occurs when a price is "unreasonable" or some vague description like that; it gives a precise definition of what constitutes fraud—namely, one-sixth above or below the market price. Notice also that it maintains that not only sellers can engage in fraud; buyers too may defraud sellers by buying a commodity for a sixth less than what they know the market price to be.

Applying this Mishnah to contemporary business is, in some ways, easier than in 200 CE, the time that the Mishnah was edited, for the Internet can supply the market range of many commodities within minutes. At the same time, markets fluctuate considerably more in our times than in antiquity, and so presuming a fixed market price against which to measure this kind of fraud may be hard to do for at least some commodities.

The paragraphs of the Mishnah that follow this one spell out in greater detail the laws governing this kind of fraud, as, for example, how long a defrauded party has to claim fraud and either have the deal canceled or adjust the price to the market value. Then, in paragraph 10 of this chapter, the Mishnah says this:

> Mishnah 10:
> Just as there is [fraud by] overreaching in buying and selling, so there is wrong (*ona'ah*) done by means of words. [Thus,] one may not say to another, "What is the price of this thing?" if he does not wish to purchase it . . .

Notice how the Mishnah shifts effortlessly from law to morality in prohibiting a person from asking the price of an object he has no intention to buy. This is clearly a moral matter, for, as the Talmud will later say in commenting on this Mishnah, only the questioner knows for sure whether he intends to buy such an object or not. Legal remedies for violating this prohibition are therefore not available; this is a moral norm, a matter of character. The Mishnah is not banning comparative shopping; as long as one plans on buying the kind of object about which he or she inquires—or even knows that a friend is in the market for that type of object—the question is perfectly fine. What the Mishnah finds fraudulent is asking a seller the price of something when he and everybody he knows has no plans to buy such an object in the near future—when, for example, he asks because he has just bought such an object and wants to find out if he got a good deal. Then he is both stealing the seller's time in asking the question, and he is also, in the Mishnah's phrase, engaged in "stealing his mind" (*ge'naivat da'at*)—that is, deceiving him—for he leads the seller to believe that there might be a sale here. If he says to the seller honestly that he just bought such an object, and he was curious to know how much it would have cost here, then the questioner is not deceiving the seller, and the seller can choose to answer the question or move on to another customer.

Mishnah 11:

> One must not mix together produce with other produce, even new [produce] with new, and much less, needless to say, new with old; [yet], in truth, they [the Rabbis] permitted [the seller] to mix strong [wine] with mild because this improves it [but only with the buyer's agreement]. A seller may not mix the lees [sediment, dregs] of [one barrel of] wine with the wine [of another barrel], but he may give him [the buyer] the lees [together with the wine of the same barrel]. If one's wine is mixed with water, he must not sell it in the shop unless he has told him [of the dilution], and he must not [sell it] to a merchant, even if he has informed him, because [the merchant would buy it] only to deceive [other consumers] with it. In a place where it is the practice to mix wine with water, however, they may do so [because the buyers can be presumed to be aware of the prevailing practice and would consequently not be deceived by such dilution].

This is the question raised by the small basket of strawberries that you buy in the supermarket. The first time you bought such a basket, you thought that all the strawberries in the basket looked as good as the ones on top. That is deception, plain and simple, for the delicious looking strawberries at the top lured you into buying the whole basket. Once you have learned that this arrangement of baskets of strawberries is common practice, however, you can no longer claim that you have been deceived. This Mishnah is making the same kind of distinction. It prohibits false presentations of products except if either that is the common custom that the buyer should know or the seller specifically tells the buyer what is in the product. Here the Mishnah is limiting the degree to which it will protect inexperienced buyers by asserting that buyers cannot claim they were deceived if the seller followed common custom.

Some Implications for Interfaith Discussions and for Government Policies

In what ways can these deliberations about business contribute to interfaith discussions and the shaping of government policies regarding business? I would suggest the following Jewish lessons:

- The importance of seeing how intimately and profoundly our business decisions affect the community and the environment.
- The use of the law to help us achieve moral goals for our society rather than just providing the minimal requirements of living together as a community.
- The positive view of work, economic development, and creativity balanced with a thick safety net for the poor, laws to prevent fraud, and rules to protect the environment.
- The need to specify in concrete terms what is required of us to accomplish these ends; general principles, while important, are not enough.

"Did You Engage in Business Honestly?"

This essay has demonstrated that the Jewish tradition takes business seriously. It does not see money in and of itself as somehow dirty; such judgments depend on how one earns and uses money. God created and owns the world, but God wants us to use it for our purposes as we simultaneously take steps to preserve it. God created us with both self-serving and altruistic drives, and we need to use and balance both to gain the values of entrepreneurship while at the same time protecting the vulnerable. To help us do that, God gives us laws, which rabbis in each generation interpret and apply to new business contexts, so that we can discern what are legitimate business practices and what are not.

The seriousness with which the Jewish tradition takes matters of business is illustrated graphically by all of the theological and legal attention Jewish sources devote to it. It is also in evidence in the Rabbinic text that will serve as a fitting end to this essay. In imagining what God asks you when you die, the Rabbis did not begin their list by depicting God as asking whether you committed murder or adultery, perhaps because they presumed that most Jews did not do such things. Instead, the very first question that the Rabbis put on God's list is this: "Did you transact your business honestly?" When God asks us these questions, then, may we all be able to answer "Yes!"

> When a person is brought before God's tribunal [after death], God asks him [or her]: Did you transact your business hon-

estly? Did you fix times for the study of Torah? Did you fulfill your duty with respect to establishing a family? Did you hope for the salvation [of the Messiah]? Did you search for wisdom? Did you try to deduce one thing from another [in study]? Even should all these questions be answered affirmatively, only if "the fear of the Lord is his treasure" (Isaiah 33:6) will it avail; otherwise it will not. (Babylonian Talmud, *Shabbat* 31a)

3

Islamic Law, Sharīʿah-based Finance, and Economics

Caner K. Dagli

Economics and Finance as a Part of Islamic Law (Sharīʿah)

Today many people in the field of Islamic finance are in an ongoing debate as to what makes a given transaction "Islamic" or "Sharīʿah-compliant" or not, one side tending to stick with the traditional forms of contracts as a guarantor of their compliance, the other side seeking to define an underlying philosophical and economic rationale for the prohibitions in the Qurʾān and *ḥadīth*. As we shall see, far from being a mere technical question, reflection upon the inner workings of Islamic law as it concerns economic matters also raises profound spiritual and moral questions applicable to our current situation.

To begin, it is helpful to remember that whether it be Islamic finance, Islamic banking, or contracts, one is speaking of a branch of Islamic law or Sharīʿah. As a developed tradition of law, one can think of Islamic law as encompassing three levels, or three intersecting dimensions.

First, one can speak of positive law, which comprises the actual rules and regulations, or 'the laws on the books.' The second level or dimension is called in Islam "the roots of the law" or jurisprudence (*uṣūl al-fiqh*), which identifies the sources of the law, as well as the methodology by which those sources are used to arrive at positive law. Different schools gave different amounts of latitude when it came to reasoning by analogy, for example, which led to a certain range of opinion on almost any matter of positive law and also on ancillary matters of theology. The third and most fundamental dimension of Islamic law encompasses the objectives of the law, dealing with the meaning or purpose of the Sharīʿah. What is the Sharīʿah there for? The commands and prohibition in the Islamic sources were generally concrete and particular, such as the prohibition against gambling, alchohol, and adultery.

While the Prophet was alive, he served as the interpreter and legislator *par excellence*, but after his death Muslims were left to take the individual rules and fit them into a larger ethical structure. The science of the "roots of the law" historically came first, in that new legal situations called for the application and reapplication of the rules laid out in the Qurʾān and *ḥadīth*. Almost always, reasoning by analogy was a one-to-one affair. Does beer intoxicate? Then it is prohibited, as is wine. If the Prophet laid down an economic rule based upon a transaction in dates or wheat, it was not unfeasible to use that rule to govern the trading of pistachios and apples. If a man who owned four hundred camels had to give ten in alms, one could extend that quite easily to llamas if the matter arose.

As the science of law progressed, however, jurists felt a need to articulate, not only the application of individual rulings to new situations, but the general objectives of these rulings themselves, their *raison d'etre*, their ultimate significance. This is not to say that jurists did not use general principles, since equity and public interest were part of the earliest discussions of law, and indeed the justifications for many rulings were provided by the Qurʾān itself, which often warns against corruption, injustice, and tyranny. However, in the absence of an explicit text, there was a natural reticence to categorically identify the "reason" why God did anything, and a more conservative approach was preferred, constructing law from precedent rather than from abstract ideas.

But as the law became increasingly complex, the moral principles which had always operated implicitly to determine and understand law were made more concrete and explicit. In its most famous form, the "objectives of the law" (*maqāṣid al-sharīʿah*), as they are usually known, are discussed as things which the law must preserve. These were categorized into those objectives that were essential, complementary, or desirable, though here we will restrict ourselves to a discussion of the essential objectives of the law.

These objectives were usually listed as 1) Religion (*dīn*); 2) Life; 3) Mind/Intelligence (*ʿaql*); 4) Lineage/Honor/Dignity (*nasab* or *ʿirḍ*); 5) Property. From the Islamic point of view, without these five things, no society could be worthy of the name, and so Islamic law seeks to uphold and protect them above all other considerations. Of course, the last of these, property, is especially relevant to the topic at hand, although each of the five objectives—or what could be called fundamental rights—is impossible to disentangle from the others.

It is not my purpose here to embark on a history of Islamic economics. The economic history of Islamdom is quite complex and multifaceted, ranging from the most basic barter systems of tribal nomads to the central planning of large empires. The Qurʾān and *ḥadīth* do not lay out the blueprint of any economic system, just as they do not describe a political system except in the most general terms that society should obey the laws of God. What one finds, rather, are commands and prohibitions regarding transactions and the accumulation of wealth. In what follows, I will discuss some of the important questions regarding Islamic banking and finance, at each of these three aforementioned levels of Islamic law: positive law, the roots of the law, and the objectives of the law. I will discuss these different levels in terms of rules and regulations, the underlying logic of these rules, and finally as aspects of a larger set of philosophical questions.

Zakāh's Role for Individuals and the Economy

One of the most significant and undoubtedly most well-known commands regarding economics in Islam is the *zakāh*. It is one of the five pillars of Islam, sometimes translated as "alms" or "poor-due." As a general rule of thumb, the rule of *zakāh* is to give 1/40th of one's accumulated liquid wealth, though this could and was subject to modification. For example, if separate from one's expenses one kept four hundred ounces of gold continuously for a year, ten ounces would be given in *zakāh* for the needy. One's other wealth, such as one's house, clothes, or furniture, are not subject to *zakāh*.

The *zakāh* can be thought of as institutionalized charity, but in practice it is a public welfare system that discourages hoarding while acknowledging that caring for the needy is an intrinsic duty and that the poor have a claim on the wealth of believers. In the Qurʾān *zakāh* often appears together with the prayer in almost a refrain: the believers are those who "offer prayer and give the poor-due"—the *salah* and *zakāh*. The *zakāh* is significant, not only because it institutionalizes charity and places an absolute value on helping the needy, but because it also closes the question, as it were, of public/private ownership. *Zakāh* demands the compulsory redistribution of wealth, yet it only functions because it presumes private property as the norm. At a strictly legal level, it enshrines a bounded welfare system and social safety net. It is the institutional expression, one might say, of the Prophet's teaching that one is not a believer if he goes to bed full while his neighbor is hungry.

Does *Ribā* Mean "Interest"?

In addition to *zakāh* there are two concepts that are crucial and worth knowing in the Arabic, and these are *ribā* and *gharar*. Lexically, *ribā* means "increase" or "growth," and *gharar* means "risk" and is etymologically related to "delusion" and "deception." Understanding the technical and legal meaning of these ideas are essential to understanding Islamic banking and finance, and an analysis of *ribā* and *gharar* will make up the core of the following pages.

Many who have only a passing familiarity with Islamic law will have heard that the distinguishing feature of Islamic banking and finance is that Islamic law forbids interest, and hence must provide for interest-free mortgages, interest-free savings, and so forth. The idea that Islam forbids interest stems from the equation of the concept *ribā* with "interest." Others will be more careful and say that *ribā* is usury or usurious interest. Much scholarly work has been done recently to show that such an easy equation between *ribā* and "interest" is almost surely mistaken. Indeed, not all *ribā* is interest, and not all interest is *ribā*.

The Qurʾān lays out a general condemnation and prohibition of *ribā*, but does not give a detailed explanation for what it is:

> O you who believe, devour not *ribā*, doubling and multiplying. (Q 3:130)

> They say, "Buying and selling are simply like *ribā*," though God has permitted buying and selling and forbidden *ribā* . . . (Q 2:275)

The *ribā* of pre-Islamic Arabia referred to charging a fee on an interest-free loan once it came due. That is, in the words of Imam Mālik, *ribā* in the pre-Islamic Days of Ignorance was that, "A man would be owed a debt by another man for a set term. When the term was due, he would say, 'Will you pay it off or give me *ribā*?' If the man paid, he took it. If not, he increased his debt and lengthened the term for him" (Mālik *Muwaṭṭaʾ K. al-buyūʿ*).

Many believe that the general prohibitions in the Qurʾān against *ribā*, allowing trade but forbidding *ribā*, refer to this practice, which was deferment on already existing loans at the time of their maturity. The deferment often led to doubling of the principal in a year, and then re-doubling when the deferment period expired and another deferment became necessary. The classical legal tradition would discuss how, under such conditions, a debtor could eventually lose all his possessions to the creditor through the doubling and re-doubling mentioned in the Qurʾān.

Complicating the definition of *ribā* as simply synonymous with interest on a loan are *ḥadīth* of the Prophet. In one example, sometimes called the "*ḥadīth* of the six commodities," the Prophet commanded:

> Gold for gold, silver for silver, wheat for wheat, barley for barley, dates for dates, and salt for salt; like for like, hand to hand, in equal amounts; and any increase is *ribā*.[1]

> Bilāl visted the Messenger of God with some high quality dates, and the Prophet inquired about their source. Bilāl explained that he traded two volumes of lower quality dates for one volume of higher quality. The Messenger of God said: "This is precisely the forbidden *ribā*! Do not do this. Instead, sell the first type of dates, and use the proceeds to buy the other.[2]

This account, and other similar ones which appear in the *ḥadīth* literature, show that an easy equation of *ribā* with loan interest is incorrect. Let us provisionally take the legal definition of *ribā* to mean "unlawful gain." Taking together the Qurʾānic injunctions against this unlawful

1. Muslim, *K. al-buyūʿ* (Gamal translation).
2. Muslim *K. al-masāqāh* (Gamal translation).

gain, which seemed to deal with debts, and the *ḥadīths* which seemed to deal with certain kinds of sales or trades, jurists came to classify two general kinds of unlawful gain, one through deferment (*ribā al-nasīʾāh*), the other through surplus (*ribā al-faḍl*). The unlawful gain by deferment came to be understood as profit from a loan, while unlawful gain through surplus prohibited trading goods of the same genus and kind in different quantities, in light of the aforementioned *ḥadīth*.

Abdullah Saeed explains the increase-*ribā* this way:

> It seems that at the time of the Prophet, some forms of sale were common in Medina and the surrounding region, in which one party sold, say, one kilo of wheat for two kilos to be received at the time of the transaction or in the future, or more wheat of inferior quality for less wheat of good quality to be received at the time of the transaction or in the future. Since most people who resorted to such transactions would be less affluent and would only do so because of necessity, there may have been injustice towards or perhaps some exploitation of the weaker party in such dealings. The economically weaker party to the transaction could have been forced to give a higher countervalue, either in terms of quantity or quality, either at the time of the transaction or in the future. In any case, it was the weaker party who suffered most from having to pay a higher value than he received. Moreover, the commodities mentioned [in the *ḥadīth* of six commodities] were essential for survival in Medina and the surrounding areas . . . The Prophet would not have tolerated the exploitation of the poor in the sale of these essential items. It seems that in line with his prohibition of certain other forms of sale, the Prophet was most probably attempting to block the potential injustice in the barter exchange of these six commodities.[3]

Another authority in Islamic finance, Mahmoud al-Gamal,[4] interprets the *ribā* of the *unlawful gain through surplus* injunctions in terms of economic efficiency and equity. According to this view, the Islamic prohibitions force the parties to acquire information about market conditions and mark the terms of trade to market prices. One could imagine that bartering dates for dates, for example, could lead to abus-

3. Abdullah Saeed, *Islamic Banking and Interest: A Study in the Prohibition of Riba and Its Contemporary Interpretation* (New York: Brill, 1996) 32.

4. See especially his *Islamic Finance: Law, Economics, and Practice* (New York: Cambridge University Press, 2009).

es which bartering dates for barley might not, in that the latter transaction would almost certainly demand that the parties have knowledge of market conditions. This would lead to fewer disadvantageous trades and greater equity and economic efficiency. The goal is to achieve a mark-to-market approach, as Gamal defines it, in establishing trading ratios.

For Gamal, understanding unlawful gain through deferment (on loans) in terms of efficiency and equity is not a great leap: it would mean that credit would have to be extended at the appropriate interest rate, no matter the financial instrument used to extend that credit. That is to say, it would have to properly reflect the cost of money at the time when one extends credit or makes an investment.

The Operative Cause of *Ribā*

When making a legal analogy, which is to say when they take an explicit ruling in the Qurʾān or *ḥadīth* and apply it to a new case, jurists must find an "operative cause" (*ʿillah*) that links the two analogous examples. This is part of the science of the "roots of the law" or jurisprudence mentioned above. In the case of wine and beer, the efficient cause common to the original case (wine) and the new case (beer) is regarded as intoxication, not that they are liquids or that they are fermented. But in the case of wine and beer one can avoid the question of why intoxication is bad or why God forbade it.

That brings us to the third aspect of the law, its objective or purpose. Jurists were and are reluctant to stick their necks out too far to speak about God's intents or purposes unless God had done so Himself in the Qurʾān or in the *ḥadīth* through His Prophet. There was thus disagreement among the jurists as to what role the "wisdom" of a ruling should have in reasoning by analogy. If intoxication by alcohol is forbidden, what about caffeine, or nicotine? A prohibition against coffee based upon the prohibition of alcohol would be based on the *moral* of the law, not the operative cause of it, in this case, a decision that the alteration of human consciousness through chemicals is always bad.

As the Islamic community moved further away from the divine revelation in time, reliance upon the "operative cause" in determining legality became increasingly difficult, especially in trade and finance, as the goods traded multiplied and the transactional forms became more complex. Rulings about gold and dates were good and well, but what about fractional reserve banking and complex derivatives? In a sense, this is where the pinch was felt in moving from the "laws on the books" to new cases for which there was no explicit precedent.

In the case of *ribā*, Muslims have a problem: while remaining systematic and loyal to the Qurʾān and the Prophet's teachings, how can Muslims arrive at rules governing other debt transactions and sales? All the schools of law were presented with the same data, as it were, but arrived at differing interpretations because of the juridical methods they used. In trying to understand the reason why the Prophet mentioned those six commodities (gold, silver, wheat, barley, dates, and salt), for example, the Ḥanafī school said the decisive attribute was that the commodity be weighable or measureable; the Māliki school said it was that they be either currency, or storable foodstuff for human beings; the Shāfiʿī school that they be either foodstuffs or currency; and the Hanbalī school that it be either currency or be measureable or weighable. A similar variety of views exists on the nature of the goods involved with *ribā* (unlawful gain) by deferment transactions.

That is why the jurists arrived at a variety of conclusions about unlawful gain through surplus: they did not agree on the essential quality that distinguished the transactions and commodities mentioned by the Prophet. Moreover, they did not agree on the "operative cause" of the unlawful gain mentioned in the Qurʾān. In some cases this led to what might seem rather illogical conclusions. Some jurists, following their reasoning to a logical conclusion, decided that the rule did not extend to apples, which could be counted but not weighed (presumably with sufficient continuity), or to cloth, or eggs, since these commodities lacked the attributes common to those items mentioned in the *ḥadīth*.

Many scholars of Islamic banking and finance have argued that the legal tradition has focused too much on the *form* of a loan or sale, while ignoring or deemphasizing the moral substance of it. In the case of deferment-*ribā*, this meant in practice that jurists, when dealing with the *ribā*-focused verse,

> And if you repent you shall have the principal of your wealth,
> and you shall neither wrong nor be wronged. (Q 2:179)

attended to the phrase "the principal of your wealth" but tended to ignore "neither wrong nor be wronged." Or they ignored the fact that in 30:39 *ribā* is compared against charity, not trade, which to some indicates that the rules of *ribā* are focused on injustice especially as it applies to the disadvantaged of society:

> That which you give in *ribā* that it might increase through other people's wealth does not increase with God. But that which you give in *zakāh*, desiring the Face of God—it is they who receive a manifold increase. (Q 30:39)

In their classical form, in general, the rules on *ribā* amounted to something like this:

1) If money is lent, compensation for this financing cannot be for a predetermined amount. Rather, it shares in the profits of the venture. Money is not a commodity, but a bearer of risk, and should be subject to the same uncertainties.

2) An investor may compensate themselves for foregone opportunities if they finance goods by sale or lease. Profits from lease payments or credit sale can even explicitly list a time factor.[5]

This last statement is important, because it may seem paradoxical that Islamic law acknowledges that there is a time factor in money.

We will see that in actually trying to structure financial transactions, Muslims in recent years, trying to come to grips with living in accord with Islam in the contemporary world of banking and finance, have run into a form-over-substance problem in trying to avoid what they considered *ribā* (which they understood to be interest-bearing loans). There are numerous kinds of financial and sale transactions in Islamic law, which I could not possibly discuss in depth here, but it is instructive to look at an example to see how form can become uncoupled from the ethical and spiritual substance of the transaction.

In a conventional mortgage, the buyer borrows money from the bank and purchases a home. He is the owner of the home, which serves as collateral, and he repays the mortgage according to a predetermined interest rate. According to the equation of *ribā* with interest, this would be the forbidden *ribā*.

5. Frank E. Vogel and Samuel L. Hayes III, *Islamic Law and Finance: Religion, Risk, and Return* (The Hague: Kluwer Law International, 1998) 2.

Now consider a transaction in Islamic finance called a *murābaḥah*. There are three parties to the sale: the property buyer, the bank, and the property seller. For example, the property buyer provides 20 percent of the sale price to the seller, and the bank provides 80 percent. At the same time, the bank agrees to sell its share of the house to the buyer at a deferred price payable in monthly installments. The difference between what the bank paid to the seller and what it receives from the buyer is the bank's profit.

So, suppose I want to buy a house that costs $500,000. I pay the seller $100,000 and the bank pays $400,000. The bank then turns around and sells its share to me for $800,000 payable in monthly installments over 30 years. This is roughly what a conventional mortgage would cost me at 5%. The question is, is this interest? Although this seems like a clear distinction between transactions based on debt (conventional mortgage) and transactions based on shared equity (*murābaḥah*), existing contemporary *murābaḥah* loans, when examined more closely, in fact become functionally equivalent to conventional mortgages, involving nearly identical allocations of capital and risk.

Gharar: The Limits and Management of Risk

Along with *ribā*, or unlawful gain, the other core concept I mentioned above is *gharar*, which means risk or uncertainty. A typical definition of *gharar* would be the following by Mustafa Al-Zarqa: "[the forbidden *bay' al-gharar*] is the sale of probable items whose existence or characteristics are uncertain, the risky nature of which makes the transaction akin to gambling."[6] Although *gharar* is not mentioned in the Qur'ān, it is mentioned in *ḥadīth* such as:

> The Prophet forbade the purchase of unborn cattle in the womb, the purchase of the milk in their udders except by a set amount . . . the purchase of spoils of war prior to their distribution . . . and the purchase of the catch of a diver. (Ibn Mājah *K. al-tijārāt*)

It should be recalled here that gambling is categorically forbidden in Islam, which is not unconnected to the spirit of the prohibition of *ribā* and *gharar*. Most jurists have argued that the meaning of *gharar* is risk

6. Cited in Gamal, *Islamic Finance*, 58.

or uncertainty as the dominant aspect of a sale. But jurists necessarily allow for minor *gharar*, since no contract could possibly be free of all risk or uncertainty, and they allow *gharar* when the need for the contract cannot be met otherwise.

Some transactions were allowed, such as forward or "prepayment" sales (*salam*) on items such as crops, since it allowed farmers access to capital for seeds and other expenses. Or in the case of the diver, one could pay him hourly for whatever he catches, but not a fixed cost for what he might catch.

One definition of *gharar* would be "the unbundled sale of risk." For example, the sale of a warranty by the manufacturer or retail seller with a product is allowed, as it is a bundled contingency claim. An obvious example of forbidden *gharar* or trading in risk would be complex derivatives. With derivatives, two parties exchange money based on an underlying asset, without having to own that asset, and often in the absence of any real asset. The most notorious of these in recent times was the "credit default swap," which was no more or less than a bet between two parties that a third party would go into default or have some other "credit event."

Applying *Ribā* and *Gharar* Prohibitions

These twin prohibitions on *ribā* and *gharar* are foundational for Islamic finance and banking. A very helpful conceptual key for trying to understand, at the very least, the economic rationale for the prohibition of *ribā* and *gharar* is given by al-Gamal:

> It is interesting . . . to note that the prohibitions of *ribā* and *gharar* are precisely restrictions on means of trading in risk (the extension of credit exposes the creditor to potential borrower default or bankruptcy, and leverage increases the borrower's own risk thereof). Thus, the spirit of Islamic jurisprudence allows the transfer of credit and risk *only if bundled* within a financial transaction such as sales, leases, and partnerships. Such bundling regulates the riskiness of financial transactions, thus allowing for necessary risk taking to encourage investment and economic growth, while minimizing individual and systemic risks of bankruptcy and wild fluctuations in economic values.[7]

7. *Islamic Finance*, 164–65.

This brings us to the form-over-substance problem with Sharīʿah-based finance today. Some have argued that, in avoiding a full-throated articulation of the moral substance of *ribā* and *gharar*, and in hewing too close to the *form* which classical jurists used in establishing fair practices (forms such as *murābaḥah*), many Islamic experts who sit on the so-called Sharīʿah boards of major banks have missed the point of the prohibition of *ribā* and *gharar*.

Many academic scholars of Islamic law and banking are quite unhappy with many of the developments in so-called Sharīʿah-compliant transactions. They have convincingly argued that many of these "Sharīʿah-compliant" financial instruments involve the *exact same transfer of credit and risk*. Despite the use of premodern Arabic names, the financial instruments are sometimes only vaguely similar to classical Islamic forms. Often the so-called rates of profit are keyed to some bank rate such as LIBOR, and the transactions often require the same kinds of insurance to back them up. Thus, in the case of a mortgage, the *murābaḥah* often functions, so far as the buyer is concerned, as a conventional secured loan. Worse, they are often more expensive, as they incur expenses from the extra administrative costs, and often do not carry the same legal protections that have accrued to conventional mortgages over the decades.

In the words of a disillusioned former member of the Islamic banking industry: "Islamic banks have arrived at a wonderland in which through their creative use of language, there exists an Islamic equivalent to almost all the major products and modes of financing of the conventional interest-based sector."[8] This is not to say that there have not been many "substance-over-form" successes, as many Muslims are organizing institutions that follow both the spirit and form of Islamic law. One way to address the need for Islamic finance with familiar institutions would be to have mutual savings banks and mutual insurance companies. In a mutual bank, the profits belong to the depositors, beyond the costs of running the bank, which is tasked with making investments of a conservative nature. Seeking greater profits could only come at the price of greater risk exposure, which would defeat the purpose of a mutual bank in the first place. Through existing structures, one could bring a nonprofit approach to credit ex-

8. Muhammad Saleem, *Islamic Banking: A $300 Billion Deception* (self-published, 2006) 23.

tension, eliminating the perverse incentives which, incidentally, many say drove us to the financial collapse of 2008.

Philosophy and Economics

To conclude I would like to reflect on some broader questions relating to the science of economics, and also to apply some of the ethical rules of Islamic law to the current situation. Much of this paper has treated the way in which Muslims have tried to use jurisprudence to apply the rulings and principles in the Qurʾān, *ḥadīth*, and the classical legal tradition to the contemporary situation. However, the legal picture would be incomplete without consideration of its nontechnical dimensions. If Islam, or any religion, is going to make a claim to being a comprehensive way of life, it must provide a clear nexus between its spiritual vision and the rules it promulgates.

All ethics exist within a worldview, which is to say that it is literally impossible to make a judgment about what is right except upon the basis of what you think reality is, and this applies to the economic sphere as well as anywhere else. Any religion—by *definition*, one could say—affirms a belief in the sacred, which is to say that no religion—at least, religion in the traditional sense—affirms that material reality *as such* is all that there is. This is certainly true for the theistic faiths such as Islam, Hinduism, and even Taoism in an impersonal mode, but it also true in nontheistic religions such as Buddhism. You will not find a traditional Buddhist who thinks that Enlightenment or Nirvana is merely—that is, purely and simply—a special arrangement of molecules in a physical brain. For Muslims, it is in relation to the sacred that good and evil have any true meaning. Even the material goods which are protected by the Sharīʿah are considered in their deepest sense to be gifts from God, *for* which we are to be grateful and *from* which we are to give to others. We are called to meditate upon creation as a collection of signs of God, and we are also called to deal justly with all creatures while here on earth. Our actions in this world are spoken of in the Qurʾān as things which our hands "send ahead" to the Hereafter.

The Qurʾān teaches that there is within man a heart capable of being whole, which must contend with a soul that wants to follow its passions. The heart, as in most traditional teachings on the true seat of consciousness, is also called the spirit, or the intellect. It is the seat of faith and of understanding. It is the most obvious fact of the human condition that we have a will in conflict with itself, and this conflict is more certain than death or taxes (see how I tied it in to economics?). In the sentence, "I discipline myself," there is an "I" and a "myself." I am aware of things, *and* I am aware of my awareness. I have thoughts, *and* I judge the goodness of those thoughts. This level of self-awareness, of wakefulness, of truly human consciousness is not always actualized, but nevertheless remains there in potency.

In the Qurʾān, true human intelligence (reason, but not merely in the sense of ratiocination), faith, and spirit are not proper to the soul insofar as they are merely a bundle of needs and impulses. Islam does not condemn hunger, sexual desire, love of family, the desire to live a dignified life, or the desire for material well-being, but even in the law it subordinates these needs to man's final ends, which are not ultimately of this world, and calls upon man to subordinate these desires to the spirit, the heart, and, yes, the reason.

By the time economics arose as a separate discipline within the eighteenth-century West, the traditional Christian view of the cosmos had been swept away, and the view of man as a being comprised of *body*, *soul*, and *spirit* had given way to, at best, the Cartesian bifurcation between a world of mathematical quantities (the objective world out there) and the world of the thinking being (the subjective world within). Although Descartes' conception was not an atheistic one, between the reduction of the human soul to *res cogitans*, and the withdrawal of God to the role of an Architect who winds up the universe and then lets it go its merry way, it wasn't long before even the soul and God both disappeared from the realm of serious consideration.

This all matters for economics because, in the main, economics could not avoid the reductionist worldview which took physics and mathematics as its pivot. The economist and philosopher E. F. Schumacher, author of the famous *Small Is Beautiful* and the lesser known but more profound *Guide for the Perplexed*, notes that "the great majority of economists are still pursuing the absurd idea of making their 'science' as scientific and precise as physics, as if there were no qualitiative difference between mindless atoms and men made in the image of God."[9] Many of the founders of neoclassical economics

9. E. F. Schumacher, *Small Is Beautiful: Economics as if People Mattered* (London: Blond & Briggs, 1973) 51.

(Jevons, Edgeworth, Pareto, Walras) drew explicit analogies between physics and economics, and the drive towards almost complete quantification and mathematization in mainstream economics certainly bears this out.

One of the important features of *classical* economics was a labor theory of value, where the value of a good was related, in some fashion, to the amount of labor required to produce it. The different versions of this theory and its development are important for our purposes only to point out that, in that classical picture, there was something intrinsic to the good or service which was taken into account in putting a value on it. Neoclassical economics, which came to the fore in the late nineteenth and early twentieth centuries and has dominated ever since, dispensed with theories of value and instead focused on *pricing*. Rather than intrinsic needs, people had preferences. There was neither a need to differentiate needs from wants, nor to distinguish goods from each other, except on the basis of their "utility."

In the classical conception, value could and often did have a decidedly earthbound nature, in that the value was measurable in terms of physical objects and processes as physical things. Even there, however, one could at least hold on to a sentimental conception of intrinsic value. However, to completely disregard *any* consideration of the intrinsic value of things in favor of their comparative utility at the margins is to eliminate questions of good and evil as far as the science of economics is concerned. There is no consideration of whether some commodity is good or bad, because no one needs to ask that question. If this conception were just a tool of analysis, a kind of technique for studying markets, it might not be so pernicious, but notice that the neoclassical conception of utility leaves no room for the kind of human being discussed above, one who possesses passions and desires but who is capable of rising above them in light of a reality that transcends this world.

Let us pause and ask: how can a rational person believe that things like hunger and sexual desire can exist on the same utility curve as generosity, appreciation for beauty, and the yearning for God? How can all of these things be grouped under the single label "utility"? What kind of picture of man could allow such a theory to carry any weight?

Part of the reason why neoclassical economics can reduce values to tastes and needs to wants (as my colleague Waleed el-Ansary so aptly puts it)[10] while continuing to retain plausibility, I believe, is Darwinism. I am not talking about "survival of the fittest," though this is the aspect of Darwinism most regularly invoked in the history of economic discourse. No, I refer to the reduction and flattening of man which Darwinism entails and indeed demands.

Let us consider the example of generosity or sacrifice. How does a Darwinist explain that most glaring human fact, that we have both an "I" and a "myself," and that the true I sometimes rises above the false one? What happens when I sacrifice my needs for the needs of another, or even my very life? Well, by some happenstance a long time ago, our ancestors were born with a mutation which—purely by accident—gave them an impulse to act for the benefit of others. Somehow that trait led to greater survival, which is to say that those poor creatures who had no impulse towards what we would call generosity or sacrifice (never mind a sense of beauty or the sacred) did not manage to survive—again purely by accident. You would not expect a creature without a sexual drive to reproduce, and for more subtle reasons a creature without the altruistic impulse would not survive long enough to reproduce, or would not be attractive as a sexual partner. And despite any protestations to the contrary, this explanation dispenses with any ideas of higher or lower faculties, or control of instincts. Rather, one has a balance or equilibrium of impulses. For the Darwinist, the desire to procreate and the desire to write poetry are both matters of the neurophysiology of the brain. There is no objective standard by which love can be placed "above" thirst. They are different arrangements of molecules in the organism.

Richard Dawkins has said that Darwin made it possible to be an intellectually fulfilled atheist. It turns out to make neoclassical economics easier, too. If the difference between a desire to eat and a desire to marry is nothing more than different arrangements of the molecules of the brain, it makes perfect sense to arrange those preferences along a single mathematical curve, or to order them in a single list, and to talk about preferences, marginal rates of substitution, indifference curves,

10. See his "The Quantum Enigma and Islamic Sciences of Nature: Implications for Islamic Economic Theory," *Proceedings of the 6th International Conference on Islamic Economics and Finance* (Jeddah: Islamic Development Bank, 2005) 143–75; "The Spiritual Significance of Jihād in Islamic Economics," *American Journal of Islamic Social Sciences* 14:2 (1997) 231–63; "The Traditionalist Critique of Contemporary Economic Theory," *Sophia: A Journal of Traditional Studies* 11.1 (2005) 115–55.

and the like. There is no need to differentiate between spiritual and material goods. Indeed, how could such a theory *not* emerge if one truly believes that the soul is the mind, that the mind is the brain, that the brain is chemicals, is molecules, is atoms, is quarks? Of course economics should be like physics; after all, it's really the study of complex physical systems—us.

For me, it has always been a paradox that economics, which speaks about "rationality," completely undermines any full account of human reason. Rationality, economically speaking, is *utility-maximizing behavior under economic constraint*. Reason was once thought of as a lofty faculty, and at the very least it was opposed to the passions, and considered superior to them. According to the Darwinian conception, reason is no better or worse than the passions, and the same is true for spirit, love, etc. They are all mutations that have survived quite without purpose in the way human beings usually understand the word *purpose*.

If one objects that this is not how most Darwinians and neoclassical economists think of themselves, I would say you were right. Even Richard Dawkins and Sam Harris and other so-called New Atheists cling tenaciously to ethics and morality. My argument is that Darwinism and neoclassical economics go together as *ideas*, and ideas do matter. It is not that Darwinians do not try to act morally or feel horrified by evil, since they most certainly do. Rather, I am arguing that joining the notions of the "sacred," or "higher" and "lower" faculties, with the Darwinian view of man is intellectually incoherent.

Moreover, it is impossible that such ideas will not eventually make their power felt. Would Alan Greenspan have acted as he did if, rather than venerating Ayn Rand, he were instead a follower of Gandhi? Is it really possible to disentangle the ideological and deliberate quantification of the social sciences, from the fact that the Wall Street "wizards" thought they could manage huge risk with their stupendously complex mathematics (which had such terrible consequences for the entire economy)? Are we supposed to believe that the efficient-market hypothesis, and the general sentiment that the market will take care of everything, does not come from the same ideological impulse that imputes god-like qualities to evolution itself?

I began by discussing the meaning and purpose of Islamic law. The five "objectives of the law" are not preferences. They are objective goods: they are good independent of us and they are good for us. When a jurist says that Islam protects wealth and says that no society can sustain itself without the protection of private property, this does not absolutize this need nor relegate it to a mere preference.

Moreover, the right to property is informed and shaped by the other rights: religion, life, intelligence, and honor. In this conception, there is no way a monomaniacal obsession with quantity and material things could take over considerations of property. Today, the objective of wealth or property, in being degraded, has mutated and now threatens to consume everything else.

From the point of view of someone outside of Islam, Islamic law and its spiritual underpinning are really only one example of the sacred worldview shared by all religious civilizations. When E. F. Schumacher wrote his famous essay "Buddhist Economics," he began by saying: "The choice of Buddhism for this purpose is purely incidental; the teachings of Christianity, Islam, or Judaism could have been used just as well as those of any other of the great Eastern traditions."[11]

We cannot solve all the problems facing us today through mere technique and nuance, and we should seek wisdom where wisdom has always been nurtured—our religious traditions. We ought not to seek for human welfare in ideas that are intrinsically dehumanizing, or seek human happiness in a system that tries to quantify happiness. The intellectual underpinnings of modern economics are intrinsically monstrous, since they eliminate, by definition, any consideration of the spiritual center that makes human beings who they are. There is no possibility of a consequential engagement by people of faith with contemporary economic realities so long as they accept the general framework and assumptions governing economic and social life today. Otherwise, we will simply be choosing between the options presented to us and trying to make some adjustments to an inherently corrupt system, at the margins and with little lasting effect.

11. Schumacher, *Small Is Beautiful*, 55.

4

Linking Ethics and Economics for Integral Development: The Need for a New Economic Paradigm and the Three Dimensions of Islam

Waleed El-Ansary

Islam, as other religions, sees the end of the human state in the perfection of our spiritual possibilities. Development must therefore address our physical, intellectual, and spiritual needs, balancing all three in such a way that no single dimension is emphasized at the expense of others. E. F. Schumacher, the renowned development economist who wrote on Buddhist and Christian economics (and who was greatly influenced by contemporary Muslim thinkers, as we shall see), discussed this integral approach to development in terms of three objectives of work: first, to provide necessary and useful goods and services; second, to enable every one of us to use and thereby perfect our gifts like good stewards; and third, to do so in service to, and in cooperation with, others, so as to liberate ourselves from our inborn egocentricity.[1]

Of course, economists recognize the first objective of work. But some recognize the second and third objectives to various degrees, acknowledging that different types of work have different effects. For

1. E. F. Schumacher, *Good Work* (New York: Harper & Row, 1979) 3–4. Regarding striving for perfection, he cites the biblical injunction: "Be ye therefore perfect, even as your Father which is in heaven is perfect." He also cites: "Whichever gift each of you have received, use it in service to one another, like good stewards dispensing the grace of God in its varied forms."

example, Adam Smith acknowledged the ongoing development of individual gifts when he argued that an extremely high division of labor employing few of man's faculties could have serious social costs by reducing certain human capabilities:

> [T]he understandings of the greater part of men are necessarily formed by their ordinary employments. The man whose life is spent in performing a few simple operations . . . has no occasion to exert his understanding . . . He naturally loses, therefore, the habit of such exertion and generally becomes as stupid and ignorant as it is possible for a human creature to become . . . but in every improved and civilised society this is the state into which the labouring poor, that is, the great body of the people, must necessarily fall, unless government takes some pains to prevent it.[2]

Other figures such as David Ricardo and James Mill, the father of John Stuart Mill, opposed this view, denying the existence of such harmful effects, and asserting that all types of work were homogeneous in terms of human development.[3] And due to an anthropology that heavily emphasized psychological hedonism, these thinkers also denied the possibility of liberation from egocentricity, leaving only the first objective, the production of useful goods, for economics. More recently, some neoclassical economists have assumed that all types of work are homogeneous on one hand, while asserting the legitimacy of all three objectives on the other.[4] These various positions clearly have important implications for the link between ethics and economics and the extent to which economic realities can be governed by their own logic.

On one hand, Islamic law establishes a minimum division of labor to fulfill the first objective of work, asserting that some members of the community must practice *each* profession to fulfill the needs of society. The division of labor is thus analogous to other collective duties (*fard kifā'i*), such as building orphanages and hospitals. If no

2. Adam Smith, *An Inquiry into the Nature and Causes of the Wealth of Nations* (Oxford: Oxford University Press, Glasgow Edition, 1976) 781–82.

3. For an excellent survey of classical and neoclassical approaches to work in the history of economic thought, see Ugo Pagano, *Work and Welfare in Economic Theory* (Oxford: Blackwell, 1985).

4. Some economists adopt this position implicitly by acknowledging the validity of religious beliefs on one hand and employing the neoclassical approach to work as "forgone leisure" on the other. On the latter point, see for instance Ugo Pagano, *Work and Welfare in Economic Theory*, 111–15.

members in the community fulfill these needs, each member of the community is held spiritually accountable. The division of labor is thus conceived of as a duty, not simply a right.

On the other hand, the division of labor must leave ample room for human creativity according to the Islamic intellectual heritage, facilitating the second objective, "to use and thereby perfect our gifts like good stewards." A too-extreme division of labor creates an unsustainable trade-off between the various objectives of work, leading to lopsided development that fails to provide people with psychological and spiritual fulfillment, and that fails to keep nature clean and self-replenishing. Such trade-offs can only exist in the short or medium-term, not the long-term, from the Islamic point of view. "Equilibrium on the socioeconomic plane is impossible to realize without reaching that inner equilibrium which cannot be attained save through surrender to the One and living a life according to the dictum of Heaven."[5]

Accordingly, only when the division of labor is above the minimum level required for the community's material needs and below the maximum level for human development, or between a "floor" and "ceiling," are all three objectives of work and integral development possible from the Islamic perspective. The balance of this chapter is therefore structured according to the famous *Hadīth* of Gabriel that has been used as a model for discussing the essentials of Islam for over one thousand years. It divides Islam into three dimensions: submission or "right action" (*islām*), faith or "right understanding" (*īmān*), and virtue or "right intention" (*ihsān*), corresponding to the legal/ethical, intellectual, and esoteric dimensions of an integral tradition.[6] As we shall see, the first and second dimensions establish the minimum and maximum levels of the division of labor, respectively, and are closely connected to the first and second objectives of work, whereas the third dimension is closely connected to the third objective. These intercon-

5. Seyyed Hossein Nasr, "Review of Ethics and Economics: An Islamic Synthesis," Rev. of *Ethics and Economics: An Islamic Synthesis*, by Syed Haider Naqvi, *Hamdard Islamicus*, Summer 1982, 89.

6. For an in-depth treatment of each dimension in the *hadīth* and corresponding Islamic sciences, see Sachiko Murata and William C. Chittick, *The Vision of Islam* (New York: Paragon House, 1994). We have adapted some of the following arguments from our article "Islamic Environmental Economics and the Three Dimensions of Islam: 'A Common Word' on the Environment as Neighbor," in *Muslim and Christian Understanding: Theory and Application of "A Common Word,"* Waleed El-Ansary and David Linnan (eds.) (New York: Palgrave Macmillan, 2010) 143–57.

nections are not reducible to a one-to-one correspondence, however, because all three dimensions are interdependent and necessary to achieve socioeconomic equilibrium from the Islamic perspective.

Objectives of Islamic Law and the Hierarchy of Needs

Islamic economic law represents one of four major areas of Islamic positive law (*fiqh*), comprising approximately one-quarter of the body of law.[7] According to Islam, every aspect of life, including the economic, is sacred, because nothing is outside of the Absolute, and no aspect of life is profane, because everything is attached to God. What would appear to be the most mundane of activities has religious significance, integrating all of life around a sacred Center. This unity of purpose is reflected in a saying from the Prophet of Islam that an individual working to feed his or her family is performing "an act of worship as if [they] were praying."[8] Such a statement may be very difficult to understand in the modern West where a large domain of human life has been secularized, and it is not possible to find religious meaning in most actions. However, the Divine Law in Islam makes the effort to earn one's daily bread a religious act as obligatory as any other specifically religious duty, to be performed with an awareness that it is pleasing in the sight of God. In fact, the Divine Law gives religious meaning to all acts that are necessary for human life, but not those that are simply luxuries.[9]

This distinction between needs and wants is particularly important in analyzing the first objective of work, "to provide necessary and useful goods and services," as well as any trade-offs between the three objectives. As Caner Dagli's chapter in this volume suggests, the objectives of the Divine Law (*maqāsid al-Sharī'ah*) are used to interpret Islamic positive law (*fiqh*) in terms of the protection of one or more

7. Other major areas of Islamic law include social and political transactions (grouped under *fiqh al-mu'amalāt*) and religious rites (under *fiqh al-'ibadāt*). For a brief overview of Islamic law, particularly in relation to Islamic finance, see Caner Dagli's chapter in this volume. For a general discussion, see Hashim Kamali, *Introduction to Islamic Law* (Cambridge: Islamic Texts Society, 1999).

8. Seyyed Hossein Nasr, *Ideals and Realities of Islam* (San Francisco: Aquarian, 1994) 98.

9. Seyyed Hossein Nasr, *Traditional Islam in the Modern World* (London and New York: KPT, 1987) 38.

interests in a hierarchy of spiritual and other needs, or *masālih*. (The intimate connection between the "right" and the "good" in this view is indicated by the fact that *masālih* [sing. *maslahah*] is derived from the root word *salaha*, which means that something has become "pure, correct, and right."[10])

Jurists generally classify these *masālih* for human society into three levels.[11] The first level concerns fundamental necessities (*darūriyyāt*), such as the preservation of religion (*dīn*), life (*nafs*), posterity (*nasl*), intelligence (*'aql*), and property (*māl*). Disregarding any of these will result in disruption and chaos. Next are complementary needs (*hājiyyāt*), which, if unfulfilled, lead to real hardship and distress but not the ruin of the community. Finally, supplementary benefits (*tahsīniyyāt*) involve the beautification of life and refinement and perfection of ethics.[12] Based on this hierarchy, priority is given to higher-level needs if there is a conflict with lower-level needs or wants. Important juristic principles that flow from this hierarchy include: "The averting of harm from the poor takes priority over the averting of harm from the wealthy," "There shall be no damage and no infliction of damage," and "The averting of harm takes precedence over the acquisition of benefits."[13] Of course, such general principles need qualification depending on the particular context.

These principles have major implications for assessing production processes, establishing a minimum floor for the division of labor in order to provide necessary and useful goods and services on one hand, and the *possibility* of a maximum ceiling for integral human development on the other. This returns us to the question of trade-offs

10. For a detailed analysis of *maslahah* in the context of Islamic economics, see Waleed El-Ansary, "The Spiritual Significance of *Jihād* in the Islamic Approach to Markets and the Environment," (PhD diss., George Washington University, 2006), chs. 1–3.

11. For a full discussion of all three levels and the philosophy of Islamic law, see Imran Khan Nyazee, *Theories of Islamic Law: The Methodology of Ijtihād* (Islamabad: International Institute of Islamic Thought and Islamic Research Institute, 1994).

12. Of course, qualitative differences exist *within* each of the three levels as well as between them. The *hājiyyāt* and *tahsīniyyāt* may also simultaneously serve spiritual as well as other needs.

13. Othman Abd-ar-Rahman Llewellyn, "The Basis for a Discipline of Islamic Environmental Law," in *Islam and Ecology: A Bestowed Trust*, edited by Richard C. Foltz, Frederick M. Denny, and Azizan Baharuddin (Cambridge: Harvard University Press, 2003) 196–97.

between potentially competing Islamic objectives of work. Although Islamic law sets certain conditions for production, it neither prescribes particular processes nor contains all the necessary information to make all-things-considered ethical judgments (*ijtihād*) regarding a ceiling to the division of labor. This requires input from the Islamic intellectual and productive sciences, as we shall see in the next section.

But economists such as Paul Heyne argue that a high division of labor makes economics *amoral* rather than immoral:

> Most of us behave courteously toward others. But we do not, because we cannot, put their interests ahead of our own. In families and perhaps in small face-to-face communities, it is possible for individuals to sacrifice their interests to the interests of others. But in the large and unavoidably anonymous societies in which we produce for others and obtain from others most of what we need to live, our moral responsibility to others cannot be much more than to refrain from doing to them what we would consider unfair if done to us.[14]

> Most of those who complain about the "immorality" of the marketplace have misread the situation. Market interactions are not less moral or more selfish than nonmarket interactions. But they are generally more impersonal. And that cannot really be changed without giving up the benefits derived from specialization: the greater range of more attractive choices that constitute an increase in wealth.[15]

In short, impersonal exchange, rather than immorality, is simply the price of high specialization and productivity.

But such arguments quickly unravel the instant one asserts that an industrial economy has already surrendered the spiritual objectives of work. Heyne is correct to argue that impersonal exchange essentially delinks ethics and economics at an individual level, and that this does

14. Paul Heyne, *A Student's Guide to Economics* (Wilmington, DE: ISI, 2000) 24. He adds,

> It is a common mistake, one unfortunately made by many economists when they are not thinking carefully, to assert that a market-coordinated economy encourages or rewards or depends upon *selfish* behavior. Markets coordinate *self-interested* behavior, which certainly may be selfish behavior, but much more frequently is not. Even to speak of self-interested behavior risks misunderstanding. Perhaps we ought to say that markets coordinate the behavior of people who are *pursuing the projects that interest them* (25).

15. Ibid, 30.

not necessarily imply immorality. But to claim that delinking ethics and economics is amoral (not immoral) at the *collective* level presupposes that either industrial production processes can accomplish all three objectives of work, or that the second and third objectives are not relevant to begin with. Economists must therefore put forward corresponding philosophical arguments to contend that conventional economic theory and praxis based on impersonal production and exchange processes are amoral, not immoral.

Some economists may nevertheless object that ethics and economics are in principle separate, regardless of the division of labor, citing Lionel Robbins' popular definition of economics as "the science which studies human behavior as a relationship between ends and scarce means which have alternative uses."[16] According to this definition, economics analyzes the (optimal) allocation of means, given some set of ends, rather than the ends themselves, which are a subject for ethics. Yet, this way of separating ethics and economics in investigating an aspect of affairs in general (economizing) rather than a particular domain of affairs (exchange) presupposes that

> . . . means and ends can be *given* and defined independently of their relationship—with the latter and not the former being the only concern of the economist. In particular, it is implicitly assumed in this definition that the variables that the economist studies show a peculiar kind of stability: they are either means or ends, and they never switch their role by crossing into intermediate stages in which they are both means and ends at the same time.[17]

Accordingly, human activities are divided into two "sets":

> 1) leisure activities, which affect social welfare but do not affect production (i.e., they are only ends);
>
> 2) work activities, which affect production but do not affect social welfare (i.e., they are only means).[18]

16. Lionel Robbins, *An Essay on the Nature and Significance of Economic Science* (London: Macmillan, 1937), 16.

17. Ugo Pagano, *Work and Welfare in Economic Theory*, 172. For an extensive analysis of alternative definitions of economics, see for instance Lindley Fraser, *Economic Thought and Language: A Critique of Some Fundamental Economic Concepts* (London: A. & C. Black, 1947), ch. 2.

18. Ugo Pagano, *Work and Welfare in Economic Theory*, 172.

Human activities do not fit this rigid definition according to the three objectives of work, because work can be both a means *and* an end (even a form of prayer). Of course, work can be meaningless if its spiritual objectives have been surrendered. But one cannot then claim that economics is amoral based on this separation of means and ends, because it is precisely the reduction of work to a means rather than an end that is morally problematic. In short, separating means and ends can itself be immoral, and arguments for the amorality of economics based on the economizing definition must therefore make the same presuppositions regarding industrial production processes as Heyne's exchange-based view, even raising the possibility that the economizing definition cannot apply in the first place. The exchange definition is, in this sense, more inclusive than the economizing definition, since it does not necessarily separate ends and means.[19]

The Islamic Intellectual Heritage and the Spiritual Significance of Art and Work

Islamic law is necessary for any integral approach to Islamic development, but it is not sufficient. Islamic intellectual and productive sciences are needed as well, for the norms and principles of Islamic art, which are also derived from the Islamic revelation, govern the making of things in an Islamic economy.[20] From this point of view, what man makes, or man's art, should communicate a spiritual truth and presence analogous to nature, or God's art. "The ethical aspect of work in this case embraces also the aesthetic."[21] The production process is thus conceived as, and elevated to the level of, a spiritual discipline in which what one makes is an instrument of livelihood and devotion. "Every

19. For a detailed discussion of these definitions of economics from an Islamic point of view, see Waleed El-Ansary, "The Spiritual Significance of *Jihād* in the Islamic Approach to Markets and the Environment," ch. 1.

20. See for instance Titus Burckhardt, *Art of Islam: Language and Meaning* (Bloomington, IN: World Wisdom, 2009); Jean-Louis Michon, *Introduction to Traditional Islam: Foundations, Art and Spirituality* (Bloomington, IN: World Wisdom, 2008), part II; and Seyyed Hossein Nasr, *Islamic Art and Spirituality* (Albany, NY: State University of New York Press, 1987).

21. Seyyed Hossein Nasr, *Traditional Islam in the Modern World*, 43. He also notes that *husn*, the root of *ihsān* in Arabic, means both "beauty" and "goodness," whereas *qubh* means both "ugliness" and "evil."

man is a special kind of artist" in this perspective; the artist is not "a special kind of man."[22]

Indeed, the link between metaphysics and cosmology on one hand and the making of things on the other hand is to be found in Islamic doctrines regarding the correspondence between the cosmos and the soul.[23] Islamic metaphysics and sciences of nature therefore transform everything in the productive sciences from architecture and urban planning to the art of dress and personal living space. The same applies to the practical sciences dealing with everything from social organization to the treatment of the environment. The link between work, spiritual education, and sacred ambiance forged by the Islamic intellectual sciences is thus crucial to fulfilling the three objectives of work and highlighting the interconnections between religion, economics, and civilization from the Islamic point of view.

In fact, the application of these principles within communities of different sizes helps explain why the classical Arabic meaning of *al-iqtisād*, the modern Arabic word for economics, is related to properly managing the affairs of one's household (consistent with the original Latin meaning of *oeconomicus*, itself of Greek origin). The word is derived from the root *qasd*, which literally means "equilibrium" or the "state of being even, equally balanced, or evenly in between."[24] Both the classical and contemporary meanings of *al-iqtisād* are therefore related

22. According to the famous quote of Ananda Coomaraswamy, "The artist is not a special kind of man, but every man is a special kind of artist." See Rama Coomaraswamy (ed.), *The Essential Ananda K. Coomaraswamy* (Bloomington, IN: World Wisdom, 2004), 124.

23. See for instance Titus Burckhardt, *Alchemy: Science of the Cosmos, Science of the Soul* (Louisville, KY: Fons Vitae, 1997).

24. For this etymology and some of its economic implications, see for instance Baqir Al-Hasani, "The Concept of *Iqtisād*," in Baqir Al-Hasani and Abbas Mirakhor (eds.), *Essays on Iqtisād: The Islamic Approach to Economic Problems* (Silver Spring, MD: Nur Corporation, 1989) 24. Abbas Mirakhor and Baqir al-Hasani also note that:

> "In one of his supplications, Imam 'Ali ibn al-Husayn, Zayn-ul-'Abidin (As) said: 'Oh God, bless Muhammad and his family. And bless me with *iqtisād*, let me be of the people of righteousness, of the guides to virtue, and of the pious servants . . .' In another supplication, he (As) said: 'O *Allāh*, bless Muhammad and his family. Restrain me from extravagance and excess. Strengthen me with generosity and *iqtisād*. Teach me the (secret of) accurate measure. Graciously restrict me from wastefulness. Let my sustenance flow from honest sources. Direct my expenditure in matters of righteousness . . .'"(i)

to exchange in the sense that it can occur outside the market *within* the household as well as *between* households within the market. Thus, Nasīr al-Dīn Tūsī wrote a widely read classical treatise on philosophical ethics divided into three parts: Part I examined the management of one's self, simultaneously establishing a hierarchy of spiritual and other needs and refuting egoism; Part II examined the management of the household, or exchange within the smallest traditional community, based on the aforementioned spiritual principles; and Part III examined the division of labor in the larger community in the context of political philosophy and management of the state.[25]

From this point of view, competitive industrial markets necessarily and systematically de-skill work for "efficiency gains."[26] In this regard, Schumacher is highly critical of industrial production processes and the reductionist approach to man and nature upon which they are based:

> . . . industrialism as such, irrespective of its social form . . . stunt(s) personality . . . mainly by making most forms of work—manual and white-collared—utterly uninteresting and meaningless. Mechanical, artificial, divorced from nature, utilizing only the smallest part of man's potential capabilities, it sentences the great majority of workers to spending their working lives in a way which contains no worthy challenge, no stimulus to self-perfection, no chance of development, no element of Beauty, Truth, or Goodness. The basic aim of modern industrialism is not to make work satisfying but to raise productivity; its proudest achievement is labor saving, whereby labor is stamped with the mark of undesirability. But what is undesirable cannot confer dignity; so the working life of a laborer is a life without dignity. The result, not surprisingly, is a spirit of sullen irresponsibility which refuses to be mollified by higher wage awards but is often only stimulated by them.[27]

Rama Coomaraswamy likewise argues that, "Only when an individual's body and soul can participate in his work—something never possible in a factory—can the medieval principle that *laborare est orare* [to

25. Nasīr al-Dīn Tūsī, *The Nasirean Ethics* (London: Allen & Unwin, 1964).

26. Also see for example Ugo Pagano, *Work and Welfare in Economic Theory*, especially ch. 1. For a useful survey of neoclassical counter-arguments and the corresponding rebuttal, see Louis Putterman, *Division of Labor and Welfare: An Introduction to Economic Systems* (Oxford: Oxford University Press, 1990), ch. 4.

27. E. F. Schumacher, *Good Work*, 27–28.

labor is to pray] fully apply."[28] What we wish to emphasize here is that the economist cannot address these questions regarding the intertwining of means and ends and the relation between ethics and economics *qua* economist. Dialogue between economists and theologians is urgently needed; one must kick this debate up to the philosophical level where it belongs.[29]

Indeed, there is an increasingly urgent debate over whether the secular paradigm that has indirectly created industrial production processes can generate new technologies quickly enough to solve the accompanying crises related to the environment, depletion of non-renewable resources, and escapism. There is no question that the technology must change. The only question is whether the paradigm within which the technology is developed must also change. If the current paradigm does not correspond to the nature of reality, then attempting to find a technological "fix" *within* this paradigm can lead to a vicious cycle of technologies that backfire, ending in a catastrophe. This point can be illustrated with the true story of a man who, having a spot of arthritis in his finger joints, was given tablets by his doctor that resulted in a stomach ulcer.[30] A subsequent operation for the ulcer in conjunction with strong antibiotics interfered with his cardiovascular system to the extent that the doctor felt an obligation to carry out a couple of minor operations. Complications from this then required a heart specialist, and in the patient's weakened condition, he contracted a lung infection. The patient died within two weeks of the operations despite the continual care of three doctors and the hospital staff. Accordingly, those who hope for technological fixes within the current reductionist paradigm are arguably substituting a secular faith for a traditional one (this is quite literally true in light of the history of the notion of progress).[31]

28. Rama Coomaraswamy, "Traditional Economics and Liberation Theology," in *In Quest of the Sacred*, Seyyed Hossein Nasr (ed.) (Oakton: The Foundation for Traditional Studies, 1987). Roger Sworder also provides a remarkable overview of critiques of industrial production processes from this point of view in "The Desacralization of Work," in Harry Oldmeadow (ed.), *The Betrayal of Tradition: Essays on the Spiritual Crisis of Modernity* (Bloomington, IN: World Wisdom, 2005), 183–216.

29. See Paul Knitter, ch. 1 in this volume.

30. Ezra J. Mishan, *Economic Myths and the Mythology of Economics* (Atlantic Highlands, NJ: Humanities Press International, 1986) 174–75.

31. For example, the positivist cult of Saint-Simon, who "envisaged an assembly

The intellectual dimension of *īmān* is also necessary to respond to the erroneous claim that modern mainstream, or "neoclassical," economic theory accommodates any set of internally consistent values or tastes.[32] In fact, neoclassical theory routinely reduces needs to wants and values to tastes by assuming a single use value devoid of any qualitative differences, i.e., a purely quantitative aggregate. This negates the distinction between needs and wants in the three objectives of work. Indeed, "'need' is a non-word" in neoclassical economics.[33] As Nicholas Georgescu-Roegen points out, it "reduces all wants to one general abstract want called 'utility.' In line with this reduction, one need not say 'these people need more shoes': instead, 'these people need more utility' should suffice."[34] Yet, common sense suggests that "he who does not

---

of 'the twenty-one elect of humanity' to be called the Council of Newton," acquired "all the paraphernalia of the Church—hymns, altars, priests in their vestments, and its own calendar, with the months named after Archimedes, Gutenberg, Descartes, and other rationalist saints" [John Gray, *Al Qaeda and What It Means to Be Modern*, (New York: New Press, 2003), 30–34]. Fortunately, the discoveries of physics over the course of the last century have prompted a search for a non-reductionist philosophy of nature that resolves quantum paradox on one hand and integrates the findings of physics into higher orders of knowledge on the other. See Wolfgang Smith, *The Quantum Enigma: Finding the Hidden Key* (Ghent, New York: Sophia Perennis et Universalis, 2005). Remarkably, Muslim philosopher-scientists such as Ibn Sīnā (d. 1037 CE), 'Umar Khayyām (d. 1131 CE), and Nasīr al-Dīn Tūsī (d. 1274 CE) anticipated a solution to this centuries earlier based on an Islamic philosophy of nature. See Seyyed Hossein Nasr, *Islamic Philosophy from its Origin to the Present: Philosophy in the Land of Prophecy* (Albany, NY: State University of New York Press), 169–83.

32. As Shaun Hargreaves Heap asserts:

> The desires (of *Homo economicus*) can be "good," "bad," "selfish," "altruistic"—anything you like. The only proviso is that those desires generate a preference ordering; that is, the person can always say whether he or she prefers one bundle to another or is indifferent between them, and that the ordering satisfies the following conditions (reflexivity, completeness, consistency, and continuity).

Shaun Hargreaves Heap, Martin Hollis, Bruce Lyons, Robert Sugden, and Albert Weale, *The Theory of Choice: A Critical Guide* (Oxford: Blackwell, 1994) 5.

33. William Allen, *Midnight Economist: Broadcast Essays III* (Los Angeles: International Institute for Economic Research, 1982), 23, as quoted in Mark Lutz and Kenneth Lux, *Humanistic Economics: The New Challenge* (New York: Bootstrap, 1988), 21.

34. Nicholas Georgescu-Roegen, "Utility and Value in Economic Thought," in *Dictionary of the History of Ideas*, ed. Philip P. Weiner, vol. 4 (New York: Scribner, 1973) 458.

have enough to eat cannot satisfy his hunger by wearing more shirts."[35] The conventional neoclassical approach assuming a single use value, or mono-utility, therefore implicitly attributes "to man 'faculties which he actually does not possess,' unless we could drink paper, eat leisure, and wear steam engines."[36]

The three objectives of work require a *multiple* utility approach in which each type of value combines an essentially useful object with the corresponding capacity to use it. Accordingly, "a mattress, knife, so much bread . . . are things that have by design particular qualities in virtue of which they are useful for particular purposes and meet particular needs, and they are inherently different."[37] At stake is the difference between a whole consisting of *qualitatively* different parts and a quantitative aggregate reducible to the *sum* of its parts.[38] The solution from the Islamic point of view is therefore *multiple* use values on one hand and a spiritual end on the other hand. Such a combination may appear paradoxical, since multiple use values would seem to imply multiple ends, but it is possible given a *hierarchy* of levels of reality, as Islam and other religions assert.[39] (This approach also differs from a lexicographic function involving *multiple* ends related to different use values, since this compromises internal unity and consistency of preferences.[40]) A mono-utility approach should only be applied *within* a given need or want, not *between* needs and wants, e.g., choices involving tastes rather than values. The incorrect application of neoclassical

35. Ibid., 457.

36. Mark Lutz and Kenneth Lux, *Humanistic Economics: The New Challenge* (New York: Bootstrap, 1988) 324.

37. Scott Meikle, *Aristotle's Economic Thought* (Oxford: Oxford University Press, 1995) 16.

38. The fundamental opposition between Islamic values and a mono-utility function is based on the polarity between "unity" and "uniformity" according to the technical vocabulary of contemporary Islamic philosophy. See for instance René Guénon's classic, *The Reign of Quantity and the Signs of the Times* (Ghent, NY: Sophia Perennis, 2001), particularly chs. 1 and 7.

39. Some economists may assume that a single end is incompatible with multiple use values, but this is only true if they are all on a single level of reality. Islamic treatises on philosophical ethics explicitly establish the ontological basis of multiple use values in the context of spiritual needs. For a classic example, see the "First Discourse" of Nasīr al-Dīn Tūsī's *The Nasirean Ethics*, translated by G. M. Wickens (London: Allen & Unwin, 1964).

40. For a detailed discussion, see Waleed El-Ansary, "The Spiritual Significance of *Jihād* in the Islamic Approach to Markets and the Environment," chs. 1 and 4.

theory therefore compromises any limit to the division of labor based on a hierarchy of spiritual and other needs.

In this sense, the neoclassical economic claim to provide a neutral theory of choice can effectively smuggle a form of psychological hedonism into economic policy while suppressing the need for substantive philosophical debate over these policies.[41] This draws the wrong welfare and efficiency implications for ethical constraints in favor of libertarian policies. To help illustrate this point, imagine that we have the authority to prevent an evil act, and someone is trying to bribe us to permit it in violation of the third objective to work "in service to, and in cooperation with, others, so as to liberate ourselves from our inborn egocentricity." Although we may be unwilling to accept any amount of money to permit the evil act, we may also have a limit on how much we would be willing to pay to stop the same event that others have the authority to prevent. The two situations are different in the sense that the former is an "act" in which we participate to accomplish an evil, whereas the latter is an "event" others perform that perhaps we cannot afford to stop. The mono-utility approach, however, requires that willingness to accept (WTA) be equal to willingness to pay (WTP) (adjusting for "income effects" is not relevant in this context and cannot account for divergences in contingent value surveys in any case[42]). This excludes the ethical values of one who "cannot be bought at any price," although it can accommodate the egoistic preferences of a miser or a hedonist. In fact, if we constrain choice to alternatives that equate WTA and WTP, no alternative is more "right" or "wrong" than any other (in the absence of special assumptions that the cost of eliminating the damage happens to equal WTA, theoretically allowing one to compensate for the damage in permitting an otherwise evil act). Unconditionally equating WTA and WTP therefore implies arbitrary choice from a normative point of view and denies a rational basis for

41. The objection that a mono-utility function does not necessarily imply psychological hedonism, because mono-utility is compatible with psychological masochism hardly rebuts the current argument regarding the neoclassical exclusion of a hierarchy of spiritual and other needs. Moreover, one could define psychological masochism as a form of psychological hedonism.

42. See for instance Mark Sagoff, *Price, Principle, and the Environment* (New York: Cambridge University Press, 2004); and Thomas C. Brown and Robin Gregory, "Survey: Why the WTA-WTP Disparity Matters," *Ecological Economics* 28 (1999), 323–35.

ethics, with all this implies for the division of labor. As John Finnis points out, "there is no difference in principle between buying the right to inflict injury intentionally and buying the right not to take precautions which would eliminate an equivalent number and type of injuries accidentally."[43] In short, a mono-utility approach ultimately substitutes technical market solutions (appropriate for tastes) for substantive philosophical debate (appropriate for values).[44]

Paradoxically, the most important economist of the twentieth century from an Islamic point of view was not a Muslim, but a Christian, namely, E. F. Schumacher.[45] His personal library reveals the immense influence of contemporary Muslim philosophers, showing that he took far more extensive notes *within* the books of René Guénon (Shaykh 'Abdul Wāhid Yahyā), Frithjof Schuon (Shaykh 'Īsā Nūr al-Dīn), and Titus Burckhardt (Shaykh Ibrāhīm) than most other authors, including leading Catholic thinkers such as Jacques Maritain. Moreover, this Islamic influence appears in Schumacher's notes for a 24-lecture course he taught at London University in 1959 and 1960 titled "Crucial Problems for Modern Living."[46] His lecture notes are highly detailed with extensive commentary and references, including notes on the perennial philosophy and Burckhardt's *Alchemy: Science of the Cosmos, Science of the Soul* in German. However, Schumacher died a few weeks before a scheduled meeting on Islamic economics in Tehran with Seyyed Hossein Nasr. Despite such profound influences, this foundation of Schumacher's work is not widely known. But it is precisely this type of interfaith intellectual collaboration that points the way forward.

43. John Finnis, "Natural Law and Legal Reasoning," *Cleveland State Law Review* 38:1 (1990) 12.

44. For a detailed exposition of this, see Waleed El-Ansary, "The Spiritual Significance of *Jihād* in the Islamic Approach to Markets and the Environment," chs. 1–3.

45. For Schumacher's biography, see Barbara Wood, *Alias Papa: A Life of Fritz Schumacher* (London: Cape, 1984).

46. See Waleed El-Ansary, *Not by Bread Alone: E. F. Schumacher and Islamic Economics* (Bloomington, IN: World Wisdom, forthcoming 2012).

Islamic Mysticism and Socioeconomic Equilibrium

The connection between religious beliefs and economic praxis is particularly clear in Islamic mysticism, the dimension of *ihsān*, or "right intention," which has always been closely wed to the Islamic productive sciences. As Yusuf Ibish points out,

> The Damascene weavers, for example, preceded their work by hours if not days of spiritual preparation: prayers, meditation and contemplation were an integral part of the creative process, at the end of which beautiful design would emerge: outwardly inspiring designs reflecting inwardly the realised harmony with the source of all inspiration. One could say the same for the calligraphers: purity of soul and nobility of character were regarded as indispensable conditions for the accomplishment of this, the sacred art of Islam *par excellence*.[47]

Greed would be inconsistent with the spiritual vision necessary to execute the art that results from this inner work, for the necessary condition in this approach to the making of things is consciousness of one's contingency and complete dependence on the Absolute, or "spiritual poverty" (*faqr*).[48] (This explains the fact that, although traditional craftsmen generally had adequate incomes, they did not amass significant wealth.[49]) *Ihsān* is thus clearly connected to the third objective of work, "to liberate ourselves from our egocentricity," although this dimension also affects the distribution of useful and necessary goods

47. Yusuf Ibish, "Traditional Guilds in the Ottoman Empire: An Evaluation of their Spiritual Role and Social Function," *Islamic World Report* (1999), 6.

48. For the man who has acquired *faqr*, its immediate consequence is "detachment with regard to all manifested things, for the being knows from then on that these things, like himself, are nothing, and that they have no importance whatsoever compared with the absolute Reality." This detachment implies "indifference with regard to the fruits of action . . . which enables the being to escape from the unending chain of consequence which follows from this action" [Rene Guenon, "*Al-Faqr* or 'Spiritual Poverty,'" *Studies in Comparative Religion*, Winter Issue (1973)].

49. "It is indeed interesting to note that, among those who had become large landowners (in Egypt) in the 19th century—perhaps the most significant sign of affluence at the time—we have not found a single shaykh [master] of a guild" [Gabriel Baer, *Egyptian Guilds in Modern Times* (Jerusalem: Israel Oriental Society, 1964), 74]. In fact, if a particular shaykh or master craftsman did happen to amass wealth, it was frequently donated to an Islamic educational or religious institution such as a *madrasah* or a *zāwiyah*.

and services in the first objective, as well as the use and perfection of our gifts in the second objective.

In traditional Islamic society, the guilds (*asnāf*, sing. *sinf*) transmitted these doctrines and practices on the division of labor, production, and market exchange that allowed man to live in harmony with himself, his fellow men, and nature.[50] Of course, we are not suggesting a replication of Islamic economic history. But this history can serve as a source of inspiration for understanding how Islamic economic principles were previously applied and how we can apply them today. Prior to the late nineteenth century, the guild system comprised practically the entire gainfully occupied population in Islamic towns.[51] The guilds themselves highlighted their religious origins with important implications for interreligious cooperation:

> . . . practically every guild identified a particular Prophet or saint as being the patron of its particular craft, thus endowing the craft with something of the sacred character of the personage. . . . For example, the carpenters took as their patron the Prophet Noah: having built the ark, he stands forth as the exemplary master carpenter. The Virgin Mary was adopted by the weavers as their patroness: it was she who wove the swaddling clothes for the child Jesus. The Persian companion of the Prophet, Salman al-Farisi, having been the Prophet's barber, was the patron of the barbers' guild. . . . The Caliph 'Umar was reputed to have said that he would have adopted perfume-

50. Brian Keeble, *Art: For Whom and For What?* (Ipswich, UK: Golgonooza, 1998), 4.

51. Gabriel Baer, *Egyptian Guilds in Modern Times*. In the case of Cairo, Baer explains:

> Not only were all the artisans and merchants organized in guilds according to their crafts and trades, but also people engaged in transport (such as donkey-drivers) and in services (such as story-tellers and other types of entertainers). The guild system embraced owners of shops . . . , owners of workshops (*karhane*) such as starchworkers, makers of wax and candles, makers of dyes, bottles, carpets, etc.; owners of large stores (*mahzen*) such as salt-merchants, corn-merchants, iron-merchants, etc. There were also guilds of people who worked in their own houses, such as painters and those who worked with sulphur ("because of the bad smell"), as well as of salaried workers (e.g., in the building trade) and government employees, such as employees of the mint. . . . Both rich and poor had their guilds: corn-merchants as well as sewermen, saddlers as well as makers of rope (5–6).

Even the *ulamā'*, or religious scholars, had their own organization that was not dissimilar to the guilds (47).

> making as his profession: if he made no profit, he would at least have with him always a beautiful scent—hence his adoption by the perfumiers as their patron.[52]

In fact, the link between the prophets encouraged the existence of interfaith guilds as well as promoting harmony between different intrafaith guilds in traditional Islamic civilization.[53] There was thus a link between members within a particular guild as well as between guilds, for all had a common origin.

This approach to production and social organization entails a system of personal exchange in which coordination between members is highly manageable. In fact, traditional craftsmen accepted the duty to supply their goods at "just" and stable prices, since the division of labor was a duty, not just a right.[54] To avoid over- or under-supply of the market at a particular time, for example, a master craftsman could postpone or accelerate taking on extra apprentices while another qualified craftsman had insufficient or excess work, respectively. Equilibrium therefore occurred by design based on spiritual principles rather than as an unintended consequence of greed.

Motivational assumptions are thus clearly important in the traditional Islamic economic system, tightly linking ethics and economics. Even if guilds became corrupt in places such as Western Europe after the Renaissance, as Adam Smith asserts, this does not imply that *all* guilds were necessarily corrupt in *all* places at *all* times. In the case of Islamic economic history, it would be incorrect to assume that greed was automatically the motivating cause of traditional production and exchange, and that the hidden purpose of the guilds was simply to serve the interests of its members by eliminating competition and increasing prices to the consuming public.

52. Yusuf Ibish, "Traditional Guilds in the Ottoman Empire: An Evaluation of their Spiritual Role and Social Function," *Islamic World Report* (1999), 6–7. He adds that "material work and holy significance were in this manner never allowed to diverge, the sacred was manifested outwardly in the work, and the work was ennobled by the inward presence of the sacred."

53. See for instance Bernard Lewis, "The Islamic Guilds," *Economic History Review* (1937), 20–37.

54. See for instance volumes 17 to 19 on prices (*al-as'ar*; sing. *si'r*) in Ali Goma'a (ed.), *Revealing the Islamic Economic Heritage* [*Takshīf al-Turāth al-Islāmī al-Iqtisādī*] (Cairo: International Institute of Islamic Thought, 1997).

Since the nineteenth century, the guild system in the Islamic world has been devastated by the advent of colonialism and by attempts to imitate Western industrialization, breaking the connection between work and spiritual education.[55] Nevertheless, some guilds survive to this day from Fez to Benares, and it is vital to carefully examine how and why they survive to help inform an integral Islamic development strategy.[56]

Accordingly, the first step in an integral Islamic development program must be recovering the Islamic intellectual heritage, shaping education accordingly, and bringing forth Islamic science and technology.[57] Education is indeed the "greatest resource," for it shapes supply and demand according to Islamic principles, so to speak. On the one hand, the contemporary Islamic educational system must integrate the findings of modern physics into higher orders of knowledge based on the traditional sciences of nature, and on the other hand, contemporary Islamic productive sciences must integrate *neutral* technologies into the making of things based on traditional metaphysical principles. We conclude with Titus Burckhardt's masterful and penetrating summation of the current situation of traditional craftsmen still left in the Islamic world:

> I knew a comb-maker who worked in the street of his guild, the *mshshātin*. He was called 'Abd al-Azīz (the 'slave of the Almighty') and always wore a black *jellaba*—the loose, hooded garment with sleeves—and a white turban with a *lithām*, the face veil, which surrounded his somewhat severe features. He obtained the horn for his combs from ox skulls, which he bought from butchers. He dried the horned skulls at a rented

55. "The conquered imitate the conquerors," as Ibn Khaldun suggested, creating an educational "domino effect." Ibish also points out:

> In many instances, the colonialists were looking for raw materials and markets and hence their first victims were the local manufacturers. The reorganization of local government under colonial rule and the introduction of new systems of taxation weakened the powers of the traditional authorities and hit the crafts severely. . . . New, oppressive taxes and duties caused many trades to be taken over by Europeans, because they were exempted from taxes by the capitulations (124).

56. Seyyed Hossein Nasr, *Heart of Islam*, 180.

57. As Schumacher argues, the modern world "has been shaped by its metaphysics, which has shaped its education, which in turn has brought forth its science and technology" (*Small Is Beautiful*, 120).

place, removed the horns, opened them lengthwise, and straightened them over a fire, a procedure that had to be done with the greatest care, lest they should break. From this raw material he cut combs and turned boxes for antimony (used as an eye decoration) on a simple lathe; this he did by manipulating, with his left hand, a bow which, wrapped round a spindle, caused the apparatus to rotate. In his right hand he held the knife, and with his foot he pushed against the counterweight. As he worked he would sing Qur'ānic sūrahs in a humming tone.

I learned that, as a result of an eye disease which is common in Africa, he was already half blind, and that, in view of long practice, he was able to 'feel' his work, rather than see it. One day he complained to me that the importation of plastic combs was diminishing his business: 'It is not only a pity that to-day, solely on account of price, poor quality combs from a factory are being preferred to much more durable horn combs,' he said; 'it is also senseless that people should stand by a machine and mindlessly repeat the same movement, while an old craft like mine falls into oblivion. My work may seem crude to you; but it harbours a subtle meaning which cannot be explained in words. I myself acquired it only after many long years, and even if I wanted to, I could not automatically pass it on to my son, if he himself did not wish to acquire it—and I think he would rather take up another occupation. This craft can be traced back from apprentice to master until one reaches our Lord Seth, the son of Adam. It was he who first taught it to men, and what a Prophet brings—for Seth was a Prophet—must clearly have a special purpose, both outwardly and inwardly. I gradually came to understand that there is nothing fortuitous about this craft, that each movement and each procedure is the bearer of an element of wisdom. But not everyone can understand this. But even if one does not know this, it is still stupid and reprehensible to rob men of the inheritance of Prophets, and to put them in front of a machine where, day in and day out, they must perform a meaningless task.'[58]

58. Titus Burckhardt, *Fez: City of Islam*, trans. William Stoddard, as cited in Ibish, 124–25.

Conclusion

Islamic intellectual and productive sciences suggest a limit to the division of labor for integral development, whereas Islamic law suggests a minimum division of labor to fulfill the material needs of the community. This combination links ethics to economics in both production and exchange, the breaking of which has dire consequences for both man and nature from the Islamic point of view. Economic realities cannot therefore be governed by their own logic and systems.

Accordingly, the opposing claim that ethics is irrelevant to economics only applies to an economic system that has already surrendered the spiritual objectives of work through an excessive division of labor based on a reductionist view of man and nature. It does not apply to choices within an Islamic (or other religiously defined) economic system based on traditional metaphysics or to choices between systems *a fortiori*. Thus, there are no economic laws separate from spiritual ones, and economics cannot be a separate science.

Linking ethics and economics therefore requires far more than Islamic law. To employ the categories of Islamic thought, knowledge, or *al-ʿilm*, must accompany action, or *al-ʿamal*. In short, integral development requires the legal/ethical, intellectual, and esoteric dimensions of an integral tradition. The *Hadīth* of Gabriel thus provides the basis for a new paradigm in economic theory and practice.

5

The Poverty of Economic Development

David R. Loy

The world's most primitive people have few possessions, *but they are not poor.* Poverty is not a certain small amount of goods, nor is it just a relation between means and ends; above all it is a relation between people. Poverty is a social status. As such it is the invention of civilization . . . It was not until culture reached the height of its material achievements that it erected a shrine to the unattainable: *Infinite Needs.*

—Marshall Sahlins[1]

In time-honored academic fashion, let me begin by problematizing the topic. *Development* is a concept that usually has positive connotations: e.g., "childhood development." Add the adjective "economic," however, and the implications become more ambivalent and controversial. *Economic development* can mean providing rural villages with access to clean water and sufficient food, but it can also mean a dam flooding large valleys in order to provide electricity that does not benefit villagers who are displaced without anywhere else to go. Even the conservative Supreme Court of India has observed that for millions of Indians, development has become "a dreadful and hated word."[2] In the "developed world"—I prefer the term "economized societies," for

1. Marshall Sahlins, *Stone Age Economics* (Hawthorne, NY: Aldine de Gruyter, 1972), 37, 39 (italics original).

2. Quoted by Pankaj Mishra in *The Guardian Weekly*, Aug. 6, 2010, 19.

reasons that will become evident—a *land developer* can be someone who drains a pestilential swamp, or who cuts down a grove of old-growth trees to build a parking lot for yet another shopping mall. This ambiguity is at the heart of religious attempts to evaluate "economic development."[3]

Buddhist emphases on interdependence and mutual causality challenge assumptions that distinguish economic transactions from other social interactions. Just as the modern notion of a private "religious sphere" of life distinct from other aspects of society has become questionable, so we should be cautious about supposing the "economic sphere" to be separable from the other dimensions of human life. From a Buddhist perspective, any evaluation of economic development should consider the linkages to all aspects of our existence.

For example, one can question the division between economic values and religious ones, a duality that is largely a legacy of the Protestant Reformation. Economics as an academic discipline aspires to be a social science, and economists emphasize its value-neutrality. But if we adopt a functionalist definition of "religion"—as what grounds us by teaching us what this world really is, and what our role in that world is—then our present economic system can also be understood as a global or globalizing religion, because it serves a religious function for us. From that perspective, economics is less a science than the theology of that missionary religion, whose God, otherwise known as the Market, offers a kind of alternative "salvation" in the form of ever-increasing production and consumption. This amounts to a world-view and set of values whose religious role we overlook only because we have learned to view them as secular.[4]

3. Buddhism can also be problematized: which one? Buddhism is a missionary "religion" (another problematized term!) that has taken very different forms in different cultures, which means that broad generalizations about Buddhism are at least as hazardous as generalities about the Abrahamic traditions. This paper will say little about actual economic practices in Asian Buddhist societies or modern developments in socially engaged Buddhism, which are addressed in two other essays included in this volume, by Donald Swearer and Christopher Ives. Instead, it offers a provocative perspective based mostly on basic teachings in the earliest texts we have, the Pali Canon, along with an eclectic appropriation of key Buddhist concepts such as *dukkha* (suffering in the broadest sense, including anxiety and dis-ease), *anicca* (impermanence), and *anatta* (not-self, insubstantiality).

4. Elsewhere I have argued that consumer capitalism is the most successful missionary religion that the world has ever known. See Loy, "The Religion of the Market," *Journal of the American Academy of Religion* 65 (1997) 275–90, also cited in

This implies that an interreligious discussion of economic development should not only consider the economic implications of religious teachings but also examine the *religious* role of consumerism and productionism, including the ways they have been institutionalized into globalizing capitalism. When perceiving "poor" people in "undeveloped" societies as miserable, are we projecting how we—addicted to consumerism—would experience their lives? This is not to minimize the importance of relieving destitution whenever and wherever it occurs, but one needs to be sensitive to the larger context to insure that economic efforts to reduce poverty do not also aggravate other kinds of *dukkha* (ill-being or suffering in the broadest sense).

Today, moreover, such discussions must also be related to other urgent issues such as ecological degradation, overpopulation, and their consequences for our values and happiness projects. Are attitudes towards economic development compatible with the implications of the eco-crisis, or do they assume models of perpetual growth and unlimited resources that are not sustainable? The best way to begin, however, is by unpacking the complex attitude of the Buddhist tradition(s) toward poverty.

Poverty

Although economic development is usually understood to be about more "developed" ("economized") societies "helping" relatively "undeveloped" (or "underdeveloped") ones, religious perspectives can help us raise awkward questions about this process, for example about the *monetarization* that this inevitably involves. The shift away from material and social self-sufficiency (or insufficiency) requires increasing reliance on monetary resources and monetary values—and therefore promotes the tendency for money to become the measure of all things.

As this suggests, religious traditions are often ambivalent about poverty. Poverty is bad because deprivation involves suffering. Yet the salvation religions offer is not material wealth, and certain types of poverty can even be beneficial in reducing distractions that otherwise interfere with living a religious life or following a spiritual path.

Perhaps this tension was less pronounced in premodern cultures, where (what we now consider) poverty was common, in fact the norm,

---

Paul Knitter's essay in this volume.

and options were more limited. Modern economized societies offer the possibility of a more secular and materialistic salvation from many of life's ills. Whether or not this deliverance actually delivers us, and from what, we now have the economic and technological resources to liberate all human beings from extreme deprivation, if we care to do so. Shouldn't that be a collective priority? But can this be done in ways that remain sensitive to other religious hesitations about wealth, ways that do not convert whole societies to consumerism and "moneytheism"?

Buddhism offers a particularly clear example of this tension. Buddhist societies make a strong distinction between the laity and a monastic *sangha* composed of mendicants (today mostly male). *Bhikkhu* monks, who engage in no productive work, are expected to live very simply with few personal possessions—mainly three robes and an almsbowl. At the same time, however, the Buddhist tradition does not encourage laypeople to be poor; on the contrary, some economic surplus is needed to support the *sangha*.

There are obvious parallels with certain forms of Christian monasticism. In some other ways, however, Buddhism provides a revealing contrast to the Abrahamic religions (Judaism, Christianity, Islam). Consider, for example, whether we have a "moral imperative" to relieve extreme poverty. In the Abrahamic faiths morality is the central theme and obligation, for it is the main way that divinity and humanity communicate; God instructs us about how to live and what will happen to us if we do not live that way. This world is the place where good and evil contend with each other, both within ourselves and collectively in history. For Buddhism, however, morality plays a more subordinate role on the path that leads to liberation, since the primary issue is cognitive: not good will versus bad will, but ignorance versus wisdom. The fundamental ignorance that causes us to suffer is unawareness of the "emptiness" of the self, and the solution is realizing something about ourselves and our relationship with the world.

This difference has consequences for how we respond to poverty. The Abrahamic response is part of its larger concern with justice, including social justice—concepts largely lacking in traditional Buddhism. For Buddhism, poverty is bad because it causes *dukkha* (suffering), but *dukkha* is also caused by delusion, including our ways of thinking about poverty and wealth. Any understanding of the Buddhist perspective on poverty must be sensitive to both dimensions.

Otherwise, the *dukkha* of poverty might be alleviated in ways that augment other types of *dukkha*.

According to the traditional myth, Shakyamuni the Buddha (literally, "the awakened one") renounced a life of wealth and pleasure for the difficult path of a mendicant forest dweller, yet asceticism did not lead to the enlightenment he sought. He eventually discovered a "middle way" that emphasizes calming and understanding the mind. Contrary to the popular stereotype of Buddhism as world-denying, its goal does not necessarily involve "transcending" this world. Buddhist philosophers such as Nagarjuna have emphasized that the liberation the Buddha experienced under the bodhi tree is better understood as *awakening* to the true nature of this world, including one's own true nature.

This awakening has important implications for how one relates to wealth and poverty. According to Sizemore and Swearer, "a non-attached orientation toward life does not require a flat renunciation of all material possessions. Rather, it specifies an attitude to be cultivated and expressed in whatever material condition one finds oneself. To be non-attached is to possess and use material things but not to be possessed or used by them."[5] The main issue is not wealth or the lack of it, but how we respond to our situation, for "the greatest wealth is contentment" (*santutthi paramam dhanam*).[6] The Buddha cautioned his followers against a life devoted to acquiring wealth: "Few are those people in the world who, when they obtain superior possessions, do not become intoxicated and negligent, yield to greed for sensual pleasures, and mistreat other beings."[7] He praised those who renounce attachment to material things in favor of a life focused on the path of liberation, by joining the monastic *sangha*.

A world in which envy (Pali, *issa*) and miserliness (*macchariya*) are prevalent is not one in which poverty has been eliminated. This is implied by the second noble (or "ennobling") truth of the Buddha: the cause of *dukkha* is *tanha*, "craving." When we develop a strong ac-

5. Russell F. Sizemore and Donald K. Swearer, eds., *Ethics, Wealth and Salvation: A Study in Buddhist Social Ethics* (Columbia: University of South Carolina Press, 1990) 2.

6. *Dhammapada* verse 204.

7. Samyutta Nikaya, *Kosalasamyutta Sutta*, 167–68, in Bhikkhu Bodhi, trans., *The Connected Discourses of the Buddha* (Boston: Wisdom, 2000) 169.

quisitive drive for something, it becomes a cause of suffering, involving much anxiety but little satisfaction.

Obviously, this has important implications for how we understand modernization and economic growth. Nevertheless, it does not mean that wealth in itself is something that should be avoided, or that could be avoided, if a society is going to be able to support monastics who do not contribute economically. As a worldview and spiritual path that advocates eliminating *dukkha,* Buddhism cannot promote poverty (Pali, *daliddiya*) that is a source of *dukkha. Daliddiya* means: lacking the basic requirements for leading a decent life free from hunger, exposure and disease. Buddhism recognizes the importance of such material needs even for those who aspire to its spiritual goal, and in fact the basic needs of a monastic provide a useful minimal standard for all human beings. The four requisites of a Buddhist monk or nun are enough food to alleviate hunger and maintain health, enough clothing to be socially decent and to protect the body, enough shelter for serious engagement with cultivating the mind, and basic health care to cure and prevent physical illness.[8] People who choose to renounce worldly possessions and pleasures in favor of a life with only these basic requisites belong to the community of "noble ones" (*ariyapuggala*).

Daliddiya makes it more difficult to follow the Buddhist path. According to one story in the Pali Canon, the Buddha could see (with his special powers) that a poor man in the village of Alavi was ready to realize the first level of enlightenment, so he traveled there to give a discourse. That very morning, however, the man lost his ox, and was hunting for it while others were eating. When he finally returned with the ox, the Buddha told the donors to offer food to him as well, and waited for him to eat. Only afterwards did the Buddha expound the Dharma, whereupon the man was indeed awakened. The monks who accompanied the Buddha were surprised that he had waited until the man was fed, and on the return he responded: "Bhikkhus! You do not understand that I came all this way because I knew that he was in a fitting condition to take in the Dharma. If he were feeling very hungry, the pangs of hunger might have prevented him from taking in the Dharma fully. That man had been out looking for his ox the whole

8. For example, see the *Sabbasava Sutta,* in *Majjhima Nikaya* I, 10; also *Anguttara Nikaya* III, 387.

morning, and was very tired and also very hungry. After all, there is no ailment which is so difficult to bear as hunger."[9]

The five basic precepts commonly accepted by all Buddhists—to avoid harming living beings, taking what is not given, improper sexual behavior, false speech, and intoxicants that encourage heedlessness—do not mention abstaining from riches or property, although the precepts do have implications for how one pursues wealth and uses it. Wealth properly acquired is appreciated as a sign of virtue, and, used properly, can be a boon for everyone, because it creates opportunities to benefit people and (often emphasized just as much) to cultivate non-attachment by developing generosity.

On another occasion the Buddha was told about a miser who had recently died without an heir to his fortune. The Buddha contrasted his unused resources with those of someone wiser who uses his riches to support his family, servants, employees and (not to be left out) religious mendicants. The miser's wealth "is like a forest pool, clear, cool and fresh, with good approaches and shady setting, but located in a forest of ogres. No one can drink, bathe in or make use of that water." The wise man's wealth "is like a forest pool not far from a village or town, with cool, clear, fresh water, good approaches and shady setting. People can freely drink of that water, carry it away, bathe in it, or use it as they please."[10]

According to another of the Buddha's metaphors, some people are completely blind because they have neither the vision to improve their material circumstances, nor the vision to lead a morally elevated life. Others can see only with one eye because, although they have the vision to improve their material conditions, they do not have the vision to live morally; of course, the best class of people have the vision to improve both.

To sum up, according to the Pali Canon it is blameworthy to gain wealth improperly, to become attached to it and not to use it for the well-being of everyone, to squander it or use it to cause suffering to others. "Wealth destroys the foolish, though not those who search for

9. This story is from the *Annataraupasakavatthu* in the *Sukhavagga* of the *Dhammapadatthakatha* Vol. III 261f, a commentary on the *Dhammapada* cited in http://departments.colgate.edu/greatreligions/pages/buddhanet/genbuddhism/dv/poverty.txt.

10. *Kosalasamyutta Sutta* I.89–91.

the goal."[11] Wealth can be beneficial, and the destitution that is *dalid-diya* is certainly *dukkha*, but when evaluating the quality of one's life it is not enough to measure the material conditions. That brings us back to the ambiguity of economic development.

The *Lack* of Economic Development

What do the above attitudes imply about economic development? Is it a requirement for social justice? Justice is not a Buddhist concept, except in the sense that karma implies that moral reciprocity is built into the way the cosmos functions. If alleviating poverty is a moral imperative, who or what requires us to do so? No one is required to take the five precepts; they are vows one makes to oneself, to train oneself in these ways, because doing so will improve one's karma and progress on the path and therefore reduce one's *dukkha*. How does this individual self-project intersect with a commitment to reduce the poverty-*dukkha* of others?

This brings us back to the contrast between the Abrahamic *moral* worldview and the more *cognitive* Buddhist worldview. Although morality is certainly important in Buddhism, the primary issue is not a struggle between good and evil but progress from ignorance to insight. What seems most distinctive about the Buddhist perspective is its emphasis on the relationship between *dukkha*, suffering, and *anatta*, the lack of self: the sense of being a self that is separate from the world one is "in" is illusory—in fact, it is our most dangerous delusion.

In contemporary terms, the Buddhist claim is that the self is a psychosocial construct: *psychological* because a product of mental conditioning, and *social* because a self develops in relation to other constructed selves. This construct is composed of mostly habitual ways of perceiving, feeling, thinking, acting, reacting, remembering, intending, and so forth. Buddhism teaches that there is always something uncomfortable about this construct, because there is *nothing* (better, "*no-thing*") substantial within or "behind" it. This means that one's constructed sense of self is ungrounded, and therefore normally haunted by a fundamental sense of insecurity and unreality—which is *dukkha*.

11. *Dhammapada* verse 355.

This has implications for how we think about poverty (and wealth, its conceptual twin) and helps us understand what motivates Buddhists to address others' poverty, a motivation that merits attention because it does not derive from considerations of justice or even moral imperatives.

The lack of a separate (*svabhava*, "self-existing") self causes anxiety that we understand as "something is wrong with me" or "there is something missing in my life." Thus the sense of self is shadowed by a sense of *lack*. What is lacking? How I understand that lack will depend upon my personality and the society in which I live. The amorphous sense that something is wrong with me needs to be given more specific form for me to be able to do something about it. Traditional Christianity provided an answer—I am *sinful*—and provided religious ways for me to atone for my sins (confession, penance, etc.). Modern secular societies do not recognize the concept of sin, so our sense of lack is usually understood as one or another secular problem: in the U.S. today, for example, I am likely to understand my lack as not having enough money, regardless of how much I may already have.

According to this way of understanding Buddhism, preoccupation with money can often be traced back to the basic discomfort of the self, due to the fact that it is an ungrounded and ungroundable construct. But if desire for wealth is in fact a symptom of something else—an attempt to fill up my sense of lack—then I can never have enough money (or possessions, or fame, or sexual conquests, or power) because none of them can resolve a sense of lack that ultimately derives from my delusion of being a separate self.

The Greek myth of Midas and his golden touch provides the classic metaphor for what happens when we become unable to distinguish between needs and wants, because what we seek symbolizes something else. Today that simple story is even more relevant than it was in ancient Greece, because the world we live in is so much more monetarized—in fact, I suspect there is at least a bit of Midas in all of us. Living in an "economized" world that emphasizes instant convertibility tends to de-emphasize our senses, in favor of the green pieces of paper in our wallets, or the magical numbers that grow and shrink in our bank accounts. Instead of appreciating fully the sensuous qualities of a glass of wine, we are conditioned to be more aware of how much it cost and what that implies about us as sophisticated wine drinkers.

This points to a "religious" function of money for us. Beyond its usefulness as a medium of exchange, a storehouse of value and capital for investment, money tends to become a society's most important "reality symbol" as it becomes more monetarized. In economized societies money is generally believed to be the best way to secure oneself, to solidify one's identity, to cope with the gnawing intuition that I do not really exist as a separate self. We used to visit temples and churches to ground ourselves in a relationship with God or gods. Now we invest in "securities" and "trust funds" to ground ourselves economically, yet there is a karmic rebound. The more we value money, the more we find it used—and the more we use it—to evaluate ourselves. We end up being manipulated by the symbol we take so seriously. In this sense, the problem is not that we are too materialistic but that we are not materialistic enough. The more we become preoccupied with money as a socially constructed symbol system, the more we live symbolically: infatuated less with the things that money can buy than with the status they confer on our always-insecure selves—not so much with the comfort and power of an expensive car as with what owning a Mercedes-Benz says about *me*. "I'm the kind of guy who drives a Mercedes."

In terms of economic development, the issue is whether the globalization of corporate capitalism adds a collective dimension to this wealth/poverty preoccupation. Should the world's *poverty problem* (underdevelopment) be understood separately from its *wealth problem* (overdevelopment)? Is a "war on poverty" the other side of our preoccupation with wealth-creation? Is that how we rationalize a way of life obsessed with economic growth, no matter what its other costs? People who are "undeveloped" must be miserable because that is how we (preoccupied with consumerism) would experience their lives. Perhaps global poverty is conceptually necessary if the rest of the world is to be commodified and monetarized. Otherwise one cannot rationalize the profound social reorientation (including monetarization) that is required. Traditional cultures must be redefined as obstacles to be overcome, and local elites must become dissatisfied with them, in order to create a consumerist lifestyle.

I am not trivializing the situation for those whose destitution needs to be alleviated as soon as possible. The larger issue is whether one of the causes of poverty today is the delusions of the wealthy—delusions with very concrete effects on the well-being of many people, including the rich themselves. Perhaps, to compensate for potential bias, we should not focus only on the poverty side of the problem, but should be as concerned about the other side: the personal, social, and ecological costs of our collective obsession with wealth-creation and perpetual economic growth. A Buddhist perspective emphasizes the importance of seeing through such dualisms if efforts to help impoverished people—and deluded wealthy people—are actually to be successful.

What motivates Buddhist efforts to relieve poverty, if not a concern for social justice or a Kantian-type moral imperative? Destitution is *dukkha*, but why should we be so concerned about someone else's *dukkha*? That brings us back to the Buddhist understanding of the self and its *dukkha*.

In the Pali Canon, Shakyamuni, the historical Buddha, does not say much about the nature of *nirvana* except that it is the end of *dukkha*, craving, and delusion. It is apparent, however, that Buddhist "awakening" involves realizing something about the constructedness of the self. Usually the self's "emptiness"—the nothingness (or "no-thing-ness") at our core—is so uncomfortable that one tries to elude it, by identifying with something that seems to offer stability and security.

What happens, then, when we do not run away from that distressed and destabilizing void at our core? Meditation is an important part of the Buddhist path because meditation involves "letting go" of the physical and mental tendencies—the habitual ways of thinking, feeling, acting, reacting, remembering, and intending—that constitute the sense of self. Inasmuch as these habits *are* the self, letting go of them—observing them without identifying with them—is letting go of one's sense of self, or "forgetting the self," as Dogen, the thirteenth-century Japanese Zen master, famously put it: "To study the buddha is to study the self. To study the self is to forget the self. To forget the self is to be actualized by myriad things [of the world]. When actualized by myriad things, your body and mind as well as the bodies and minds of others drop away."[12] We are enlightened by the myriad things of this world when we realize our nonduality with them. Awakening is realizing that the sense of separation between me "inside" and the

12. This is the beginning of *Genjo-koan*, the first fascicle of Dogen's *Shobogenzo*, trans. by Dan Welch and Kazuaki Tanahashi in *Moon in a Dewdrop: Writings of Zen Master Dogen*, ed. Kazuaki Tanahashi (San Francisco: North Point, 1985) 70.

objective world "outside" is the basic ignorance at the root of our most troublesome *dukkha*. This does not involve getting rid of the self, because there never has been a separate self, but simply "awakening" to what has always been the case.

This clarifies the Buddhist motivation for relieving poverty. Waking up to my nonduality with the world is realizing my responsibility for it. I naturally want to take care of "other" beings for the same reason that I naturally want to take care of my own leg. My own well-being cannot be pursued indifferent to their well-being. The Buddhist tradition emphasizes compassion as much as wisdom because compassion is how one's awakening manifests in daily life.

According to a traditional (although misleading) stereotype, a monastic in the Theravada tradition of Buddhism aspires to become an *arhat*: someone who dwells in perfect serenity because he or she has put an end to craving. For Mahayana Buddhism, however, the spiritual goal is to become a *bodhisattva* selflessly devoted to helping all living beings awaken to their true nature. This is usually understood as a personal sacrifice, but I believe that this mythological way of understanding the bodhisattva path misses the main point: the bodhisattva has realized that he (or she) cannot be fully enlightened until everyone is. Any sense that my own *dukkha* can be resolved without also addressing the *dukkha* of others is a delusion, indicating that one's enlightenment is incomplete.

Needless to say, this describes the ideal, not the way most Buddhists actually live, in Asia or anywhere else. But this principle remains essential for understanding the Buddhist perspective on economic development.

What, if anything, does this imply about priorities? Should our main concern be the most extreme poverty, no matter where it may be, or should we focus instead on the less extreme poverty within (or near) our own communities? Although I am not aware of any Buddhist text that addresses this issue directly, one could draw on elements within the tradition to argue for either side. The bodhisattva vows to save all living beings, anywhere, suggest a universalism that would want to alleviate the worst *daliddiya*. By being so universal, however, such a concern also becomes abstract, tending to draw attention away from our immediate situation, from those we personally (and nondually) encounter in our daily lives. Perhaps the Mahayana principle of *upaya kausalya* (skill-in-means) implies that no generally applicable, definitive answer can be given to this dilemma, for we need to be sensitive to each individual situation and decide on a case-by-case basis. The same applies to issues of short-term pain for the sake of long-term gain—a favorite strategy of the World Bank and IMF—with the caveat that those with the most to gain should not be inflicting pain on those who have little to gain.

The Role of Institutions

Who or what has the greatest responsibility for alleviating poverty? The Pali Buddhist text that has the most to say about this issue is the *Lion's Roar on the Turning of the Wheel* (*Cakkavatti-Sihanada Sutta*).[13] It offers a myth that implies a causal relationship between material destitution and social deterioration, and attributes responsibility for that relationship to the ruler—in contemporary terms, I would argue, to the state.

The Buddha tells the story of a monarch in the distant past who at first followed the advice of his sage: "Let no crime prevail in your kingdom, and to those who are in need, give property." Later, however, he began to rule according to his own ideas and did not give property to the needy, and poverty became widespread. One man "took what was not given" and was arrested; when the king asked him why, the man said he had nothing to live on. So the king gave him some property, saying that it would be enough to carry on a business and support his family.

Exactly the same thing happened to another poor man who stole. When other people heard about this they too decided to steal so they would be treated in a similar way. Then the king realized that if he continued to give property to such men, theft would continue to increase. So he decided to get tough on the next thief: "I had better make an end of him, finish him off once and for all, and cut his head off." And he did. At this point in the story, we might expect a moralistic parable about the importance of deterring crime, but it goes on to make a very different point:

13. *Digha Nikaya* iii 65 ff, in Maurice Walshe, trans., *The Long Discourses of the Buddha* (Boston: Wisdom, 1995) 396–405.

> Hearing about this, people thought: "Now let us get sharp swords made for us, and then we can take from anybody what is not given, we will make an end of them, finish them off once and for all and cut off their heads." So, having procured some sharp swords, they launched murderous assaults on villages, towns and cities, and went in for highway robbery, killing their victims by cutting off their heads.
>
> Thus, from the not giving of property to the needy, poverty became widespread, from the growth of poverty, the taking of what was not given increased, from the increase of theft, the use of weapons increased, from the increased use of weapons, the taking of life increased . . .[14]

Despite its mythic elements, this fable has some interesting implications. Poverty is presented as a root cause of immoral behavior such as theft and violence. The solution has nothing to do with accepting our (or others') "poverty karma." The problem begins when the king does not give property to the needy—in modern terms, when the state neglects its responsibility to maintain a minimum of what we now call distributive justice. The *sutta* argues, in effect, that social breakdown cannot be separated from broader questions about the benevolence and distributive justice of the social order. The solution to poverty-induced crime is not to punish severely but to enable people to provide for their basic needs.

Although the *sutta* is not clear on this point, contemporary comparisons suggest that when the king "began to rule according to his own ideas," he may have adopted policies that exploited the poor, which made it more difficult for them to provide for their own needs. This issue is quite relevant today, especially in the U.S., where the percentage of poor people is increasing and the middle class is under threat, due to government policies that favor corporate power and those who are already wealthy. In this context, then, perhaps the *sutta* implies not only the importance of avoiding policies that harm those who are already disadvantaged, but that governments should be proactive in addressing their plight—because it is not desirable nor possible to be "neutral" about distributive justice.

As this *sutta* suggests, *dana*, "generosity," is the most important concept in traditional Buddhist solutions to poverty and social responsibility, because it is the main way non-attachment is cultivated and

14. Ibid., 399–400.

demonstrated. Buddhists are called upon to show compassion to those who need help. Even if those who suffer are reaping the karmic fruit of their previous deeds, Buddhism does not teach that their lot should be understood in a punitive way. Although they may be victims of their own previous selfishness, the importance of generosity for those on the Buddhist path does not allow indifference to their situation.

Notice, however, that the appeal is not to justice for a victim. Despite the prudential considerations expressed in this *sutta*—what may happen if we are not generous—the karma and spiritual progress of the *giver* is what is usually emphasized. No one can evade responsibility for his or her own deeds and efforts, yet for those following the Buddhist path generosity is not optional: we are obligated to respond compassionately to those in need.

Conclusion

Whether or not the number of impoverished people in the world is growing, the gap between rich and poor has certainly been increasing dramatically in the last few decades, including within the United States. No one knows how many Buddhists there are, but four hundred million may be a reasonable estimate. A large majority live in "underdeveloped" countries and many of them are poor—by modern Western standards, at least.

Poverty is one of a cluster of economic and social issues that are not culturally neutral. Absolute deprivation—Buddhism emphasizes insufficient food and water, clothing, shelter, and access to basic medical care—needs to be addressed wherever it occurs, but beyond that development agencies should be careful not to assume that "we know what you need, and what you need to do to get there." Buddhist worldviews are becoming more relevant as the globalization of corporate capitalism becomes more problematic. Buddhism's implicit critique of consumerism, in particular, challenges the "moneytheistic" values that often accompany a "higher standard of living." What is most important, I have argued, is the connection Buddhism emphasizes between one's sense of being a separate self—an individual whose own well-being can be pursued apart from the well-being of others—and *dukkha*, one's basic dissatisfaction and sense of *lack*. If such a self *is dukkha*, and if "awakening" involves realizing our interdependence with others, there are profound implications for how we understand and address poverty.

In response, one might argue that the perspective offered in this essay is unrealistic: people everywhere want to consume more, in fact as much as they can, and it is unfair for those of us in economized societies to deny that possibility to those who live in poorer ones. There is obviously at least a grain of truth in that, but the important question is *why*. Is the inclination to want more and more simply human nature, or is it because economic and media globalization are conditioning almost all of us in similar ways? We should not underestimate the extraordinary psychological effects of pervasive advertising and exposure to the glamorous lifestyles promoted on television, etc. If widespread consumerist values are a delusive construct that causes *dukkha*, they amount to a type of missionary religion that needs to be challenged. Recent economic and psychological studies support the notion that, once a minimal level of subsistence is available, what really makes people happy is not more consumption but *relationships*.[15] The Buddha would not be surprised.

Another reason moneytheistic values need to be challenged is that they themselves are unrealistic, given the ecological limitations of the earth, which are already strained by a human population rapidly approaching seven billion people. Today any approach to economic development needs to keep firmly in mind that the world's global economy is a wholly owned subsidiary of a very finite biosphere. This is not an argument against addressing impoverishment, but rather calls our attention to the fact that the relationship between the world's few wealthy people and its many poor is unjust, no matter how their wealth was accumulated. Buddhist emphasis on impermanence and interdependence suggests that henceforth the focus of economic development should be on *undeveloping* in the sense of emphasizing sustainability, simplicity, localism, and so forth. Of course, most of the world's people already live simple and local lives, which means that the finger is pointing at those of us who do not.

15. See, for example, Richard Layard, *Happiness: Lessons from a New Science* (New York: Penguin, 2005); and Matthieu Ricard, *Happiness: A Guide to Developing Life's Most Important Skill* (New York: Little, Brown, 2007).

6

Liberation from Economic Dukkha: A Buddhist Critique of the Gospels of Growth and Globalization in Dialogue with John Cobb

Christopher Ives

Since the publication of E. F. Schumacher's *Small Is Beautiful* in 1973, writers have advocated "Buddhist economics" as an alternative to dominant economic systems.[1] Others have marshaled Buddhist critiques of consumerism, commercialization, globalization, the growing power of corporations, and the environmental destruction wrought by human economic activity. As Buddhist ethicists respond to these issues, they can benefit from dialogue with Christian theologian John B. Cobb Jr. Over the past twenty years, from the perspective of Whiteheadian process philosophy, Cobb has built on his earlier explorations of religion and ecology[2] to investigate issues surrounding "economism," globalization, and sustainability.

This paper, and the interests behind it, grew out of my own interreligious dialogue with John Cobb.[3] While a graduate student in the

1. See, for example, Padmasiri de Silva, *The Search for Buddhist Economics* (Kandy: Buddhist Publication Society, 1975) and Prayudh Payutto, *Buddhist Economics: A Middle Way for the Market Place*, 2nd ed. (Bangkok: Buddhadhamma Foundation, 1994).

2. See Charles Birch and John B. Cobb Jr., *Liberation of Life: From the Cell to the Community* (New York: Cambridge University Press, 1981).

3. I thank John for commenting on a earlier draft of this essay.

1980s at Claremont Graduate School, having followed Masao Abe there from Japan, I was first exposed to Cobb's work on economic issues.[4] Since then I have tracked Cobb's work on sustainability, and his writings, in conjunction with my doubts about Abe's largely metaphysical approach to dialogue (in terms of the doctrine of emptiness), have influenced my previous writing on issues of dialogue. In 2003, I argued that

> even though Buddhists might have much to teach about the psychology of *dukkha*, sin, and other existential issues, they have much to learn about the socio-political facets of *dukkha*. And Buddhists *need* to learn from thinkers like [Paul] Knitter, whose "soteriocentric" model focuses on "the welfare of humanity and this earth, the promotion of life and the removal of that which promotes death"[5] and lifts up "the 'salvation' or 'well-being' of humans and Earth as the starting point and common ground for our efforts to share and understand our religious experiences and notions of the Ultimately Important."[6] Dialogue with Knitter and other liberation theologians (as well as Cobb and his recent writings on "economism," globalization, and sustainability) might be the *most transformative* dialogue for Buddhists at present.[7]

In this essay, my concern is to see not just what Buddhism can learn, but also what Buddhism might have to offer in a dialogue with Cobb's critique, as we evaluate and formulate alternative approaches to economics, development, and globalization. For a number of years Cobb and many others have analyzed in detail the negative impact of certain economic practices on the poor, on the environment, on all of us, and there is little I can add to these assessments. In some respects it might be safest simply to argue that because of the suffering caused by those

4. His influence at that time appears in my 1988 dissertation, published in 1992 as *Zen Awakening and Society* (London: Macmillan) in which I examine several economic issues.

5. Paul F. Knitter, "Interreligious Dialogue: What? Why? How?" in *Death or Dialogue? From the Age of Monologue to the Age of Dialogue*, ed. John B. Cobb Jr. et al. (Philadelphia: Trinity, 1990) 37.

6. Paul F. Knitter, *Jesus and the Other Names: Christian Mission and Global Responsibility* (Maryknoll, NY: Orbis, 1996) 17.

7. Christopher Ives, "Liberating Truth: A Buddhist Approach to Religious Pluralism," in *Deep Religious Pluralism*, ed. David Ray Griffin (Louisville: Westminster John Knox, 2005) 189–90.

practices and the structures supporting them, Buddhists should affirm Cobb's criticisms and, with informed wisdom and active compassion, participate in the various organizations trying to ameliorate that suffering.

But perhaps there is something Buddhism can add to ongoing critical and constructive efforts, and I will argue here that although Buddhists—rich and poor—might feel moved to direct their efforts primarily at poverty, perhaps the more distinctive contribution they can make is a Buddhist response to wealth, or to those of us with comfortable, middle-class lifestyles in consumerist societies. In particular, Buddhist doctrines lend themselves to analyzing how it is that so many people get caught up in consumerism and the gospel of open-ended economic growth and globalization, and to offering a vision of fulfillment that diverges from and ultimately subverts the material "happiness" that is celebrated in consumerist ideologies and the growth paradigm. That is to say, in principle if not always in actual practice, Buddhism rejects the consumerism and materialism woven into dominant economic systems and offers in their stead a path of simplicity that leads not to deprivation but to a more fulfilling form of "wealth," a state of well-being that is not dependent on overconsumption or the accumulation of possessions, capital, and power by those who have more than met their basic survival needs.

Cobb argues that in the eighteenth and nineteenth centuries, theism or "Christianism" was largely supplanted by nationalism, which, in turn, was replaced by "economism," "the belief that the economy is the most important dimension of human life, that the whole of society should be organized around it."[8] In this subordination of social, political, and cultural life to economic values, concerns, and activities, "the national good is measured by economic growth,"[9] and people buy into the view that "our well-being is a function of total production or consumption."[10] With the "subordinating [of] all other interests to the

8. John B. Cobb Jr., ed., *Resistance: The New Role of Progressive Christians* (Louisville: Westminster John Knox, 2008).

9. John B. Cobb Jr., *Sustaining the Common Good: A Christian Perspective on the Global Economy* (Cleveland: Pilgrim, 1994) 28.

10. Ibid., 37. Cobb's analysis echoes that of Karl Polanyi in *The Great Transformation,* who wrote, "instead of [the] economy being embedded in social relations, social relations are embedded in the economic system" (Polanyi, *The Great Transformation: The Political and Economic Origins of Our Time* (Boston: Beacon,

goal of economic growth,"[11] the pursuit of that growth trumps the development and maintenance of just and sustainable societies and the preservation of resource bases and healthy environments. Moreover, economic indicators like GDP fail to take into account a multitude of costs, and may actually treat positively some of the negatives of economic activities, such as when a toxic spill that is causing disease and death prompts expenditures for the clean-up.[12]

The problems resulting from economism are exacerbated by globalization. Cobb decries the degree to which economic globalization has shifted wealth and power to elites, unaccountable transnational corporations, and the Bretton Woods institutions (the World Bank, the International Monetary Fund, the General Agreement on Tariffs and Trade (GATT), and now, having replaced GATT, the World Trade Organization).[13] The current form of economic globalization can destroy local economies (which may have had diversified economic production and non-monetary exchanges); deregulate corporate activities in ways that undermine local labor and environmental laws; contribute to the overexploitation of nonrenewable resources; promote monoculture agriculture geared toward exporting specific crops for which the country has competitive advantage but thereby cause vulnerability to global price fluctuations and a decrease in biodiversity (as well as a number of other environmental problems); promote the privatization of government services (which, though in some cases improving efficiency and, like other "structural adjustments," satisfying the IMF as it restructures loans, may decrease the availability of those services and increase their cost); support the privatization and commodification of elements of the world that formerly were part of the commons; centralize and concentrate economic power; weaken

1957) 57; quoted by Loy, *The Great Awakening: A Buddhist Social Theory* (Boston: Wisdom, 2003) 67).

11. Cobb, *Sustaining the Common Good*, 114.

12. See Herman E. Daly and John B. Cobb Jr., *For the Common Good: Redirecting the Economy toward Community, the Environment, and a Sustainable Future*, 2nd ed. (Boston: Beacon, 1994).

13. For a concise summary of Cobb's critique, see his "Globalization as an Enemy of the Common Good," *Journal of Globalization for the Common Good* (Spring 2007); online: http://lass.calumet.purdue.edu/cca/jgcg/2007/sp07/jgcg-sp07-cobb.htm.

communities; and sacrifice the common good on the altar of growth and shareholder profit.[14]

Hovering over these immediate problems is the further question of sustainability. Cobb and economist Herman Daly view sustainability as the issue of "the optimal scale of the macro-economy relative to the ecosystem,"[15] and affirm that "sustainability is really justice extended to the future."[16] Given the ecological devastation they have wrought, recent human economic activities are not sustainable. This becomes clear when we look at the depletion of natural resources, the destruction of ecosystems, the disruption of biogeochemical processes on which economic activity ultimately depends, and pollution beyond the capacity of natural sinks to absorb it, as seen in the destruction caused by increased levels of carbon dioxide and other greenhouse gases in the atmosphere.

As Buddhists collaborate with people of other religious traditions to address the economic problems analyzed by Cobb, they can draw from several core doctrines and values in their tradition to provide a framework for their critical reflection and constructive praxis. Though speaking about "Buddhism" in the singular is problematical, the various forms of the tradition do focus on suffering, its causes, and its elimination, as first delineated in the Buddha's four "ennobling truths," and Buddhist ethicists can effectively reinterpret those truths in social, political, and economic terms.[17] Not that such reinterpretation would come easily to Buddhism. Historically, the Buddhist focus has been on suffering in the narrower sense of existential anguish,[18] and despite

14. In this list I am pulling from Cobb's writings and an article by Jerry Mander, founder and president of the International Forum on Globalization: "Economic Globalization and the Environment," *Tikkun* 16:5 (2001) 33–40.

15. Daly and Cobb, *For the Common Good*, 145.

16. Ibid., 146. This stance echoes the Brundtland Commission's assertion that development is sustainable when it "meets the needs of the present without compromising the ability of future generations to meet their own needs," World Commission on Environment and Development, *Our Common Future* (Oxford: Oxford University Press, 1987) 8.

17. See Christopher Ives, "Deploying the Dharma: Reflections on the Methodology of Constructive Buddhist Ethics," *Journal of Buddhist Ethics* 15 (2008) 23–44; online: http://blogs.dickinson.edu/buddhistethics/files/2010/05/ives-article.pdf.

18. Even though early doctrinal treatment of *dukkha* encompasses such "mundane" forms of suffering as physical pain.

textual references to social welfare activities and to the compassionate provision of materials and conditions that satisfy basic needs,[19] the tradition tends to regard suffering and the path to its resolution as matters that are relatively independent of particular social and economic conditions. In the case of Zen, for example, the general attitude is that "one can awaken in any and all circumstances."

That being said, we can safely argue from a Buddhist perspective that economism—or what we could call "growthism"—stands in stark tension with the Dharma. First, the anthropology behind regnant economic systems contrasts sharply with Buddhist presuppositions. As Simon James has pointed out, "One could argue . . . that capitalism takes selfishness to be a fact of human nature rather than a problem to be solved; that it encourages excessive consumption, rather than regarding greed as a vice; that it tranquilizes its citizens through the media and through an education system that upholds the value of instrumental rationality to the detriment of training in character."[20]

Dominant economic approaches also foster a set of values contrary to Buddhist teachings. As Cobb has pointed out, religious values get replaced by corporate values, such as the value placed on continued growth of the economy even though it may hurt the vulnerable or undermine communities, on short-term profits for shareholders rather than long-term interests of stakeholders, and on individual material acquisition rather than communal well-being. In particular, economies that take growth as the highest value, and transnational corporate attempts to foster a uniform consumer population across the globe, promote not only ever-increasing levels of consumption but the ideology and practices of consumerism. We can define "consumerism" as both the belief that possessing or simply being able to purchase certain things will make a person happy, and the actions based on that belief, including certain consumer behaviors and the ascription of high status to those who possess wealth or desired consumer goods. From a Buddhist perspective then, "the key question is what values and prac-

19. See Stephen Jenkins, "Do Bodhisattvas Relieve Poverty? The Distinction between Economic and Spiritual Development and Their Interrelation in Indian Buddhist Texts," *Journal of Buddhist Ethics* 7 (2000); reprinted in *Action Dharma: New Studies in Engaged Buddhism*, edited by Christopher Queen, 38–49 (New York: RoutledgeCurzon, 2003).

20. Simon P. James, *Zen Buddhism and Environmental Ethics* (Hampshire, UK: Ashgate, 2004) 125.

tices would convince people to consume and reproduce less when they have the technological ability to consume and reproduce more."[21]

Buddhism offers a set of values—and a notion of human flourishing—that can serve as an alternative to consumerist values. Of particular relevance are the core Buddhist virtues of restraint, non-harming, compassion, generosity, and what we might call "enoughness."[22] As Theravada ethicist Padmasiri de Silva puts it, "A simple way of life no longer satisfies most people; they demand that a wide range of goods and services be available at all times. Buddhism calls for a modest concept of living: simplicity, frugality, and an emphasis on what is essential—in short, a basic ethic of restraint."[23]

What Buddhist practice aims to restrain are destructive actions and, more crucially, the mental states and dispositions that lie behind them, such as the "three poisons" (ignorance, greed, and ill will). Consumerism exacerbates the poison of greed, the fundamental craving and clinging[24] that characterize ordinary human existence, the desire for and attachment to the things that give us a false sense of self and security but ultimately cause anguish, as becomes abundantly clear when those things change, as they inevitably will. Though Buddhism sees this clinging as coupled with ignorance of impermanence, empirically we can also note cases where this desire for security results from a basic fearfulness caused by the recognition—or partial recognition, or perhaps repressed recognition—that everything is changing[25] and we are vulnerable and possibly insignificant, even when we think we have a permanent soul. Consumerism offers salves for this fear, sending the message that material acquisition and possessions can comfort us or provide a wall to ward off vulnerability and change. In particular, the indulgence in and intoxication with the things we consume help

21. Rita M. Gross, "Toward a Buddhist Environmental Ethic," *Journal of the American Academy of Religion* 65 (1997) 335.

22. Ives, *Zen Awakening and Society*, 129–30, 134.

23. Padmasiri de Silva, "Buddhist Environmental Ethics," in *Dharma Gaia: A Harvest of Essays in Buddhism and Ecology*, ed. Allan Hunt Badiner (Berkeley: Parallax, 1990) 15.

24. For an analysis of the four main types of clinging relative to consumerism, see Stephanie Kaza, "How Much Is Enough? Buddhist Perspectives on Consumerism," in *How Much Is Enough? Buddhism, Consumerism, and the Human Environment*, ed. Richard K. Payne (Somerville, MA: Wisdom, 2010) 48–49.

25. Granted, in arguing this way I am diverging from certain traditional Buddhist claims about how we are ignorant of change.

distract us from the fact of our mortality. And even when we are not denying death, we may feel insignificant—especially in "advanced" capitalist societies that champion individualism, celebrity, wealth, and power—and desire recognition from others if not fifteen minutes of fame, or even infamy.

David Loy understands these issues in terms of a basic human problem: the misguided attempts to fill the lack, the void or absence of any permanent self, at the base of our existence. "The problem," he writes, "is 'thirst'—not the emptiness [or lack of soul] at the core of our being but our incessant efforts to fill that hole up, because we experience it as a sense of lack that must be filled up. The problem is not that I am unreal but that I keep trying to make myself real in ways that never work."[26] Needless to say, consumerism is there to serve this misdirected attempt to deal with our lack. Advertizing can prey upon and increase the sense of lack and the desire that accompanies it. As Loy puts it, "By manipulating the gnawing sense of lack that haunts our insecure sense of self, the attention economy insinuates its basic message deep into our awareness: the solution to any discomfort we might have is consumption."[27] Seen from another angle, those who benefit financially from our consumerism are capitalizing on what we could call the "if only" trap: the notion, as cultivated by ads, that "if only" I had this product (for example, a fancy car) or the things the ad indicates that the product will deliver to me (a beautiful woman who will be attracted to me with that car), then I would be happy. Expressed differently, the "if only" trap is when we look "horizontally" (our *having* or *doing* certain things) for fulfillment rather than vertically (in terms of our *being*, our letting go and waking up in the moment). In a vein similar to what I am sketching here, Buddhist thinker Ken Jones has noted that although in the past many cultures placed a premium on "valued skills and knowledge, integrity and wisdom, as well as a rich and varied popular culture," now most of us lead our lives in a "consumer culture in which this richness and diversity has been so diminished that the commodity market (which now packages experi-

26. Loy, *The Great Awakening*, 27. Loy also writes, "Buddhism shifts our focus from the terror of death (our primal repression, according to [Carl] Becker) to the anguish of a groundlessness experienced here and now. The problem is not so much that we will die, but that we do not feel real now" (ibid., 22).

27. Loy "Consciousness Commodified," in *Hooked! Buddhist Writings on Greed, Desire, and the Urge to Consume*, ed. Stephanie Kaza (Boston: Shambhala, 2005) 100.

ences as well as things) comes to bear a disproportionate weight of the human need for meaning, significance, status, and belongingness."[28]

As seen in acts of giving (*dāna*) to monks, a central goal of Buddhist practice is, in addition to acquiring merit, the uprooting of the acquisitiveness and attachment that characterize human existence generally and are exacerbated by particular configurations of consumerism. Contrary to messages that cause us to misperceive certain "wants" as "needs" and advertisements that tell us what we must purchase to be more attractive, popular, successful, or happy, Buddhist approaches to economic life tell us to focus on real *need*, not greed, and to direct ourselves, as Thai Buddhist Sulak Sivaraksa has put it, toward "more being," not "more having." Sivaraksa has also argued that "contrary to the rationale of consumerism, where *more* is considered *better* and where the amount of personal gain and possessions marks the goodness of one's life, one learns from the Buddha to constantly reduce one's attachments and to envision the good life as the successful overcoming of attachment to gain."[29] In terms of economic development, "From the usual standpoint, when desires are increased and satisfied, development can proceed. From the Buddhist standpoint, when there are fewer desires there can be greater development. It is the reduction of desires that constitutes development,"[30] and "[t]he goals of Buddhist development are equality, love, freedom, and liberation."[31] That is not to say that wealth per se is an issue in Buddhism, for the tradition has not condemned wealth but, rather, has emphasized the obligation to earn it morally and then, rather than hoarding it, share it in ways that promote the well-being of others.

Of course, some consumers would argue that they are not caught up in active greed or believe that possessions or the ability to acquire things makes them happy. But many of us do exhibit greed or clinging insofar as we are attached to our lifestyles (in the United States, for example, where disproportionate consumption leads to disproportionate pollution relative to the rest of humanity), and many of us are resistant

28. Ken Jones, *Beyond Optimism: A Buddhist Political Economy* (Oxford: Carpenter, 1993) 22.

29. Sulak Sivaraksa, *Conflict, Culture, Change: Engaged Buddhism in a Globalizing World* (Somerville, MA: Wisdom, 2005) 37.

30. Sulak Sivaraksa, *Seeds of Peace: A Buddhist Vision for Renewing Society* (Berkeley: Parallax, 1992) 44.

31. Ibid., 47.

to simplifying our lifestyle to the extent necessary for overall global sustainability. We may also be reluctant to share as generously as we could with those in need, or to work as hard as we could to eradicate the root causes of chronic poverty.

Buddhists have viewed the "poison" of ill-will as an underlying cause of violence to other people, other species, and the environment in general. Ill-will can be generated in the economic arena, where the selfish pursuit of individual or group interests can lead to conflict if not violence, or simply the anger, envy, and resentment that can occur between neighbors or across class lines. Over the centuries Buddhists have remedied ill-will and these related mental states by engaging in religious practice to cultivate their opposites—loving-kindness and compassion—and by avoiding unnecessary harming, as advocated by the first of the five Buddhist moral precepts.[32] Recently, in part to respond to the ill-will and violence that can be caused in the economic arena, Buddhist thinkers and groups have reinterpreted the precepts. For example, Thich Nhat Hanh's Tiep Hien Order has laid out fourteen "mindfulness trainings," the eleventh of which reads, "Aware that great violence and injustice have been done to our environment and society, we are committed not to live with a vocation that is harmful to humans and nature," and the thirteenth, "Aware of the suffering caused by exploitation, social injustice, stealing, and oppression, we are committed to cultivating loving kindness and learning ways to work for the well-being of people, animals, plants, and minerals."[33]

Buddhist criticisms of greed and ill-will, as well as the ethical thrust of Buddhist precepts, finds expression in E. F. Schumacher's declaration, "The keynote of Buddhist economics . . . is simplicity and non-violence" and "the aim should be to obtain the maximum

32. The Five Precepts entail vows to restrain from 1) taking life, 2) taking what has not been given, 3) engaging in improper sex, 4) lying, and 5) using intoxicants.

33. Thich Nhat Hanh, *Interbeing: Fourteen Guidelines for Engaged Buddhism*, 3rd ed. (Berkeley: Parallax, 1998) 20, 21. Christopher Reed has crafted a list of five "eco-precepts":

1. I vow to recycle everything I can;
2. I vow to be energy efficient;
3. I vow to be an active and informed voter;
4. I vow to be car conscious;
5. I vow to exercise my purchasing power for the benefit of all sentient beings (Christopher Reed, "Down to Earth," in *Dharma Gaia*, 235).

well-being with the minimum of consumption."[34] (Or as P. A. Payutto writes, "in contrast to the classical economic equation of maximum consumption leading to maximum satisfaction, we have moderate, or wise, consumption, leading to well-being."[35]) Richard Hayes echoes Schumacher in claiming that "the Buddhist ideal of a life of simplicity, non-violence towards all living beings, and non-acquisitiveness is one that human beings must learn to follow very soon if they have any interest in the continued survival [sustainability] of their own and countless other species."[36]

Current economic activity is also colored by the poison of ignorance, understood traditionally as ignorance of impermanence and, as a corollary, ignorance of the fact that one lacks any permanent selfhood or soul. Relevant here is a form of ignorance highlighted especially by Zen Buddhists: the sense of being a separate entity that only secondarily enters into relationships with other people and things, as opposed to being an ever-changing series of events constituted through interrelationship and mutual causality.[37] Connecting this Buddhist doctrine to the issues we are examining here, Joanna Macy writes, "It is a delusion that the self is so separate and fragile that we must delineate and defend its boundaries, that it is so small and so needy that we must endlessly acquire and endlessly consume, and that it is so aloof that as individuals, corporations, nation-states, or species, we can be immune to what we do to other beings."[38]

But Buddhists can also expand their traditional treatment of ignorance to include ignorance in the sense of denial (ignor-ance), a lack of knowledge about the negative impacts of economic practices (or the imperialism backing them[39]), or the fallacious belief that economic

34. E. F. Schumacher, *Small Is Beautiful: Economics as if People Mattered* (New York: Harper & Row, 1973) 57. Schumacher also declares, "The Buddhist sees the essence of civilization not in multiplication of wants but in the purification of human character" (ibid., 55).

35. Payutto, *Buddhist Economics*, 69.

36. Richard P. Hayes, "Towards a Buddhist View of Nature," *ARC* 18 (Spring 1990) 23.

37. We usually construe ourselves as having been born into the world from the outside and then doing our thing in the world as opposed to the world doing its thing in and through us.

38. Joanna Macy, "The Greening of the Self," in *Dharma Gaia*, 57.

39. See the late Chalmers Johnson's *The Sorrows of Empire: Militarism, Secrecy, and the End of the Republic* (New York: Metropolitan, 2004) and John Cobb's essay,

growth is the key to broad, sustainable happiness and that current globalization is a process that serves the common good.[40] For example, when it comes to climate chaos, arguably the biggest problem caused by the high levels of economic activity made possible by cheap sources of energy (coal, oil, natural gas), we see ignorance operating in such forms as 1) the lack of knowledge about human impacts on the environment; 2) incorrect knowledge or disinformation, as disseminated, for example, by the American Petroleum Institute, backed by funding from big oil, with its portrayal of recent temperature increases as primarily a function of natural cycles; 3) ignorance or denial of what we are doing to climate systems, achieved and maintained in many cases by distracting ourselves, blurring the distinction between reality and illusion,[41] or slipping into psychic numbing; 4) ideas justifying the continuation of our destructive lifestyle or justifying our doing nothing, such as the idea that Christ is coming soon and the vast array of problems we are currently facing is part of a divinely orchestrated process described in the book of Revelation; or the idea that a technological fix driven by market forces will solve our problems; or the idea that "there is no reason we should make sacrifices if the Chinese and Indians aren't going to"; and 5) unawareness of, and psychological disconnection from, nature.

In conjunction with a critique of ideology,[42] meditation can help dissolve certain of these forms of ignorance. What meditation cultivates in their stead is, according to many Buddhists, a greater awareness of oneself and one's world, as well as a relational way of knowing, a recognition that we are constituted through relationships with other things and exist thoroughly interconnected with them. Martin Pitt claims that "meditation is at the heart of a true ecological awareness. It is a powerful tool for taking us beyond our obsession with the foreground and into appreciation of the wide scale of space and time. Loosening our chains to fixed objects, meditation cultivates noncon-

---

"American Imperialism," in *Resistance*.

40. David Loy expands the traditional treatment of the three poisons when he delineates how they can become institutionalized and find expression in collective egotism, or what he terms the "wego" (*The Great Awakening*, 40, 48).

41. See Chris Hedges, *Empire of Illusion: The End of Literacy and the Triumph of Spectacle* (New York: Nation, 2009).

42. See my "Not Buying in to Words and Letters: Zen, Ideology, and Prophetic Critique," *Journal of Buddhist Ethics* 13 (2006).

ceptual awareness of context—profoundly ecological, and giving rise to vision on a global scale."[43]

Buddhist meditative praxis also purportedly leads to an insight into *pratītya-samutpāda*, interrelational arising.[44] This doctrine maintains that all things emerge through conditioning factors in a web of interrelationship with other things and hence do not have any unchanging essence or soul. Insight into this metaphysical truth is said to generate both a keener recognition of how our actions affect the world around us and a stronger sense of responsibility.[45] Along these lines Allan Hunt Badiner contends, "With its emphasis on cooperation and interdependence, Buddhist practice can inspire the building of partnership societies with *need*-based, sustainable economies rather than *greed*-based, growth economics."[46] Of course, although exponents of "free trade" celebrate how people around the world are becoming "interdependent," Buddhists need to be vigilant that they do not uncritically join this celebration, for as Cobb points out (and as dependency theorists have highlighted in their analyses of *dependencia*), "careful analysis shows that interdependence as it develops out of free trade means the dependence of all on those who control the movement of capital and the terms of trade,"[47] and an "interdependent global economy will reduce the power of everyone except a few manipulators of capital."[48]

His analysis of forms of dependence has led Cobb to argue for the value of subsidiarity, the principle in Catholic social teaching that, as expressed by Pius XI, "It is an injustice, a grave evil and a disturbance of right order for a larger and higher organization to arrogate

43. Martin Pitt, "The Pebble and the Tide," in *Dharma Gaia*, 104.

44. Buddhists often render *pratītya-samutpāda* as "interdependence" and in some cases this translation has led to arguments about how "everything is dependent on everything else." To clarify that although we interrelate with or are affected by all things our well-being is not necessarily dependent on everything else, Buddhist discourse in English can benefit from a different translation of *pratītya-samutpāda*—such as "conditioned arising" or "interrelational arising."

45. And this is not simply responsibility as moral or legal accountability for something I have done but responsibility in the sense of an obligation to care for someone or some situation, as in the claim, "Parents are responsible for the well-being of their children."

46. Allan Hunt Badiner, "Introduction," in *Dharma Gaia*, xvii.

47. Cobb, *Sustaining the Common Good*,16.

48. Ibid., 42.

to itself functions that can be performed efficiently by smaller and lower bodies."[49] For all the Buddhist talk of interdependence, the principle of subsidiarity points to the need for independence from certain forms of transnational or highly centralized power at the top. Though Buddhists have not traditionally considered in detail what forms of interrelationship are optimal, they can follow Cobb's lead and affirm the importance of decentralizing power and keeping it as local or individual as possible while allowing, as he does, for the necessity of allocating power (or the responsibility to handle certain tasks) at broader, more centralized levels in certain limited cases. Buddhist advocacy of subsidiarity, however, while justifiable in terms of reducing suffering, does stand in tension with traditional Buddhism, where criticisms of self-interest, nervousness about power, and institutional symbiosis with central governments have generally subverted Buddhist affirmation of the allocation of power to individuals or their local groupings.

Given the above issues, Buddhist thinkers need to clarify what forms of interconnection and interrelationship are optimal, both for particular "things" (albeit transient and more accurately described as "events") and for larger and larger wholes, whether families, organizations, communities, societies, the international community, ecosystems, or the biosphere. Some of us "green Buddhists" who live comfortably with all of our needs and most of our wants met can slip into privileging wilderness or pristine ecosystems over social wholes or individual humans. Here, too, dialogue with Cobb can prove useful, especially for those of us who are drawn to deep ecology. He writes that "what is called 'deep ecology' usually begins with the condition of the earth and moves from that to the well-being of the human species and its members. This is a rational approach to be fully respected. But it is not the Christian one. Christians typically begin with the 'neighbor' who is in need."[50] This concern for one's fellow humans should not sound foreign to Buddhists, for it accords with the bodhisattva ideal and such core values as the four "divine abodes,"[51] especially loving-kindness as "extended" to others.

49. Pius XI, *Quadragesimo Anno* (1931); quoted by Daly and Cobb, *For the Common Good*, 17.

50. Cobb, "Protestant Theology and Deep Ecology," in *Deep Ecology and World Religions: New Essays on Sacred Ground*, ed. David Landiss Barnhill and Roger S. Gottlieb (Albany: SUNY Press, 2001) 220.

51. Loving-kindness, compassion, sympathetic joy, and equanimity.

Historically, however, the need or plight of the neighbor that Buddhists have taken seriously is less the "mundane" suffering of poverty, political oppression, other forms of injustice, and more the existential, "religious" suffering (albeit with some attention to unmet basic needs). As a result, Buddhism has usually not grappled critically with issues of poverty and exploitation. More often than not, class differences and the suffering associated with poverty have been viewed as the result of karma from past lifetimes,[52] and rather than attempt to ameliorate poverty, Buddhist clerics have often advocated acceptance of one's karmic lot and the performance of good deeds (such as giving alms to monks) as the way to better one's prospects in the future, usually a future lifetime. Even contemporary "engaged Buddhists," while making strong and convincing arguments for reducing consumption and pollution, tend to overlook distributive justice, or at least give it far less attention than Cobb and many other Christians—and Jews and Muslims—do in their writing and activism.

A valuable Buddhist resource that can be tapped in this regard is the traditional emphasis on giving to others and thereby cultivating the virtue of generosity as the antidote to the "poison" of greed. Groups like the Sarvodaya Movement in Sri Lanka have expanded the traditional connotation of *dāna*—the meritorious giving of food and money to the monastic community—to include the giving of one's time, energy, and talents to the broader community. Also pointing in the direction of expanded sharing and distributive justice is the fifth of the Tiep Hien mindfulness trainings:

> Aware that true happiness is rooted in peace, solidity, freedom, and compassion, and not in wealth or fame, we are determined not to take as the aim of our life fame, profit, wealth, or sensual pleasure, nor to accumulate wealth while millions are hungry and dying. We are committed to living simply and *sharing our time, energy, and material resources with those who are in need.* We will practice mindful consuming, not using alcohol, drugs, or any products that bring toxins into our own and the collective body and consciousness.[53]

52. And wealth has been seen in many Buddhist societies as the result of meritorious actions in a previous lifetime.

53. Thich Nhat Hanh, *Interbeing*, 18; emphasis added.

Of course, "justice" derives in large part from Western monotheistic traditions and talk of it in relation to Buddhism may sound inappropriate. Some Buddhist apologists have lifted up karma as a form of justice, at least in the retributive and compensatory senses, but historically Buddhists have not given much thought to justice as fair treatment or as the protection of human rights. Cognizant of these lacunae, and of how the naturalistic fallacy—the derivation of an "ought" from an "is"—hangs over well-intentioned affirmations of interdependence, twenty years ago, at Cobb's urging, I gave some thought to what might constitute optimal participation in communities and came up with a working construct: "participatory justice."[54] As I wrote back then, "'To be' means to be in relationship, to participate in—contribute to and receive from—the whole of which one is part. The social 'good' is achieved to the extent people actualize optimal participation and mutually supportive interaction in society."[55] Optimal participation requires the ability to participate—to give and receive—in a fulfilling way, which includes such things as education, rewarding work, the right to vote, the ability to run a viable campaign for political office, and basic freedoms of speech and assembly. Needless to say, current economic systems can limit such forms of participation and, more broadly, local self-determination.

This brings us to the question of community. From the angle of process philosophy, and in a way congruent with Buddhist perspectives, Cobb has criticized the individualism that is presupposed and promoted by current economic systems: "What troubles me most about economic theory is that it abstracts from the social or communal character of human existence and fails to notice that it does so. Underlying its neglect of motives other than self-interest is a radically individualistic view of human beings."[56] Sounding like a Buddhist, Cobb notes that in contrast to the desiring, self-interested individual presupposed by mainstream economic theories, "Most of us today believe (I am even inclined to say 'know') that human beings do not exist in isolation. We are largely constituted by our social relations. The health of the community in which we participate is crucial to our own well-being. We are persons-in-community rather than isolated individuals unaffected

54. *Zen Awakening and Society*, 124.

55. Ibid., 123–24.

56. Cobb, *Sustaining the Common Good*, 33.

by our relations to others."[57] And instead of a unified global market controlled by a handful of corporations with annual economic activity much greater than that of most countries, Cobb calls for decentralization of power (again, in terms of subsidiarity) with a "community of communities"—or "community of communities of communities"—forming the larger blocks in the global economical and political arena.

Sharing these sorts of insights, A. T. Ariyaratne and his followers have since the 1950s formulated an alternative approach to economic development. Their Sarvodaya Movement envisions development as a process of empowering local communities—as opposed to international corporations and organizations—while preserving a healthy environment and core religious and cultural values.[58] In its approach to development, Sarvodaya aims at six types of goals: social, economic, political, moral, cultural, and spiritual. The core social goals are equality, solidarity, education, and health. Economic activity is oriented toward cooperative methods in the production of goods, the preservation of resources, and appropriate consumption. The political goals include decentralized decision making, nonviolence, and freedom from coercion, while the moral goal is adherence to the five Buddhist precepts. Cultural goals include artistic expression in various media and harmonious relationships, and the spiritual goal is to extricate oneself and others from the three poisons and awaken together (hence the name "Sarvodaya," the awakening of all).[59] In response to "decadent" villages, mired in stagnation, poverty, and conflict, Sarvodaya strives to create villages characterized by cooperation, sharing, equality, selflessness, and love.[60] Similarly, Sulak Sivaraksa has claimed that the ideal Buddhist society would "function only to the degree that the people were honest, moral, generous, tolerant, and confident. It was important that they be energetic, industrious, and skillful; live in a good environment; associate with good people; have a balanced livelihood; and direct themselves."[61]

57. Ibid.

58. See Joanna Macy, *Dharma and Development: Religion as Resource in the Sarvodaya Self-Help Movement*, rev. ed. (West Hartford, CT: Kumarian, 1985); and George D. Bond, *Buddhism at Work: Community Development, Social Empowerment, and the Sarvodaya Movement* (Bloomfield, CT: Kumarian, 2004).

59. Macy, *Dharma and Development*, 35.

60. Ibid., 34.

61. Sulak Sivaraksa, *Seeds of Peace*, 109.

In Thailand, Samana Bodhirak and the Santi Asoke reform movement he started back in the 1970s offer another example of a Buddhist alternative to dominant approaches to development. Rejecting development schemes that emphasize foreign expertise, industrialization, and export-oriented production, Santi Asoke has sketched an approach to development that is "1) culturally/locally situated, 2) focused on livelihoods instead of macroeconomic growth, 3) environmentally 'sustainable,' and 4) endogenously inspired, implemented, and maintained."[62] In its seven intentional communities, the movement has emphasized hard work (as meditation), reduced consumption, sharing, strict adherence to Buddhist precepts, serving broader society, and the three core ethical values of self-reliance, moderation, and interdependence.[63] Championing small-scale subsistence economies with appropriate technology, it has recently lifted up "Three Professions to Save the Nation": natural agriculture, waste management, and chemical-free fertilizing.[64] As Juliana Essen comments, "these occupations are more suitable for Thailand's land and climate than industry, provide food for the nation, solve problems of overflowing garbage, do not create pollution, improve people's health, economize, and enable self-dependence."[65]

Along the lines of the advocacy of Sarvodaya, Sulak Sivaraksa, and Santi Asoke, Buddhists can affirm as their *telos* the sort of sociopolitical arrangements that Cobb's fellow process theologian Jay McDaniel envisions in his call to "create communities that are just, compassionate, nonviolent, participatory, and ecologically wise,"[66] and, we might add, autonomous and oriented toward fostering true well-being rather than material acquisition and open-ended growth.

But how might we measure the degree to which we have moved in the direction of such communities? Back in the 1980s, Cobb, his son Clifford, and several of Cobb's graduate students came up with an Index of Sustainable Economic Welfare (ISEW), which subtracts

62. Juliana Essen, *"Right Development": The Santi Asoke Buddhist Reform Movement of Thailand* (Lanham, MD: Lexington, 2005) 151.

63. See Juliana Essen, "Sufficiency Economy and Santi Asoke: Buddhist Economic Ethics for a Just and Sustainable World," *Journal of Buddhist Ethics* 17 (2010).

64. Essen, *"Right Development,"* 111.

65. Ibid., 115.

66. Jay McDaniel, "A Process Approach to Ecology," in *A Handbook of Process Theology*, ed. Jay McDaniel and Donna Bowman (St. Louis: Chalice, 2006) 241.

from GDP all expenditures that are regrettable necessities and do not increase overall welfare (like having to deplete one's retirement savings to pay for a home security system to maintain a constant level of safety as crime in one's neighborhood increases) and such costs as pollution; decreases in air, water, and land quality; and the loss of nonrenewable resources, species, and wilderness areas.[67] Building on this work, I proposed an Overall Quality of Life Index, which would also bring into the calculation such elements of the Physical Quality of Life Index (used by some developmental economists) as infant mortality rates, life expectancy at age one, and literacy rates, while also considering physical health, crime rates, the degree to which civil rights are protected, and the frequency of military conflict.[68]

Regardless of what we include in the calculation, at the very least the Buddhist commitment to reducing suffering and cultivating conditions necessary for well-being and awakening points to the need for an indicator that measures overall human welfare rather than simply the gross amount of economic activity. Such a social index should focus first on whether survival needs—for healthy food, potable water, appropriate clothing, adequate health care, safe housing—of the greatest number of people are met, followed by other basic needs. Helpful in this regard is the Sarvodaya Movement's identification of ten basic needs: water; food; housing; clothing; health care; communication; fuel; education; a clean, safe, beautiful environment; and a spiritual and cultural life.[69]

But regardless of the indicator, how might Buddhists act to eliminate the problems caused by current economic systems and bring about the sorts of conditions and practices sketched here? Prominent Buddhists like Sulak Sivaraksa and A. T. Ariyaratne have written and spoken at length about the problems of globalization and the negative impacts of standard approaches to economic development, but traditional Buddhism is not positioned for broad mobilization of adherents. Separate from such organizations as Sarvodaya and Santi Asoke, Buddhist denominations and individual temples in Asia are not in-

67. For the ISEW, see Daly and Cobb, *For the Common Good*, 443–507. In concert with others at the think tank Redefining Progress, Cliff Cobb reworked the ISEW into the Genuine Progress Indicator.

68. Ives, *Zen Awakening and Society*, 132–33.

69. Macy, *Dharma and Development*, 27.

stitutionally or sociologically oriented toward launching coordinated campaigns in response to contemporary issues, whether economic problems, climate crisis, or military conflict, and in general such activism is foreign to their religious life.[70] Further, until very recently, Buddhism has lacked any tradition of prophetic critique. Quite to the contrary, in most Asian countries Buddhist institutions have acquiesced to actions, policies, and structures that might be denounced as contrary to Buddhist ethical values, in part because of the degree to which they have pursued their interests symbiotically with ruling elites.

At the very least, with their focus on human suffering and its alleviation, what Buddhists need to do is promote the prophetic—or bodhisattvic—voice that has recently appeared in several of their prominent leaders, and speak out more often about the suffering caused by current economic structures and practices and complement that critical stance with further constructive efforts to provide a counter-discourse, a vision of flourishing that can subvert the sort of materialist and consumerist discourse about well-being that legitimates current economic practices and guides many of our decisions. And then, as a next step, following the lead of Sulak Sivaraksa, A. T. Ariyaratne, Samana Bodhirak, and Thich Nhat Hanh, they can elaborate that vision of flourishing beyond such traditional elements as wisdom, compassion, peace of mind, moderation, contentment, joy, and equanimity by giving it greater social, political, and economic specificity, as seen in the UN's Millennium Development Goals, "deep economy,"[71] "natural capitalism,"[72] and what Cobb is doing when he writes,

> Some features of a hopeful future can be suggested. It would be a future in which we learned to do more with less. Technology would be tamed to serve human need. Human need would be

70. Granted, there are exceptions, as we saw in Burma several years ago, or in Vietnam during the Diem regime.

71. Bill McKibben, *Deep Economy: The Wealth of Communities and the Durable Future* (New York: Times Books, 2007).

72. Paul Hawken, Amory Lovins, and L. Hunter Lovins, *Natural Capitalism: Creating the Next Industrial Revolution* (Boston: Little, Brown, 1999). According to these authors, "natural capitalism" employs four main strategies: radical resource productivity, biomimicry as a way to reduce waste, a shift from an economy of goods and purchases to one of service and flow, and investing in natural capital (10–11).

> reconceived less in material ways and more in terms of human relations, art, and wisdom. Unlike previous subsistence societies, the amount of physical labor involved would be adjusted to the requirements of health and enjoyment. Differences of wealth would be minimized, while opportunities to excel would be defined in terms of service instead. There would be maximum participation in the making of the decisions that governed the shared life. Population would be limited by individual choices in the context of social policy rather than by pestilence, war, and famine . . . enormous changes could be made in the reduction of waste and greater efficiency in the use of resources. Energy consumption could be reduced, and energy sources could be shifted toward solar energy and other less-polluting and non-exhaustible forms . . . Military expenditures could be shifted to production oriented to human needs . . . Pride in ownership of new manufactured goods could be replaced by pride in frugality and workmanship. Prizing of individual autonomy could give way to prizing of communal sharing and mutual support.[73]

By cultivating the kind of insight evident in Cobb's statement, refining their distinctive analysis of our entanglement in economic problems, formulating an alternative vision of human wealth and flourishing, and engaging in concrete action to actualize that vision, Buddhists can join Cobb in his "earthist challenge to economism."[74] Given their privileged position and all of the costs that it has entailed for other people and the biosphere, affluent Buddhists in dominant countries in particular need to shoulder the responsibility for this work and think critically about how they might deploy their wealth and power, but treatment of this issue will have to wait for another occasion.

73. John B. Cobb Jr., *Sustainability: Economics, Ecology, and Justice* (1992; reprinted, Eugene, OR: Wipf & Stock Publishers, 2007) 31–33.

74. See John B. Cobb Jr., *The Earthist Challenge to Economism: A Theological Critique of the World Bank* (New York: Palgrave Macmillan, 1999).

7

Buddhist Economics and Thailand's Sufficiency Economy

Donald K. Swearer

The shadow of Max Weber's characterization of early Indian Buddhism as an expression of an otherworldly mysticism ideal type of religion continues to shape the popular view of Buddhism in the West. Consequently, pictures of Thich Quang Duc's self-immolation during the Vietnam War or Burmese monks protesting the ruling junta in front of the Schwedagon Pagoda in Yangoon are interpreted as political rather than religious acts. After all, should the Buddhist monk not dedicate himself to the pursuit of Nirvana, the practice of meditation, and the study of religious texts? Such a view of Buddhism may be a reasonable characterization of an ideal type, but it does not correspond to historical reality.

Buddhism, like other religious traditions, is embedded in particular contexts, times, and places. Hence, like all historical religions, Buddhism should be seen as plural rather than singular, as multiplex and multivalent. Historically conditioned and culturally embedded, Buddhism(s) address a wide range of human issues and problems while at the same time connecting the human condition to universal principles and ultimate goals. The Buddhist Dharma charts a path to the resolution of the deeply felt problem of suffering, but at the same time offers practical advice to kings, merchants, fathers, wives, and children.

Contemporary Buddhists have looked to their textual traditions to formulate a wide-ranging social ethic relevant to the major issues of the day—be they political, economic, biomedical, environmental. In the course of this essay I reference three Pāli narrative texts from the Theravāda canonical tradition used by contemporary Buddhists in their construction of an economic ethic. However, a word of caution is in order in regard to the use of classical texts for contemporary purposes: crafting an ethic relevant to the pressing issues of the day from texts written in times and places vastly different from our own should be understood as an interpretative act of constructive hermeneutics, rather than a normative representation of the tradition. To use an illustration from politics, there is no clear sense in which the early Buddhist teachings regarding kingship, or the iconic example of King Asoka, can be applied to the politics of modern nation-states. I do not mean to imply that the teachings of Buddhism and other world religions are completely bound by time and place. However, their historical relativity cautions against easy generalizations about their relevance to today's contentious issues and problems.

Constructing a Buddhist Economic Ethic

There is a substantial literature on Buddhist economics and related subjects written by Buddhists, and a considerable body of scholarly work by both Buddhologists and economists. The most notable of the latter is the work of the British economist, E. F. Schumacher whose 1973 book, *Small Is Beautiful: Economics as if People Mattered*, has been and continues to be one of the most influential books in the field.

My remarks will rely on several contemporary writers on Buddhist economics and economic ethics. I am especially indebted to Buddhadāsa Bhikkhu (d. 1993) and P. A. Payutto, two Thai monastic scholars I have had the privilege of knowing personally and whose writings have influenced my understanding of Buddhism and economic matters, and to Sulak Sivaraksa, the noted socially engaged Buddhist activist and cofounder of the International Network of

Engaged Buddhists.[1] I have organized my reading of this literature around three broad topics:

(1) The Middle Way and the Value of Moderation

(2) Consumerism, Wealth, and the Value of Generous Giving

(3) Right Livelihood and Well-Being

Since 1997 the concept of Sufficiency Economy (SE) has become a widely discussed and debated practical philosophy in Thailand. It has been applied to everything from individual lifestyles (*chiwit setakit pho phieng*) and to farming methods (*kasaet pho phieng*). As will be seen in the concluding section of this paper, SE is consistent with the principles of moderation, sharing, and right livelihood.[2, 3]

The Middle Way and the Value of Moderation

The theme of moderation, an economic ethic of non-excess, reflects Buddhism's self-identification as a *Majjhima Patipadā,* or Middle Way. The Buddhist Middle Way has two primary dimensions, philosophical and practical. The former charts a modal, dynamic, causally interdependent worldview that rejects metaphysical absolutes, on the one hand, and nihilism, on the other. The practical interpretation of *Majjhima Patipadā* designs a moderate monastic lifestyle between the conventional life of the householder and the ascetic practices of renunciant movements contemporary to the time of the Buddha. Although Middle Way in this sense is identified, in particular, with the Buddha's life story and the rules of the monastic order, or Sangha, it is also applicable to the ethical code and moral values (*sīla*) of Buddhist laity as well. For example, P. A. Payutto refers to the principle of moderation as

1. Sulak Sivaraksa, *The Wisdom of Sustainability: Buddhist Economics for the 21st Century* (Kihei, HI: Koa, 2009).

2. In a recent article Juliana Essen examines Thailand's Sufficiency Economy and the Santi Asoke movement as two examples of Buddhist economics. Juliana Essen, "Sufficiency Economy and Santi Asoke: Buddhist Economic Ethics for a Just and Sustainable World," *Journal of Buddhist Ethics* 17 (2010) 70–99.

3. Although there is an extensive body of work in Thai on Sufficiency Economy, for the purposes of this essay I am relying primarily on the 2007 UNDP report on human development in Thailand. *Thailand Human Development Report 2007: Sufficiency Economy and Human Development* (Bangkok: United Nations Development Programme, 2007).

the "heart of Buddhism" that directs human interest toward the attainment of well-being rather than maximum satisfaction.[4]

David Kaluphana, emeritus philosopher at the University of Hawaii, defines the Noble Eightfold Path, the fourth of the Four Noble Truths taught by the Buddha, as a Middle Way between sense indulgence and self-mortification, whether one is a monk or a layperson.[5] The list of the eight components of the path begins with right view (*sammaditthi*) and concludes with right mindfulness (*sammasati*) and concentration (*sammasāmadhi*); but at the center, at the very fulcrum of the path, are the moral values of right speech, right action, and right livelihood. Right livelihood figures prominently in a Buddhist economic ethic, and, together with right speech and right action, is an essential component of the path to the highest level of human flourishing, namely, Nirvana. I want to emphasize that the ethical factors of right speech, action, and livelihood are linked to right view—understanding the fundamental truth that the world is dynamic, modal, and causally interdependent—and to the goal of the Buddhist path, Nirvana, conceived by Buddhists as *vimutti* or in Thai terms, *cit wang* (liberated heart-mind).

Another value associated with moderation or non-excess is non-greed. In Buddhist ethics greed (*lobha*) results from obsessive desires (*tanhā*) and blind attachment. In the Pāli Aggañña Sutta (The Sutta on Origins), obsessive desire is depicted as the instrumental cause of the decline of the natural, harmonious order of things. Numerous teachings in the Pāli texts describe the unlimited nature of obsessive desire. One such tale is the Mandhātu Jātaka.[6]

In the ancient past there lived a king named Mandhātu. He was a very powerful ruler who was known for having lived a long life. Mandhātu had all the classic requisites of a king. He was an exceptional human being who had everything that anyone could wish for.

4. P. A. Payutto, *Buddhist Economics: A Middle Way for the Market Place,* 2nd ed. trans. Dhammavijaya and Bruce G. Evans (Bangkok: Buddhadhamma Foundation, 1994) 42.

5. See David J. Kalupahana, *Ethics in Early Buddhism* (Honoloulu: University of Hawai'i Press, 1995).

6. *The Jātaka or Stories of the Buddha's Former Births,* ed. E. B. Cowell, vol. 1, no. 216–226 (New Delhi: Low Price Publications, 1997 reprint edition). Adapted from Payutto, *Buddhist Economics,* 31–32.

One day, after having ruled for 84,000 years, King Mandhātu began to shows signs of boredom. The great wealth that he possessed was no longer enough to satisfy him. The king's courtiers, perceiving his disquiet, asked what was bothering him. His majesty replied, "The wealth and pleasure I enjoy here is trifling. Tell me, is there anywhere superior to this?" "Heaven, Your Majesty," they replied. So King Mandhātu then used his royal gem wheel to travel to the Heaven of the Four Great Kings (*lokapala*). The Lokapalas came out to greet him and, on learning of his desire, invited him to take over the whole of their heavenly realm.

King Mandhātu ruled over the Heaven of the Four Great Kings for a long time until one day he began to feel bored again. The pleasures from the wealth and delights of this heavenly realm no longer satisfied him. Conferring with his attendants, he was told of the superior enjoyments of Tāvatimsa Heaven. So King Mandhātu ascended to that realm by his magic gem wheel where he was greeted by its ruler, Lord Indra, who gave him half of the kingdom. King Mandhātu ruled over Tāvatimsa Heaven with Lord Indra for a very long time until Indra was replaced by another Lord Indra and so on until, all in all, thirty-six Lord Indras had come and gone while King Mandhātu enjoyed the pleasures of his position. Finally, however, he began to be dissatisfied—half the kingdom was not enough—so he plotted to depose the reigning Lord Indra, but because human beings cannot kill heavenly beings, his craving caused him to fall down to earth where, upon his deathbed, he confessed that his insatiable desires remained unfulfilled.

Contextually, the Jātaka depiction of King Mandhātu represents a satirical critique of kingly power; however, the story also illustrates the general moral principle that desire and greed can never lead to a state of true happiness. Buddhadāsa Bhikkhu proposes that Buddhism's Middle Way of non-excess reflects the natural order of things (Pāli: *pakati* = Thai: *thammachat*), one of balanced distribution and sustainability:

> Nature would have each of us use no more than we actually need. For years people have failed to heed the way of nature, competing with one another to take as much as they can, causing the problems that we live with to this day. If we were to take only what is enough, none of these problems would exist. The question is, then, how much is enough. These days it seems that nothing is ever enough. There is a Buddhist saying,

> "Even two entire mountains of gold are not enough to satisfy the desires of a single person." What is needed is an approach that emphasizes not taking more than is needed and that at the same time accords with the laws of nature for then people would share their excess out of loving kindness and compassion (Pāli, *mettākaruṇā*) . . . The highest law of nature is to take for ourselves only what is needed, and to accumulate or produce beyond that for the benefit of society. This is not an artificial, human-made socialism, but the socialism of nature.[7]

In practical terms, A. T. Ariyaratna, founder of the Sarvodaya Shramadana movement in Sri Lanka, employs the principles of Middle Way and non-excess in the more than 11,000 village development projects Sarvodaya has promoted on the island. The Middle Way translates into what Ariyaratna terms a "no-poverty society." Sarvodaya rejects the goal of affluence for everyone on practical grounds. It should be obvious to any reflective person that wealth as measured by the standards of Western industrial societies cannot be achieved by all. The world simply does not have sufficient resources. The social, environmental, moral, and cultural costs would be too great.

In the case of Sarvodaya's village development projects, a no-poverty society is defined in terms of meeting ten basic needs: a clean and attractive physical and psychological environment; a clean and adequate supply of water; balanced food requirements; adequate clothing requirements; simple but adequate housing; basic health care; basic communication facilities; minimum energy requirements; comprehensive education; and meeting cultural and spiritual needs.[8] Income and employment are only part of a no-poverty economy. The aim of production in a village economy is not to accumulate profit but to satisfy the needs of a community, and in doing so to engage all members of the community in the process of solving common problems.[9]

7. Buddhadāsa Bhikkhu, *Me and Mine: Selected Essays of Bhikkhu Buddhadasa*, ed. Donald K. Swearer (Albany: SUNY Press, 1989) 174.

8. A. T. Ariyaratna, *Buddhist Economics in Practice: In the Sarvodaya Shramadana Movement of Sri Lanka* (New York: Sarvodaya Support Group, 1999) 36–37.

9. Ibid., 38.

Consumerism, Wealth, and the Value of Generous Giving

A contemporary Buddhist economic ethic critiques consumerism as the commodification of cultural and religious values. Sulak Sivaraksa characterizes consumerism as the new demonic religion; Pracha Hutanuwatra, Sulak's colleague and director of the Wongsanit Ashram on the outskirts of Bangkok, contends that even many monks are "obsessed with raising money from their newly rich parishioners to build ever-bigger Buddha statues and superfluous religious halls,"[10] and Phra Phaisan Visalo, the prominent abbot of Wat Pa Sukhato in Chaiyaphum, laments:

> The distinction between religious faith and consumerism is becoming increasingly vague these days . . . Nowadays, religious faith has been altered to the degree that it means purchasing auspicious objects to worship. One's faith (*saddha*) is no longer measured by how one applies it, how one lives [one's] life, but by how many holy or sacred articles one possesses.[11]

Although contemporary socially engaged Buddhists attack consumerism as the new global religion, Buddhism's Middle Way ethic does not reject the accumulation of wealth. It does, however, establish guidelines for its acquisition and use. Wealth honestly gained is praiseworthy, but attachment to wealth, even when honestly and lawfully gained, is blameworthy, as is stinginess—not to share one's resources for the benefit and well-being of others. Acquiring wealth is acceptable then, if at the same time, it promotes the well-being of a community or society.[12]

One of the most praiseworthy moral values is the act of generous giving (*dāna*), incumbent particularly on people of means. In the Theravāda tradition of Southeast Asia the prominence of the moral perfection of generosity is celebrated by the story of the noble prince Vessantara. Its importance is signaled by its inclusion as the penulti-

10. Pracha Hutanuwatra and Jane Rashbash, "No River Bigger than *Tanha*," in *Hooked! Buddhist Writings on Greed, Desire, and the Urge to Consume*, ed. Stephanie Kaza (Boston: Shambhala, 2005) 106.

11. Phra Phaisan Visalo, "Spiritual Materialism and the Sacraments of Consumerism: A View from Thailand"; online: http://bpf /phaisan1.htm1.org/ tsangha.

12. Phra Rajavaramuni (aka P. A. Payutto), "Foundations of Buddhist Social Ethics," in *Ethics, Wealth, and Salvation: A Study in Buddhist Social Ethics*, ed. Russell F. Sizemore and Donald K. Swearer (Columbia: University of South Carolina Press) 42.

mate tale in the collection of Jātakas recounting the many lives of the Buddha. Second in popularity only to the story of Prince Siddhartha's achievement of Buddhahood, Vessantara personifies virtuous generosity. As the story begins, Vessantara, prince of Sivi, offers his kingdom's white elephant with magical rain-making powers to the neighboring territory of Kalinga to end their drought. The citizens of Sivi, incensed by this generous act that could jeopardize their own material welfare, call for the banishment of Vessantara and his family to the jungle. Before his departure he arranges a *dāna* or gift-giving ceremony, wherein he gives away most of his possessions. Upon leaving the capital city, a group of Brahmins request his horse-drawn chariot, which he willingly surrenders, whereupon Vessantara proceeds on foot with his wife and two children into the forest. As we might expect, and as the logic of true *dāna* as absolute moral principle requires, soon after Vessantara and his family are happily settled in their simple jungle hut, the prince is asked to give up his children to serve Jujaka, an elderly Brahmin. When Indra appears in human disguise and Vessantara accedes to the god's demand that he surrender his wife, Maddi, the prince's trials come to an end. Having successfully met this ultimate test of generosity—the sacrifice of his wife and children—Vessantara's family is restored to him and he succeeds his father as ruler of Sivi.

Although Buddhists in Southeast Asia celebrate Vessantara as the epitome of generous giving, the story contains several moral ambiguities, not the least of which is the apparent dismissive treatment of his wife and children as chattel. Such issues aside, however, at the story's conclusion, Vessantara is rewarded for his generous nature and charitable gifts. What he freely gives is returned and even multiplied; furthermore, readers of the Jātaka tale know that in his next life Vessantara will achieve Buddhahood as Siddhartha Gotama.

Although the story celebrates *dāna*, on another level, one particularly relevant to an economic ethic, the story depicts a conflict between unstinting adherence to an absolute moral principle—in this case the principle of generosity—and the duties attendant to one's station in life. Vessantara's commitment to *dāna* conflicts with the duty to fulfill his responsibilities as a head of a state, as a husband, and as a father. This reading of the story suggests that in terms of an economic ethic, while one is expected to share generously, it should not come at the expense of the well-being of self and others—both those near and dear as well as the stranger. In Niebuhrian terms, we might say that although the attitude toward and use of goods is deemed most worthy when measured in terms of *dāna* as an absolute principle, *dāna* as a universal moral principle *nonetheless* cannot, and perhaps should not, be realized in history. From this perspective, the just distribution of goods should be tempered by one's duties and responsibilities in society.

Within the customary ritual practices of Theravāda Buddhism, *dāna* is most germane to *puñña,* or merit-making.[13] Three basic Theravāda attitudes toward wealth are central to the value of generosity as seen from the vantage point of *puñña*. First, the concept of *dāna* reflects a critique of craving and hoarding. Buddhism puts the greatest emphasis on cultivating and expressing the attitude of non-attachment. Since, at least ideally, the monk represents the value of non-attachment, giving to the Sangha, when matched by the purity of the donor's attitude, is most meritorious for the giver. Second, *dāna* affirms that the amount of wealth possessed and its distribution is morally secondary to the attitude one has toward wealth and the way one uses it. Third, as a moral principle, the practice of *dāna* flows from a vision of material wealth—even wealth that benefits both the individual and her community—as provisional in nature.

In an essay critical of popular Thai practices of giving to holy monks for purposes of self-benefit, spiritual or material, in this or future lifetimes, Buddhadāsa Bhikkhu advocates for what he terms "the gift of emptiness":

> Thais usually interpret the benefit of giving to the Sangha as a future reward, a better life in the future or rebirth in heaven. Such a belief is childish. One still remains stuck in the cycle of rebirth . . . The best *dāna* is the gift of *emptiness*. This means to give away oneself or to give up all one's selfish interests. Indeed, if we really give this kind of *dāna* there is no self which gives it. If you ask what is given the answer is—the self (Thai: *tua ku*). What is given up is attachment to the notion of a self. What is left is freedom, consciousness constituted by awareness, wisdom, and purity.[14]

13. Sizemore and Swearer, *Ethics, Wealth, and Salvation*, 13.

14. Buddhadāsa Bhikkhu, "True Giving" [Hai Dana Thi Mai Sia Ngen], trans. Donald K. Swearer, in Donald Lopez Jr., ed., *Buddhism in Practice* (Princeton: Princeton University Press, 1995).

Consideration of economic distribution in traditional Theravāda sources is less a matter of rationally calculated fairness in a Rawlsian sense, and more a matter of duty and responsibility. It is the duty of the king to provide for the material well-being of the citizenry—hence the moral dilemma in the story of Prince Vessantara between duty and adherence to an absolute moral principle. This duty is illustrated in a satirical critique of responsibilities of kingship in the Pāli discourse, "The Lion's Roar on the Turning of the Wheel" (*Cakkavatti-sihanada Sutta*).

Embodied in this narrative of universal Buddhist kingship (*cakkavatti*) is advice on just and righteous governance that includes looking out for the well-being of all, including the poor. One *cakkavatti* ruler, however, fails to provide materially for the poor which leads to poverty. Stealing, then, arises from poverty, which requires that the king make a judgment regarding the thief. Standing before the king, the thief pleads that he stole because he was so poor. The king in his naïve ignorance gives the thief the material goods necessary to provide for himself, his family, and his business with no punishment. When the word gets around that the king, in effect, rewards stealing, thievery increases. The king then goes to the other extreme by executing the next person caught for stealing which, in turn, caused thieves to arm themselves with weapons, which produces violence and social chaos. The Buddha sums up what amounts to a sardonic critique of royal stupidity as follows: "thus, from not giving to the needy, poverty became rife, from the growth of poverty, the taking of what was not given increased, from the increase of theft, the use of weapons increased, from the increased use of weapons, the taking of life increased, and from the taking of life, people's lifespan and their beauty decreased."[15]

The moral of the story is obvious, that rulers have the responsibility to provide for the material well-being of the poor, and that if they do not, then they sow the seeds of crime and social conflict. Systemic poverty threatens law and order and thus inhibits social harmony and personal morality.

In a manner resonant with current discussions on the innateness of altruism,[16] Buddhadāsa Bhikkhu interprets the distribution of

15. D.iii.68. Peter Harvey, *Introduction to Buddhist Ethics* (Cambridge: Cambridge University Press, 2000) 197.

16. Sarah Coakley and Martin A. Nowak, *Evolution, Games and God: The*

wealth and the treatment of the poor as a norm of the "law of nature" (Thai: *kot thammachat*) exemplified by moral agents in an idealized past, rather than a function of duty:

> Our ancestors taught that we should do what we can to promote the co-existence of all beings. All living beings are able to exist to the degree that they form a society, a mutually beneficial cooperative. This is the handiwork of nature. If nature lacked this character we would all die. Those who know this principle hold fast to it. Even the rice paddies are planted for the benefit of wild animals who feed on it, as well as for their own consumption. They grow as much as they can to share with all forms of living beings.[17]

Right Livelihood and Well-Being

Right livelihood denotes the Buddhist understanding of work or labor. E. F. Schumacher delineates the Buddhist view of work into three aspects: an opportunity to develop human faculties; to overcome egocenteredness by joining with others in a common task; and to bring forth goods and services needed for a satisfying life.[18] For purposes of argument, Schumacher draws a sharp contrast with modern Western economists who, he contends, look at work as a necessary evil. For employers, labor is a matter of cost to be reduced to a minimum; for workers, labor may be perceived as a sacrifice of leisure and wages as compensation for the sacrifice.[19] Modern economics, Schumacher argues, considers consumption to be the primary purpose of economic activity, and ties the maximization of human satisfactions to an optimal pattern of consumption linked to the optimal pattern of productive effort.[20] From the standpoint of Buddhist economics, this approach does not lead to happiness and certainly is not conducive to virtue. In contrast to the modern Western economist who measures wealth by

---

Principle of Cooperation (Cambridge: Harvard University Press, forthcoming).

17. Buddhdāsa Bhikkhu, "A Socialism Capable of Benefiting the World," in Donald K. Swearer, ed., *Me and Mine: Selected Essays of Bhikkhu Buddhdasa* (Albany: SUNY Press, 1989) 12; see also, 196.

18. E. F. Schumacher, *Small Is Beautiful: Economics as if People Mattered* (New York: Harper Colophon Books, 1953) 51.

19. Ibid., 53.

20. Ibid., 55.

GNP and standard of living by the amount of annual consumption, for Buddhist economics consumption should be viewed in terms of the realization of human well-being. Maximum well-being is related to minimizing rather than maximizing consumption or, if you will, in terms of "sufficiency." From the perspective of Buddhist economics, the argument of political economists that increasing consumption is the solution to the current prolonged economic crisis brought on by deficit spending (i.e., overconsumption), is irrational and based on the principle of "want" rather than "need."

From Schumacher's perspective, Buddhist economics postulates that the essence of human flourishing is not in the multiplication of wants but in the purification of human character. It is, if you will, a view of economics from the perspective of the maximization of human flourishing rather than consumption. Above all, work should promote human dignity and freedom. To organize work primarily for efficiency and profit even though the work may be boring or nerve-racking is a calculus that assigns greater value to goods than people. Hence, the subtitle of Schumacher's book: "economics as if people mattered."

Buddhist economics is not an attitude of ascetical hair-shirt denial. The Middle Way should not be seen as antagonistic to physical well-being. It is not wealth, in and of itself, that stands in the way of human flourishing, but attachment to wealth that leads to increasing disparity between the wealthy and the poor. The keynote of Buddhist economics, therefore, values moderation and simplicity rather than the multiplication of wants. Since material resources are limited, a modest rather than maximal use of resources promotes the likelihood of the achievement of a greater common good, and a more just and equitable distribution of goods and services. In particular, great attention should be given to the conservation of nonrenewable resources like oil. From the point of view of Buddhist economics, therefore, the production of local resources for local needs becomes the most rational way of life.[21]

For P. A. Payutto, the separation of work and leisure has two detrimental consequences: work becomes something we are compelled to do in order to obtain money for consumption; and the separation promotes an association of happiness and satisfaction with leisure time, so that work and satisfaction are seen as opposed. Buddhism, Payutto contends, holds the view that when work stems from the desire for

21. Ibid., 57.

true well-being, then there is satisfaction in the direct and immediate results of the work itself.[22] Payutto illustrates his argument with two examples—a Mr. Smith who is motivated by *chanda*, a desire for well-being, and a Mr. Jones who is motivated by *tanhā*, a desire to consume:

> Let us imagine two research workers. They are both investigating natural means of pest control for agricultural use. The first researcher, Mr. Smith, desires the direct fruits of his research—knowledge and its practical application—and takes pride in his work. The discoveries and advances he makes afford him a sense of satisfaction.
>
> The second, Mr. Jones, works primarily for money and promotions. Knowledge and its application, the direct results of his work, are not really what he desires; they are merely the means through which he can ultimately obtain money and position. Satisfaction associated with a sense of well-being is not his concern.[23]

For both Schumacher and Payutto, economics as a field has been overly narrow and fragmentary. Schumacher suggests that it should be transformed by "metaeconomics." [24] Metaeconomics derives its objects from the study of what it means to be human and the natural and social environments in which human beings are situated.[25] Payutto contends that "economics has become a narrow and rarefied discipline; an isolated, almost stunted body of knowledge having little to do with other disciplines or human activities."[26] Buddhist economics, by contrast, offers a different approach not as a self-contained science or discipline but "one of a number of interdependent disciplines working in concert toward the common goal of social, individual, and environmental well being."[27] Taking a cue from the situatedness of right livelihood in the Noble Eightfold Path, Buddhist economics not only "casts a wider, more comprehensive eye on the question of ethics"[28] than does neoclassical economics, it grounds Buddhist social ethics in

22. Payutto, *Buddhist Economics*, 47.

23. Ibid.

24. Schumacher, 49.

25. See also, Stephen A. Marglin, *The Dismal Science: How Thinking like an Economist Undermines Community* (Cambridge: Harvard University Press, 2008).

26. Payutto, *Buddhist Economics*, 19.

27. Ibid.

28. Ibid., 27.

Buddhist Dharmic epistemology and soteriology, namely, the *paticca-samuppāda* view of the world as interdependent and co-arising, and the Buddhist path to the full realization of human flourishing.

Thailand's Sufficiency Economy

The origin of the term *Sufficiency Economy* (SE) is attributed to Thailand's King Bhumibol Adulyadej's birthday address to the nation on December 4, 1997, delivered on the heels of the Asian economic crisis and the collapse of the baht:

> Recently so many projects have been implemented, so many factories have been built, that it was thought Thailand would become a little tiger and then a big tiger. People were crazy about becoming a tiger. Being a tiger is not important. The important thing for us is to have a sufficient economy. A sufficiency economy means to have enough to support ourselves.

Sufficiency Economy as a worldview and way of life—as much or more so than as an economic philosophy—has been legitimated not only by King Bhumibol's address to the nation, but by his rural development initiatives and speeches going back to the early 1970s in which he has promoted balanced economic development at the local level. His Majesty's imprimatur is one of the significant features of the widespread propagation of the philosophy of SE in Thailand. During the past decade hundreds of SE agricultural projects have been launched, an SE school curriculum is being developed, and an extensive, primarily laudatory, literature on the Thai SE has emerged. For example, articles in both Thai and English on the SE website (www.sufficiency economy.org) include, "Sustainable Economic Development through the Sufficiency Economy Philosophy," by Chirayu Isarangkun, Kobsak Pootrakool and the Bank of Thailand; "Sufficiency Economy and a Healthy Community," by Dr. Suthawan Sathirathai and Dr. Priyanut Piboolsravut, the director of the Sufficiency Economy Research Project of the Bureau of Crown Property; "Development of the Sufficiency Economy Philosophy in the Thai Business Sector: Evidence, Future Research & Policy Implications," by Sooksan Kantabutra, an advisor to the Sufficiency Economy Research Project; "The Balanced Economy at the Edges of Standard Economics," by Professor Peter Calkins, Faculty of Economics, Chiang Mai University and Cornell.

The literature on SE has emphasized the role of the king in the promulgation of the philosophy of SE, and through the efforts of the Sufficiency Economy Research Project of the Crown Property Bureau, the reach and application of SE has been greatly expanded.[29] "Sufficiency" (*pho phieng*), rather than "economics" in a narrow sense, has become the operative term and is applied to individuals and communities as well as agriculture, industry, and national policy.[30] The development of a nationwide SE curriculum from nursery school through high school places a strong emphasis on the development of character values that stress moderation, saving, sharing, and cooperation.[31] My current research on Sufficiency Economy focuses on the multidimensional significance of the concept *pho phieng* (sufficiency) and the problematic of its singular association with the economy as in *setakit pho phieng*.

Currently, one of the most useful documents in the burgeoning genre of SE literature available in English is the 2007 UNDP Thailand Human Development Report.[32] The report offers an analysis of the causes of Thailand's 1970s economic crisis; the development of the philosophy of SE; and several examples of SE projects. The following brief discussion of SE has been adapted from the UNDP report. A

29. See Chaiyawat Wibulsawasdi, Priyanut Piboolsravut, Kobsak Pootrakook, *Sufficiency Economy Philosophy and Development* (Bangkok: Sufficiency Economy Research Project, Bureau of The Crown Property, 2010). See also Chirayu Isarangkun, *Phophieng: Kankhapkhuen Pratya Khong Setakit Phophieng Nai Khruenkhai Kansuksa* [Sufficiency: The Power of the Philosophy of Sufficiency Economy in the Educational Network] (Bangkok: Center for the Development of Education, 2005).

30. The first principle of SE ascribed to King Bhumibol is: "Sufficiency Economy is an approach to life and conduct which *is applicable to every level from the individual through the family and community to the management and development of the nation.*" Italics mine. *Sufficiency Economy Philosophy and Development*, 1. The 2008 biography of Dr. Kasem Watannachai, a distinguished national leader, former rector of Chiang Mai University, and member of the Privy Council is titled, *Chiwit Phophieng* [A Life of Sufficiency] (2008). Examples of Sufficiency Economy communities are presented in: Churairat Saenchorat, *Chumchon Phophieng: Tuayang Chumchon Thi Prasop Qwam Sumret Tam Pratya Setakitphophieng* [Sufficiency Economy Communities: Examples of Successful Sufficiency Economy Communities] (Bangkok:Wailai, 2010).

31. For example, publications of the SE program at the Prince Royal's College school in Chiang Mai include *Kansang Nitsaya Phophieng* [Building a Sufficiency Character] (2010).

32. *Thailand Human Development Report 2007: Sufficiency Economy and Human Development* (Bangkok: United Nations Development Programme, 2007).

subsequent fuller exposition and analysis awaits the completion of my current research.

The UNDP Report points out that for forty years, Thailand's economy had an average growth rate of 7.6 percent a year, one of the fastest in the world: "In the early 1990s a new Japanese factory opened in Thailand every three days and around one million people moved from agricultural to urban jobs every year."[33] This rapid growth created significant socioeconomic problems, however, phenomena not unique to Thailand: top-down development generated primarily by the global market economy; local economies determined by outside forces rather than local needs; growing disparity between the rich and poor; the accumulation of significant indebtedness;[34] migration from rural communities to cities, particularly Bangkok; the disruption of family life and consequent personal stress and feelings of material vulnerability; and environmental degradation.

Even before Thailand's 1997 financial crisis and the collapse of the baht, however, several sectors of Thai society, concerned about the "destructive, divisive, unsustainable, and disempowering by-products of growth," looked for ways to rebuild a sense of community and greater economic self-reliance.[35] Some, including NGOs and a group of "development monks" (*phra nak phattana*), looked to Buddhism with its stress on moderation and spiritual well-being as an antidote to the emphasis on maximizing growth and consumption, and encouraged the creation of horizontal networks to mitigate the dominance of top-down economics. These local initiatives included rice and cattle banks, micro-saving schemes, community forest projects, and self-reliant mixed farming. The philosophy of SE grew out of these conditions. By the 1990s SE was integrated into national development plans, and a Sufficiency Economy Unit of the National Economic and Social Development Board was created with a focus on the development of human resources through education, health care and social welfare, and more equitable sharing through regionalization and rehabilitation of the environment.[36]

33. Ibid., 21.

34. In the northeast, the poorest section of the country, 78.7 percent of households were indebted. *Thailand Human Development Report 2007*, 9.

35. Ibid., 25.

36. *Thailand Human Development Report 2007*, 25.

The UNDP Report describes several SE projects, reporting at some length on an agricultural cooperative in northeast Thailand, known as the Inpaeng Network, consisting of nearly nine hundred villages in four provinces with activities that include agriculture, community enterprises, health care, environmental conservation, and education. Three principles are at the basis of the network: "growing what we eat and eating what we grow, community enterprises, and networking locally and regionally."[37]

In 1999–2000 a working group drew up a tripartite characterization of SE: (1) SE is an approach to life applicable at every level—individual, family, community, nation; (2) it promotes a middle path in an era of economic globalization; and (3) it requires sound judgment in planning and the implementation of economic development theory. Later these three principles were further elaborated to include the following: moderation (*pho phraman),* reasonableness (*mi het phon*), self-immunity (*phumikhumkan nai tua),* wisdom and insight (*khwam ru*), and integrity (*khunatham*) in responding to the rapid and widespread changes in the economy, society, environment, and culture.[38]

On the one hand, the philosophy of SE is not based in Buddhism, per se, nor, on the other, should it be seen as an economic theory or policy. The operative term is *sufficiency* (*pho phieng*), a guide to human flourishing that has as much or more to do with the development of character as with economic sustainability. As an ethic, worldview, and way of life, SE calls for a radical transformation of an economy governed by the norms of the global marketplace and a culture determined by the values of consumerism (*poripok niyom).* The fundamental teachings of sufficiency (*pho phieng*)—enough, in the sense of not too little and not too much; a Middle Way between want and extravagance—resonates with Buddhist teachings: *mi het phon*—the natural law of *idapaccayata*, the cause and effect that structures all things; *phumikhumkan nai tua*—the truth that in the face of *dukkha*, or suffering, each person has the potential to develop the mental ability to understand (*quam ru*) and overcome *dukkha*; and *khunatham*—the insistence that such knowledge entails the moral qualities of empathy, compassion, fairness, and generosity.[39]

37. Ibid.

38. Ibid., 29–30.

39. Ibid., see 31–35.

Sufficiency Economy has not been without its critics. Criticisms include debunking SE as a political strategy employed by the military and Democratic Party to discredit the former Prime Minister, Thaksin Shinawatra, and the Thai Rak Thai Party; as a class response to the economic crisis of the past decade; as a theory that misunderstands the nature of rural livelihood; and as a disguised tool of economic neoliberalism. Such critiques have been articulated by Danny Unger at Northern Illinois University ("Sufficiency Economy and the Bourgeois Virtues"), Peter Bell at the University of New York, Purchase ("Sufficiency Economy: Economic Theory or Class Politics?"), Andrew Walker at the Australian National University ("Royal Sufficiency and Elite Misrepresentation of Rural Livelihoods,"), and Jim Glassman at the University of British Columbia ("The Sufficiency Economy as a Neo-Liberalism").[40]

To actualize the broad scope of sufficiency (*pho phieng)* from individual lifestyles to national economic policy would require a fundamental paradigm shift. Moreover, practitioners of SE are well aware of the challenges of transforming theory into practice even on the local level. Small farmers who have successfully adopted the "new theory" (*tisadi mai*) of SE propounded by King Bhumibol based on the principles of moderation, diversification, and stage-by-stage development, are not blind to the inconsistencies between the philosophy and practices of SE and the economic interests of corporate global capitalism. Whether SE as an economic program will be able to gain meaningful traction in Thailand over the long run will depend on corporate Thailand offering more than lip service to the principles embodied in SE, such as "enough to eat, enough to live on" (*pho kin-pho yu*).

Although the principles of SE were developed in Thailand, SE shares much in common with similar movements elsewhere in Buddhist Asia. One thinks of the previously mentioned economic philosophy of A. T. Ariyaratna and Sarvodaya Shramadana in Sri Lanka, as well as Gross National Happiness, the guiding philosophy of Bhutan's development process which emphasizes human and spiritual development over commercial and material values, and was first enunciated by the King of Bhutan soon after he ascended to the throne in 1972. Sufficiency Economy, Sarvodaya Shramadana, and Gross

40. Papers presented at the 10th International Conference of Thai Studies, Thammasat University, Bangkok, Thailand, January 9–11, 2008.

National Happiness emerged as responses to the impact of global forces on their respective economies, societies, and cultures. Buddhist principles and values inform each of them, not in narrow, parochial terms, but as foundational values for a paradigm of an ecology of human flourishing.[41]

41. Donald K. Swearer, "An Ecology of Human Flourishing," *Harvard Divinity Today* 4:3 (2008) 9–12.

8

Rethinking Hinduism for Socioeconomic Empowerment and Ecological Engagement

Siddhartha

This paper reflects on my experience working with poor communities to renew and reinterpret aspects of Hindu religious practice in order to promote social and environmental justice. Hundreds of millions of people in India live below the poverty line, and climate change threatens to deepen this misery. In response, Fireflies Ashram, located near the city of Bangalore in southern India, is evolving a participatory process in which religious faith contributes to sustainable development, interreligious dialogue, and interreligious conflict transformation.

Poverty and Religious Tensions in India

As an organization active in the social empowerment process, it is clear to us at Fireflies that economic development in India is creating new forms of social injustice. To understand why the poor are excluded and to develop strategies to confront discrimination, our method of analysis has had to be structural, integrating the social, religious, economic and political factors that legitimize an unjust system. We are today at a crucial juncture in human history where, in addition to the endemic problems of social injustice, the survival of the species itself has been placed in question as a result of climate change. Issues related to social exclusion and injustice have always been with us in India, and some of us mistakenly believed, in the seventies and eighties, that we would live to see the day when civil society would have eliminated the most degrading forms of social inequality. Ecological issues were not at the fore then.

According to a study done by Oxford University and the United Nations Development Report (UNDP), about one-third of the world's poor live in India. Using a household income of US$2 per day as the poverty benchmark, the study revealed that India not only has more poor people than sub-Saharan Africa, but also has a higher level of poverty. In India, 75.6 percent of the population, or 828 million people, live below the US$2 per day line as compared to 72.2 percent, or 551 million people in sub-Saharan Africa.[1] At the other end of the scale, the wealthy few in India have amassed great riches. The number of US dollar billionaires in India on the Forbes list was fifty-three in 2008.[2]

Climate change is already creating havoc in several parts of the country.[3] Heavy floods are resulting in loss of crops, property and life. Drought is a recurring phenomenon. Fluctuating weather patterns mean that food production will be badly affected. The retreating Himalayan glaciers will eventually take a heavy toll in the agricultural areas where the Ganges and Brahmaputra flow. The Intergovernmental Panel on Climate Change states that about twenty million people in Bangladesh will be forced to migrate by 2050 due to rising sea levels. Many of these people are likely to move into India. We will witness the emergence of millions of climate change refugees. Professor Myers of Oxford University estimates that we will touch two hundred million climate migrants by 2050. This has become a widely accepted figure.[4] The issue of climate justice will need to be raised rather strongly, for countries like Bangladesh will have to pay for the sins of the United States, China and others (India is also playing no small role).

1. Study conducted by Oxford University and UNDP. Oxford Poverty and Human Development Initiative (July 2010); online: http://www.ophi.org.uk/wp-content/uploads/Country-Brief-India.pdf.

2. *Indian Express*, March 6, 2008: online: http://www.indianexpress.com/news/meet-indias-53-forbes-billionaires-19-newc/281437/.

3. For a brief statement on the implications of climate change in India see: http://uk.oneworld.net/guides/india/climate-change.

4. Nicolas Stern, *The Economics of Climate Change: The Stern Review* (Cambridge: Cambridge University Press, 2006) 3.

It is clear that the religions of the world have largely acquiesced with a market fundamentalism that has legitimized the systemic creation of poverty and ecological degradation. We know that a bogus understanding of the sacred is often "manufactured" to serve the dominant economic interests of society, and presents itself as false consciousness, as objects that are at once electrifying and numbing. Divine grace assumes the form of consumer products and financial success. In the dominant understanding of the good life our inter-connectedness with other human beings and the earth is of little consequence.

There have been radical voices of dissent, such as the liberation theology movement, the various networks of engaged Buddhists, the Gandhian movement and a small band of engaged Hindu thinkers, as well as protests from within Islam (such as the writings of Asghar Ali Engineer in India). But the religious call to social justice and ecological renewal seems to have weakened in the past two decades, liberal secularism has temporarily won the day, and the vast majority of human beings have been left in deep anxiety about their future.

We are also witnessing the activities of extremist religious groups in India who resort to brutal methods. A minority of Hindu and Muslim religious activists have exploded bombs and used other forms of violence in their efforts to create serious conflict between the two religious communities. Some secular people also hold deeply prejudiced views of the religious "other." Yet, in spite of this negative public face, religions continue to posses a great potential for liberation from social and economic oppression and from the threat of ecological disaster.

Hinduism and Social Engagement

Hinduism represents a family of traditions. But within this diverse family we can still speak broadly of a dominant stream and a countercultural one. The dominant stream is based on a worldview legitimating a hierarchical caste system. But there are many instances in Indian history where the countercultural movements challenged the caste system and even patriarchy. The Buddha spoke about human beings "being equal, not unequal."[5] The eleventh-century Basava movement had a strong egalitarian vision. And the fifteenth-century spiritual

5. Nalin Swaris, *Buddhism, Human Responsibilities and Social Renewal* (Bangalore: Pipal Tree, 2008) 25.

leader Kabir developed his own view of the unity and equality of all human beings. From the late nineteenth century onwards, a number of political and religious figures espoused social equality. Today we have a vibrant Dalit movement in India, part of which is neo-Buddhist. It has been advocating for the past forty years for the social and economic empowerment of the former "untouchables."

Despite its contradictions, the dominant stream also holds a strong message of compassion and a call to action. The wellness of others cannot be separated from spiritual liberation. The expression used to convey these values in the Bhagavad Gita is *Lokasamgraha,* which suggests that a person must work for the well-being of all.[6] The true believer, whether following the transcendent or the immanent path, is one "who has good will for all, who is friendly and has compassion, who has no thoughts of 'I' or 'mine', whose peace is the same in pleasures and sorrows, and who is forgiving."[7] Perfection can be reached through the path of action, provided that the aim is for the good of all.[8] God does not have to act, but in his compassion he continues to act in the world to prevent destruction and confusion.[9] In the religious life outlined by the Bhagavad Gita, greed, the foundation of our neoliberal paradigm, is the cause of all evil.[10] The path of action involves two simultaneous movements: acting for the well-being of all human beings, and surrendering to the divine. One acts because it is right to act, and not necessarily to see the fruits of one's action.[11] Social activists can learn much from this attitude, known as *nishkama karma*, which helps to prevent triumphalism in success and despair in failure. It would be arrogant to believe that success or failure will come from us alone. Success or failure emanates from the divine, whether it is a personal god or the non-dual spiritual energy that pervades the universe.

Very much in line with liberal economic theories, Professor A. K. Saran argues that invention, innovation and individualism are essential to economic development. To a great extent these orientations

6. *The Bhagavad Gita*, trans. Juan Mascaro (India: Penguin, 1994), chapter 3.25, p. 58.

7. Ibid., chapter 12.13, p. 97.

8. Ibid., chapter 3.20, p. 58.

9. Ibid., chapter 3.24, p. 58.

10. Ibid., chapter 3.37–41, p. 59.

11. Ibid., chapter 2.47, p. 52.

were not possible in traditional India, where occupations were embedded in caste, and individualism in the modern understanding of the term did not exist. Besides, there was no sacred/profane dichotomy; everything was considered sacred. And since everything was considered sacred, the modern scientific tendency to see nature as dead matter that needed to be studied and exploited for human progress was largely unknown to the Indian mind.[12] But modern economic development is wedded to universal doubt and an experimental-empirical approach to reality—a frame of mind that Jawaharlal Nehru, India's first prime minister, called the "scientific temperament." Nature is to be studied, manipulated and exploited for scientific progress and material development.

Nehru himself believed that religion would weaken in India as the scientific temperament consolidated itself. But this has not happened. Rather, India has today reinvented religion, caste and family values with a strong dose of individualism that is sadly weak as far as social and ecological commitments are concerned. This is very much evident in the dynamic economic sectors of service and manufacturing in urban India. In fact, the competitive values of capitalist individualism and the interdependent and relational values of religion, caste and family form a continuum from urban to rural India, with the former being stronger in the urban context.

India is the second fastest growing economy in the world. But, as mentioned earlier, it is also the largest poverty area in the world. The gap between the rich and the poor is very wide and continuously increasing. The callousness of the rich and the powerful is substantial. Individualism, blending with aggressive market fundamentalism, has contributed to this lack of social concern. Making the first buck in the fast lane has become the mantra for many urban Indians. The individualism encouraged in the modern economic process also leads to a lack of concern for the environment. The earth is referred to as real estate, property, resource, minerals, raw materials, etc. The sacredness of the human-earth relationship is lost. Climate change is a direct result of this loss of sacredness. As stated earlier this individualism partially operates within the parameters of religion, caste and family. Many of our religious leaders and ashrams emphasize pathways to peace that are highly individualistic and do not consider questions of social justice.

12. A. K. Saran, *Archives des sciences sociales des religions*, 15:15 (1963) 87–94.

Hinduism and Interreligious Dialogue

Hinduism has been characterized as one of the most open and tolerant of the major world religions. The Rig Veda is often quoted, stating that "the Truth is one. The sages call it by different names."[13] Similarly, the *Bhagavad Gita* states, "They worship me as One and as many, because they see that all is in me."[14] Later in his life, when Mahatma Gandhi was asked whether he was a Hindu, he replied: "Yes I am. I am also a Christian, a Muslim, a Buddhist and a Jew."

Ramakrishna Paramahamsa insisted that all religions were like rivers that flowed into the sea. Each river has its characteristics, but it was the journey to the sea that was important. The sea was common to all human beings. At one point in his life Ramakrishna immersed himself in studying the Koran and other Islamic teachings. He emerged from this stating that he was now fully a Muslim. Later he underwent the same experience with Christianity, declaring himself a Christian.[15] Recognition of the equality of all religions does not deny their differences. Gandhi, for example, insisted that "the need of the moment is not one religion but mutual respect and tolerance of the devotees of different religions. We want to reach not the dead level but unity in diversity. Any attempt to root out traditions, effects of heredity, climate and other surroundings is not only bound to fail but is a sacrilege. The soul of religion is one but it is encased in a multitude of forms. The latter will persist to the end of time. Wise men will ignore the outward crust and see the same soul living under a variety of crusts."[16]

Broadly speaking there are two kinds of interreligious dialogue. One variety is concerned with promoting mutual understanding and trust between the different religions, and the other goes on to include efforts to combat poverty and fight social injustice and ecological destruction.

This second variety of dialogue has two objectives. The first is to understand and empathize with the problems of the excluded sections of society; the second is to address these problems as they relate to the emerging ecological crisis. Often these encounters bring together

13. Rigveda 1:164: 46.

14. The Bhagavad Gita (1994), chapter 9.15, p. 81.

15. See Ananda Coomarasamy, online: http://religioperennis.org/documents/acoomaraswamy/ramakrishna.pdf.

16. *Young India* [weekly journal], Sept. 25, 1925.

theologians and open-minded religious leaders from the different faith traditions. A deep common bond is established in these encounters because of their deep mutual concern for social justice and climate justice. Many in these gatherings feel closer to each other than with their fellow believers from their respective faith traditions. It brings to mind what Ernst Simon said: "The people I can pray with, I can't talk to, and the people I can talk to, I can't pray with."[17] At Fireflies our interreligious meetings also include secular activists. In India, many of these secular activists are also deeply spiritual, inspired by an old Indian tradition of secular spirituality with roots in Buddhism and Advaita Vedanta. The inspiration for social action is often drawn from different religious traditions, as has been the case in other social movements in different parts of the world. Gandhi drew from Hinduism, Buddhism, Jainism and Christianity in practicing his *satyagraha*, or truth force. The liberation struggle of fishermen on the west coast of India drew from the Latin American experience of combining Christian inspiration and Marxist social analysis. And Socially Engaged Buddhism in Thailand was influenced by Marx, Paulo Freire and liberation theology, although it anchored itself in Buddhist *karuna*, or compassion. In turn, many of the secular social justice–oriented social movements in contemporary India (e.g., the Narmada Bachao Andolan, led by Medha Patkar, or Ekta Parishad, led by P. V. Rajagopal) have been deeply influenced by Gandhian thought and practice.

Dialogue and Development at Fireflies Ashram

Fireflies is an intercultural ashram (community) located in a village outside Bangalore, in South India. This is where I live along with a small group of social, cultural and environmental workers. An ashram is normally a place where a guru (a spiritually enlightened person) and his followers live. In the past a guru was never self-made. Seekers of truth always discovered such a person, finding in him or her great sensitivity, understanding and compassion. At Fireflies, there is no guru. Or, put differently, the guru is the earth, from which we have all evolved. The earth stands for the immanent spiritual energy that permeates the universe. Both *nirguna* (the impersonal understanding of the divine, without qualities) and *saguna* (the appreciation of a per-

17. J. Clammer, ed., *Socially Engaged Religions* (Bangalore: Pipal Tree, 2010) 17.

sonal God, with qualities) understandings of spirituality blend in our approach.[18]

At a general level all our efforts to integrate spirituality with social and ecological concerns go under the rubric of Communities of Faith and Action (CFA). This program of faith and action endeavors to combine inner spiritual transformation with societal change. Personal change entails moving from selfishness to kindness, from pointless self-indulgence to an authentic celebration of life. It means being positive and compassionate in our thoughts and emotions. Despite a corrupt and often ruthless political context in India, we still believe that efforts at personal transformation which are other-oriented and earth-centered can help create the nonviolent synergies needed to bring about changes in our communities and in the environment. In this pursuit, we attempt to re-establish a harmony among the four traditional Hindu *purusharthas*, or human goals: *dharma* (ethical conduct and duties for a stable and moral social order), *artha* (worldly goods, wealth, instruments of livelihood and welfare), *kama* (desire for sensual pleasure and for the comforts that material goods bring), and *moksha* (release from attachment, God realization, spiritual liberation). Some would argue that in today's capitalistic world we tend to overemphasize *artha* and *kama* and have almost completely sidelined *dharma* and *moksha*. These goals were developed in ancient India to give people an ethical and spiritual orientation without sacrificing material goals. They must work in harmony if one is to live a meaningful life.[19] Action without a deep spiritual basis, whether derived from religious or secular sources, will end up being incomplete and even superficial. Overemphasizing spiritual liberation, or *moksha*, might also lead a person into a comfortable personal spirituality that overlooks social responsibilities. The CFA program, as the name suggests, aspires to change oneself and change society as well.

Apart from the *purusharthas*, the Bhagavad Gita ideal of *Lokasamgraha*, working for the well-being of everybody, is the guiding inspiration of CFA. But working for the well-being of everybody also entails giving priority to the poor and excluded. This ideal is integrated

18. Hinduism embraces thousands of deities, which makes it primal and polytheistic. But the divine is also seen as one unified consciousness, similar to the monotheistic understanding of God. At the same time some might find the absence of distinction between God and the universe as pantheistic or even atheistic.

19. M. V. Nadkarni, *Hinduism: A Gandhian Perspective* (India: Ane, 2006) 32–38.

within a matrix of personal, social and ecological renewal. Everybody can participate, irrespective of religious or spiritual orientation. Even people who are nonreligious are welcome, as the CFA process creates a sense of community fellowship and responsibility. The program has been taking root for the past few years among the poor villagers around Fireflies, and also in the Kabini area of Mysore district, where we work with many thousands of landless laborers and small farmers. Social activists, teachers, intellectuals and business professionals are also showing interest in the process.

Once a week, the CFA group participates in a *satsang* (a session that entails prayer, meditation and *bhajans*). After the *satsang*, which has an interreligious flavor, the village group discusses the social problems it faces. One woman may bring up the issue of alcoholism and how it is ruining her husband and impacting the family negatively, another may bring up the non-implementation of the government employment program. Yet another may talk about the corruption of the local government officials and the exorbitant bribes demanded from poor people. One village wants the government bus service to change its route marginally so that it may also pass through their village. Any problem that a person, or the community as a whole, faces is brought up for discussion. After studying the problems, solutions are discussed. Some remedies may be found without too much difficulty; others may take more time and entail systemic change.

Every month or so, the village officials are invited to participate and respond to the demands of the villagers. Approximately every six months, senior politicians and officials are invited to participate in the development of solutions. Nonviolent protests are possible wherever there is no response from government.

The CFA initiative helps give substance to the notion of citizenship. Ideally speaking, a citizen must feel empowered enough to contribute to changes in the local and national context. This is the basis of any meaningful participatory democratic process. Eventually it must lead to a more transparent and accountable practice of governance.

New Meanings of Traditional Rituals

Basava, the eleventh-century religious reformer and poet, wrote about his understanding of Shiva: "Things standing shall fall, but the moving ever shall stay." An understanding of Shiva that is fixed, rigid and "standing" will crumble, while that which is living and "moving" will remain.[20] This approach is very much in line with contemporary hermeneutics, which recognizes the dynamic nature of the understanding and interpretation of texts. For the philosopher Heidegger, hermeneutics was "an engaged appropriation of what is significant from the past, growing out of present concerns, in anticipation of a meaningful future."[21] For us, however, "the hermeneutics of hope" is about the transformation of religious and cultural practice in order to evolve fresh insights for democratizing society and creating a socially and ecologically sensitive citizenry. In this process, religions and spiritualities stop becoming ways for people to merely cope with their lives. There is a shift from coping to transforming.

"The hermeneutics of hope" is not so much a scholarly practice as it is a participatory process, involving the poor, that empowers while it re-visions. It involves an interaction between the traditional cultural and religious life of the people, on the one hand, and the social and environmental challenges they face, on the other. Here, people from villages and urban communities, particularly the poor and the excluded, reflect on the deeper meaning of their existence in relation to social and environmental issues. There is no guru or religious authority to tell them what they should believe. This is essentially a dialogical process where people discover the meanings that are most appropriate to their personal and social context. Understanding, imagination and explanation are vital if the festival or religious symbol is to be made contemporary and meaningful, and connected with real problems and issues.The "hermeneutics of hope" is thus a participatory and democratic process where people think for themselves and refuse ideological manipulation.

The challenge is to re-vision cultures and democratic practices as deeply as possible. Critical openness is important to this process, and goes hand in hand with respect and empathy for cultures. Above all, this is an approach which takes the wisdom of ordinary people seriously, whether they are "educated' or "uneducated," "literate" or

20. A. K. Ramanujan, *Speaking of Shiva* (India: Penguin, 1973), 1.

21. T. R. Quigley (1998); online: http://homepage.newschool.edu/~quigleyt/vcs/surber2.html.

"illiterate." Most of the people who participate in this process are peasants and the rural poor.

The goals of the process are: to promote a respectful and sensitive process of cultural reappropriation; to integrate the cultural and religious convictions of people; to strengthen citizenship, pluralism, participatory democracy and sustainable development; to reinterpret festivals and religious symbols with respect, imagination and critical openness; and to create a common ground for both religious and secular people to celebrate festivals that lead to social and environmental action.

I would like to now relate two specific examples of participatory hermeneutics—our celebration of the Ganesh festival and our efforts to envision Sita Devi as a figure to inspire ecological renewal.

The Ganesh Festival and Ecological Awareness

Ganesh, perhaps the most endearing God in the Indian pantheon, is half elephant (the top half) and half human (the lower half). He is at once a philosopher and a merry, childlike God. He is the God of knowledge and the remover of obstacles. According to some devotees, he, not Brahma, is the creator of the universe. He is the God to be propitiated before beginning a new venture. He protects the threshold of the house, keeping away evil influences. He is also popular as the deity who bestows material riches and worldly success. Despite his apparent weight, he does not add pressure on the earth; he is carried by a mouse. Some see him as their *ishta devata*, or personal god.

Each September, for the past eight years, we have held a weeklong celebration of the Ganesh festival at Fireflies. Initially, our decision to celebrate the Ganesh festival evoked considerable skepticism from our secular and left-wing friends. For them, Ganesh was a God used by Hindu nationalist bigots to preach hatred against the Muslims. Even our pleas that there was nothing intrinsic about Ganesh that lent itself to this purpose fell on deaf ears. They argued that history could not be changed, citing that even the nationalist freedom fighter Bal Gangadhar Tilak had used Ganesh as a symbol of Hindu renaissance, alienating the Muslims with his rhetoric, although Tilak's main purpose was to get the British to quit India. To his credit, Tilak saw the enormous potential of integrating religion and social transformation, even if his vision was a flawed one.

Tilak's use of the festival as a rallying point for Hindus is nevertheless worth mentioning. On September 8, 1866, Tilak wrote in the Marathi newspaper *Kesari*: "These festivals have two main roles. The first is mass recreation and the second is mass education . . . Why shouldn't the fairs organised in conjunction with festivals be used for political purposes? . . . Why shouldn't those who call themselves educated remind the people of the atrocities committed by the government? Or, why shouldn't they awaken the religious sense in the people and as a result strengthen their national pride?"[22]

Our own experiences of celebrating the Ganesh festival are very different from that of Tilak's. One such experience has to do with a Hindu-Muslim communal riot that took place in the poor section of Thilaknagar in Bangalore. A Hindu religious procession was disrupted after an altercation between Hindu and Muslim youths. All hell broke loose and several people were seriously injured from stone-throwing and stabbing. The police had to arrest more than one hundred people. When the violence subsided, the seriousness of the neighborhood tragedy became apparent. Many of the breadwinners were in jail and small businesses were ruined. But more notably Hindus and Muslims began to view each other with suspicion and even hatred.

We invited a group of Hindu and Muslim youth from the area to our ashram to discuss the events and see if things could be improved between the two communities. The Muslim youth did not turn up. However, we persisted and met them later in their own neighborhood. The discussions with the youth brought home the point that they were all losers in the conflict and that something had to be done to set matters right. It was the beginning of a slow reconciliation process. But what became a turning point was when the Hindu youth celebrated the Ganesh festival in a big way and invited the Muslim notables of the area to be seated on the dais, beside the statue of Ganesh. The Muslims shed some of their dislike of being too closely identified with Hindu festivals, and the Hindus shed some of their prejudice against Muslims by seating them next to their deity. This was the first time that such an honor was bestowed on the local Muslims by the Hindus of the locality. It played an important role in the reconciliation process. This

22. N. C. Kelkar, ed., *Lokmanya Tilakace Kesartil Lekh* (Pune, 1922) 566–68.

experience brought home the point that the Ganesh festival need not be biased against the Muslim community, but could actually play a role to promote communal harmony. Festivals are always grounded in a worldview. If the worldview is right then the festival helps create a sense of community and collective well-being.

Our experience of the Ganesh festival in the villages around Fireflies was focused on different objectives and a strong methodology of participation. Most of the people in the villages belong to different castes, but there are also communities of tribals who are nominally outside the caste system. (There is speculation that Ganesh originated from ancient animistic traditions as a pre-Aryan elephant deity. Over a few generations the tribals integrated some Hindu practices within their belief system.) Several years ago we formulated three questions along with some of the villagers. These questions were to be discussed in the villages before the festival began. The questions ran as follows:

(1) If Ganesh is the God of knowledge, and if true knowledge is synonymous with vision, what is the kind of vision we wish for our family, for the village, for the country, for the world? Are kindness, compassion and openness part of this vision?

(2) If Ganesh is the remover of obstacles, what are the difficulties and obstacles in our villages and how are we co-responsible with Ganesh to remove them? What is our own responsibility as citizens to overcome these social obstacles?

(3) If Ganesh is half-nature and half-human, he represents the bond between the natural world and the human world. So, what are we doing to preserve our environment? Instead of nurturing our environment are we polluting and destroying it? What is the role of chemical pesticides and fertilisers in polluting our water table? Are we growing more trees instead of cutting them heedlessly? Are we protecting our lakes?

The questions were phrased in a simple way. The discussions were uneven, with some people able to deal with the personal, social and environmental dimensions better than others. But most people took an active interest in the discussions. On the first day of the festival we placed an unpainted five-foot Ganesh statue at Fireflies. The statue was unpainted because of the toxicity of the paints, which contain lead and other carcinogenic chemicals. In the first year, people asked why the Ganesh was unpainted. Our response was that the poisonous chemicals in the paint would insult and humiliate Ganesh by polluting the lake he was going to be immersed in at the end of the festival. Over the years people in the villages around Fireflies have begun to purchase unpainted Ganesh statues. For those who want color an artist at Fireflies helps paint the statues with natural dyes.

During each festival, a few days after installing Ganesh at Fireflies, he is carried in a bullock cart through the neighboring villages and eventually immersed in a lake. In the first year of the festival, the school headmaster remarked that he was deeply moved when the statue was being carried in a bullock cart. "These days," he said, "we are used to Ganesh being carried in tractors. Now it's like the old times are back again." As the Ganesh procession winds through the village streets each family brings a plate of fruit, betel leaves and flowers to be consecrated before the deity.

Obviously the experiences outlined above cannot be carried out as mere tasks, but should be deeply respectful and participatory in nature. I was once asked if I believed that Ganesh was God, and if I was not a believer, could I claim any legitimacy in participating in such a sacred event? I responded that there was often a common meeting ground between the sacred and the secular. In the celebration of the Ganesh festival, any secular person maintaining a stance of openness could completely share in the vision that the villagers were trying to develop, could empathize with the desire to overcome difficulties and obstacles, and could be in complete solidarity with efforts to create ecological awareness. The secular and the sacred could meet over a vision to create sustainable communities.

Sita Devi as Earth Mother

We now move to our participatory reinterpretation of Sita Devi, daughter of Mother Earth (or Mother Earth herself, according to some). At Fireflies, our quest to unearth all the sacred meanings associated with the earth led us to rediscover Sita Devi. Our purpose here is to show that Sita Devi represents Earth Mother, and our veneration of her is a commitment to practice forms of development that are sustainable and lead to reduced carbon emissions and other kinds of pollution. It is also an acknowledgement that our earth is indeed sacred, and that we cannot continue to despoil her soil, water, air, trees, mountains and glaciers.

Let us briefly recall the story of Sita Devi. Sita is the wife of Lord Rama (known as "*maryada purushottam*," or the ideal human being). The story of Sita is known to every woman, man and child in India. As a baby, Sita was found by Janaka, King of Mithila, in a furrow in the earth and was raised as his own daughter. At the end of her days Sita called upon the earth to receive her. The earth opened, embraced Sita, and gently allowed her to descend.

After her marriage to Lord Rama, Sita was abducted by Ravana. She was eventually rescued and returned to the side of Rama. She had to undergo the fire sacrifice to prove her chastity while she was with Ravana. She underwent this ordeal successfully. But when an unfair rumor went around questioning her chastity Rama felt obliged to separate from her. Many have criticized Rama for his insensitive behavior. Others have argued that Lord Rama represented the principle of righteousness and he could not set a different set of rules for himself. In any case Sita went into the forest where her two sons, Lav and Kush, were born. In all her ordeals Sita carried herself with great dignity and never once demeaned herself.

To this day Sita is a symbol of the ideal woman, wife and mother. She is compassionate and forgiving, principled and courageous, and free of selfishness. The scriptures refer to her as the daughter of Mother Earth. The writer Madhu Kishwar states that "while for women Sita represents an example of an ideal wife, for men she is Sita *mata* (*jag-jannani*), not just the daughter of earth, but Mother Earth herself who inspires awe and reverence."[23]

At Fireflies we have built a Sita Devi temple, where prayers are offered every day and bhajans sung on Sundays and full moon nights. Sita Devi is venerated here as Earth Mother, who watches over her human and nonhuman offspring. Those who nurture the earth and those who go about their livelihood without endangering the planet are precious to her. Sita Devi is also the goddess who watches over and protects women and children. Women in our villages take their

23. Madhu Kishwar, "Yes to Sita, No to Ram: The Continuing Popularity of Sita in India"; online: http://www.ninapaley.com/Sitayana/Manushi_YesSitaNoRam.html. Issue No. 98, January–February 1997.

problems to her and find comfort. Traditionally, there has been little effort to connect Sita Devi with the environment, or even to see her as a patron of women and children. In fact there are hardly any temples in honor of Sita Devi. She is always found beside her husband Rama, but almost never on her own. The reinterpreted Sita Devi, however, is not a religious construction that emanates from Fireflies. It is the result of long interactions and discussions with farmers, women and youth. It is a process that we have already referred to as "a participatory hermeneutics of hope," where sacred tradition is reinterpreted and re-experienced in personal, social and ecological terms.

The Sacred Song Movement

In 2009, we helped start a discussion on the importance of songs within the women's self-help groups in the villages. These groups were concerned with violence against women, alcoholism among the men, learning of new skills, and exploring small income-generating activities. As a result of these discussions, the women expressed a desire to sing *bhajans* (sacred songs) at their meetings. They started to sing old songs and learn new ones. The songs included old Vedic songs, Gandhian *bhajans* and new eco-social songs.

Although there are different approaches to religion in India, from the theistic to the nontheistic, the most popular one is the tradition of *bhakti*, or devotion to a personal God. Some of the *bhakti* traditions also carry with them a strong message of social equality. *Bhakti* saints also included "untouchables" like Ravidas and Chokamela. For most people *bhakti* represents a deep feeling of love to their personal god. *Bhajans*, or sacred songs, are a way to express this love.

For a time, our song movement became a small force to be reckoned with in the local context. The women not only sang the songs but discussed the values behind them. As a result of the song movement they developed the courage to solve difficult local issues. One case in point was a land shark from Bangalore who bought a few acres next to Fireflies and illegally fenced-in one of the village lakes, partly filling it with earth, using a bulldozer. There are four small lakes in the village and he had partially covered one of them. This was a social and ecological crime, since the village is seriously short of water for agriculture and livestock. The people were too scared, or too indifferent, to protest.

The Panchayat (local elected body) members were also paralyzed, or partially bribed. The "shark" also managed to bribe some of the local government officials.

We tried to initiate a discussion on the responsibilities of citizenship and local self-governance. People were informed that a village losing a lake was like a human being losing a lung. The water in the lakes percolated slowly and recharged the aquifers. (In the villages around Fireflies the groundwater table had declined alarmingly in the past fifteen years from about 150 feet to 600 feet or more.) Many of the people realized how serious an issue it was, but they were still not motivated to act. Eventually about twenty people (mainly women), associated with the sacred song movement went to meet with the local Member of the Legislative Assembly (MLA). They explained the problem to him and asked him to visit the village, which he did a few days later. When he came, the women took him to the partially filled lake and pointed out how the village officials had connived with the land shark. The MLA asked to see the village maps, and when he realized that the lake had indeed been fenced-in and filled-up, he asked the people to bring crow bars and demolish the fence poles. The people did exactly this. The MLA then asked the people to be responsible for their lakes. He also promised financial help to restore the lakes.

The song movement combines the "truth" of the objective conditions of social and environmental degradation with the spiritual "meanings" that provide meaning and vision. The transformation of society through democratic practice and good governance need not be hampered by cynicism and hopelessness if the wellsprings of cultural and spiritual creativity begin to flow again.

This is a challenge that confronts all societies today: how do we move out of the limitations of a purely logical social discourse that is unable to overcome the indifference and cynicism of our age? If the transformation process does not connect with our deepest emotions, feelings and sense of wonder, then it cannot charge and motivate us. A transformative social, cultural and spiritual praxis must integrate the sacred and the secular, the rational and the intuitive, prose and poetry, the festival and the negotiation, talking and singing.

9

African Indigenous Spirituality, Ecology, and the Human Right to Integral Development

Laurenti Magesa

Two opinions dominate discussion on the health of the world in our time. There is, on the one hand, the position that through current human industrial, agricultural, and economic action, the life of the Earth, and consequently that of humanity, is endangered. This conviction suggests that limitless economic growth is ultimately incompatible with a sustainable world. The Intergovernmental Panel on Climate Change (IPCC), the World Conservation Union (IUCN), the Brandt Commission and Global 2000 are among numerous independent scientific research and advocacy bodies maintaining that ecological degradation is mainly due to the excessive and inconsiderate exploitation of the Earth's resources. In particular, they argue that lethal environmental pollution stems from excessive fossil fuel–burning machines, as well as from the use of chemicals in intensive commercial farming all over the world. According to the United Nations *Human Development Report* of 2007/2008, "Global warming, a result of human activity, continues to have a devastating impact on our environment . . . often negatively impacting the lives of the poor who are most vulnerable to the 'natural' environmental disasters."[1]

1. Quoted in Kevin Ahern, ed., *The Radical Bible* (Maryknoll, NY: Orbis, 2009) 14–15.

On the other hand, however, there are individuals and groups arguing that conservationist concerns are not only alarmist, but factually baseless. According to this position, no human action whatever poses any permanent danger to Earth's existence. There is, therefore, no need to regulate the processes of industrial production, mass consumption, and economic growth, for example, in the name of protecting the environment. In this view, regulation is ultimately self-defeating because it breeds universal underdevelopment and social disorder,[2] which does not benefit anyone. On the contrary, the pursuit of unlimited economic growth in terms of production and consumption is the answer to many of the social ills facing the world today, among them poverty, unemployment, and environmental degradation. Apart from the fact that no question is raised regarding any "downward spiral of diminishing resources" in nature, which, according to this view, are inexhaustible, no human activity can ever cause irreversible damage to the environment or put the planet in harm's way. If the universe's natural, built-in mechanisms for self-sustenance and regeneration are somehow exhausted, something that is unlikely, this view argues that there is now increasing scientific know-how to fix any potential damage.[3]

The Role of Spirituality or Religion in the Debate

Whether in an overt or subtle way, spirituality and religion play a crucial role in this debate. As Ronald M. Green has shown, "religion has its basis in a process of moral and religious reasoning"[4] based on

2. This argument fails to consider the discontent and disorder caused by some of the means currently employed in poor countries to generate wealth for the rich. For example, see the documentation by the Secretary General of Amnesty International, Irene Khan, *The Unheard Truth: Poverty and Human Rights* (New York: Norton, 2009). Also, Charles Karelis, *The Persistence of Poverty: Why the Economics of the Well-off Can't Help the Poor* (New Haven: Yale University Press, 2007); Dambisa Moyo, *Dead Aid: Why Aid Is Not Working and How There Is a Better Way for Africa* (New York: Farrar, Straus & Giroux, 2009); and Jonathan Glennie, *The Trouble with Aid: Why Less Could Mean More for Africa* (London: Zed, 2008).

3. This is the position of the U.S. Chamber of Commerce, which lists what it calls 10 Myths propagated by environmentalists. © 2004 by the U.S. Chamber of Commerce.

4. Ronald M. Green, *Religion and Moral Reason: A New Method for Comparative Study* (New York: Oxford University Press, 1988) xi.

a certain perception of reality. Thomas Berry describes religion as "humanity's ultimate confrontation with chaos."[5] Although religious reasoning about reality is not uniform, and may produce either human solidarity or conflict, Green asserts nevertheless that spiritualities or religions "have a common message of human brotherhood or sisterhood." He calls this the "'deep structure' of thought underlying historical religious traditions."[6] Deep structures have much to do with issues of human development and ecology. The deep spiritual-religious structure undergirding human perceptions of life in the world is what has to be investigated if it is to be shown how spirituality influences the various practical expressions of life. These expressions inform and shape prevailing human attitudes towards the Earth.

Since they are foundational dimensions of human societies' understandings of order, faiths and religions are inevitably part and parcel of the debate on the state of the Earth. "[T]he question of humanity's future," according to Berry, "is not something to be dealt with simply in its economic and political aspects" or its exclusively material level. Berry notes that this would be a dangerous "mistake" of restriction or reduction. Any conversation about the state and future of the Earth and the human community on Earth has to include the spiritual dimension. As he puts it, "The ideal ecological process . . . must be a complete process, one that includes the physical and the spiritual as well as the human dimensions of reality."[7]

This view is affirmed by a variety of religious groups. The World Council of Churches, the Anglican Communion, and the Catholic Church have at various times issued statements relating to the relationship between the Christian faith and ecology. The statements of Pope John Paul II in this regard may be considered among the most daring. In 1979, he proclaimed St. Francis of Assisi, a lover of nature, patron saint of animals and ecologists. Further, in his 1990 Message for the World, he emphasized that "care for all creation is a serious obligation" for all Christians. He explained that "the commitment of believers to a healthy environment for everyone stems directly from their belief in God the Creator." Therefore, "Respect for life and for the

5. Thomas Berry, *The Christian Future and the Fate of the Earth*, ed. Mary Evelyn Tucker and John Grim (Maryknoll, NY: Orbis, 2009) 1.

6. Green, *Religion and Moral Reason*, xi.

7. Berry, *The Christian Future*, 2.

dignity of the human person extends also to the rest of creation, which is called to join man in praising God."[8] The gist of the body of literature in the Catholic Church called the Social Teaching of the Church takes this responsibility as one of its central points.

In 2007, the Catholic Bishops of the United States, in a document titled *Forming Conscience for Faithful Citizenship*, likewise insisted that "Care for the earth and for the environment is a moral issue." For them, "Protecting the land, water, and air we share is a religious duty of stewardship and reflects our responsibility to born and unborn children, who are most vulnerable to environmental assault."[9] In a word, care for the environment is a matter of justice. Recently, the Second Special Assembly for Africa of the Synod of Bishops (or the Second African Synod of 2009) took for granted the integrity of creation as an element in the demand of universal justice.

Criteria of Development

It should be clear that the environment, economics and development are intrinsically related issues. The two basic expressions of economic arrangement in the world today, the "regulated" economy and the "liberal" economy, both operate from fundamentally *similar* criteria of industrial and technological production first set in motion by the European industrial revolution of the eighteenth century. "No revolution," writes Andre Bieler, "has so radically and permanently transformed the social order, habits, morals, mentalities and economic and political structures of all human societies as the industrial and technological revolution."[10]

Arising from this transformation in human consciousness and activity, both liberal and regulated economic systems (or what Bieler

8. See http://www.humanesociety.org/about/department/faith/francis_files_francis_of_assisi.html.

9. In Ahern, *The Radical Bible*, 26–27. The Catholic hierarchies all over the world have, of course, issued various documents that touch on this concern. One other interesting document from the American Bishops from the Appalachian region is *This Land Is Home to Me* (1975), rereleased twenty years later in 1995 as *At Home in the Web of Life*.

10. Andre Bieler, "Gradual Awareness of Social, Economic Problems (1750–1900)," in Julio A. Barreiro et al., *Separation without Hope? Essays on the Relation between the Church and the Poor during the Industrial Revolution and the Western Colonial Expansion* (Geneva: World Council of Churches, 1978) 9.

calls "private" and "state" systems, respectively) define the meaning of development today, the criteria of which are perceived to consist of income per head and the level of material consumer goods and social services. Theirs are predominantly quantitative indices of growth. They presume material incremental processes that can be quantifiable and assessable. Qualitative aspects of human betterment such as equity, justice and human rights appear secondary by these criteria. Accordingly, "something is uneconomic when it fails to earn an adequate profit in terms of money."[11]

Inadequacy of "Coins" and "Calories" as Sole Indices of Human Development

More and more people are arguing today that exclusively economic indices do not suffice as adequate criteria of human development. For instance, according to Pope Benedict XVI in a recent Encyclical Letter called *Caritas in Veritate*,

> . . . it should be stressed that *progress of a merely economic and technological kind is insufficient.* Development needs above all to be true and integral. The mere fact of emerging from economic backwardness, though positive in itself, does not resolve the complex issues of human advancement, neither for the countries that are spearheading such progress, nor for those that are already economically developed, nor even for those that are still poor, which can suffer not just through old forms of exploitation, but also from the negative consequences of a growth that is marked by irregularities and imbalances.[12]

To a certain extent, President Barack Obama may be interpreted as pointing to the same distinction when he noted in Ghana on July 11, 2009, that real development is "about more than growth of numbers on a balance sheet." Indices of growth, he said, are also "about whether a young person with an education can get a job that supports a family; a farmer can transfer their goods to the market; an entrepreneur can start a business."[13] Most crucially, it is about those things that recognize

11. E. F. Schumacher, *Small Is Beautiful: Economics as if People Mattered* (New York: Harper & Row, 1973) 42.

12. Pope Benedict XVI, *Caritas in Veritate* (June 29, 2009) §23 (italics original).

13. Online: http://www.huffingtonpost.com/2009/07/11/obama-ghana-speech-full-t_n_230009.html

a person's dignity and offer opportunities to realize it. Thus, according to Vigdis Broch-Due and David Anderson, "Quantifiable measures of poverty, defined usually by incomes ['coins'] or nutrition ['calories'] . . . are often both inadequate and misleading when detached as raw statistics from the context of their cultural moorings." Yet, on account of their simplicity, "they give comforting appearance of objectivity and seem to travel with ease across cultural and historical boundaries."[14]

When Engelbert Mveng speaks of "anthropological poverty," "indigence of being," or "anthropological annihilation,"[15] he is referring to more than economic poverty. When Amartya Sen talks about "capacity deprivation," the "deprivations that are *intrinsically* important" (such as freedom) and not only those that are *"instrumentally* significant" (such as "low income"), he goes beyond economic criteria as a basis of human growth.[16] To revert to Mveng, "There are other goods—spiritual, moral, cultural, sociological and so on—the privation of which engenders other types of poverty: spiritual, moral, cultural, and sociological poverty . . . These kinds of poverty are just as devastating for a human being as is simple material poverty."[17]

But the economic solution is the one currently propagated by the globalization movement. It originates from "a particular economic culture, neo-liberal capitalism, a thoroughly materialistic worldview." As Albert Nolan sees it, this worldview is "based on the principle of the survival of the fittest, a culture that destroys other cultures and indigenous wisdom, making the rich richer and the poor poorer around the world."[18] The subversion or loss of local cultures poses a danger to the environment because it diminishes awareness of human proximity to the Earth. For within local communities, "the consequences of our actions become more readily apparent: for example, pollution and

14. Quoted in Agbonkhianmeghe E. Orobator, *From Crisis to Kairos: The Mission of the Church in the Time of HIV/AIDS, Refugees and Poverty* (Nairobi: Paulines Publications Africa, 2005) 183.

15. Engelbert Mveng, "A Theological Approach for Africa and the Third World," in Rosino Gibellini, ed., *Paths of African Theology* (Maryknoll, NY: Orbis, 1994) 156.

16. See Amartya Sen, *Development as Freedom* (New York: Knopf, 2000) 87ff.

17. Mveng, "A Theological Approach," 156–57.

18. See Ahern, *Radical Bible*, 57. Also Lewin L. Williams, "A Theological Perspective on the Effects of Globalization on Poverty in Pan-African Contexts," in Peter J. Paris, ed., *Religion and Poverty: Pan-African Perspectives* (Durham: Duke University Press, 2009) 88–107.

poverty can no longer be exported out of sight." Furthermore, it becomes easier to "persuade people to do what is right because it is more immediately apparent that this is in their own personal and their own community's self-interest." As a rule, "A better knowledge of place and a closer connection to the land . . . creates a spontaneous ecological awareness from which the new ethics [of ecology] can flow."[19]

The Practice of the Churches

Although I have noted that various faiths and churches have tended to be pro-ecology and pro-environment *in theory*, many have been much less so *in practice*. Among others, Bieler has noted that a "clandestine identification of the Christian message with the ethics of the Western middle classes" has been so deep as to distort in practice what Christians have gradually developed to profess in theory through the centuries.[20] There is a view among some church leaders that ecological changes are problems not of the church but of the state. Truman B. Douglas criticizes this perception as "essentially a transcendentalist view of the church."[21]

Transcendentalist views of existence usually create dangerous dichotomies between rhetoric and pragmatism, thought and action, or even spirit and matter. Thought and rhetoric may be positive and full of hope while action may be lacking in the face of destitution and death. A purely transcendentalist perspective is characterized by a discourse that, among other things, purports to stand for life, freedom, equality, and justice, but is functionally indifferent towards the death of the oppressed, inequality, and injustice in society.[22] Religious tran-

19. Mark Hathaway and Leonardo Boff, *The Tao of Liberation: Exploring the Ecology of Transformation* (Maryknoll, NY: Orbis, 2009) 360. On the significance of culture, Hathaway and Boff (ibid.) quote Marcia Nozick thus: "Culture ['as a way of life'] is the *glue* that holds communities together and makes them last over generations, even more than political and economic power. *Culture is the soul and life force of a community*—the collective expression of values, perceptions, language, technology, history, spirituality, art and social organization in a community." Italics in original. As an African, I could not agree more.

20. Bieler, "Gradual Awareness," 8.

21. See Truman B. Douglas, "Ecological Changes and the Church," in Richard D. Knudten, ed., *The Sociology of Religion: An Anthology* (New York: Appleton-Century Crofts, 1967) 149.

22. See Mveng, "Impoverishment and Liberation," 160.

scendentalism is what Bishop Oscar Romero criticizes when he speaks of those who "want to keep a Gospel so disembodied that it does not get involved at all in the world it must save."[23] That is not the gospel of Christ, Romero declares.[24] For Mohandas (Mahatma) Gandhi, likewise, involved religion is the only true one: "I do not know of any religion," he avers, "apart from human activity."[25]

A Third Model

For this discussion, I wish to propose a third model of economic life, beyond the regulative and liberal models. It arises from a spirituality which has not received much attention in shaping the world's order due primarily to historical subjugation.[26] Let us characterize this as the communitarian model.[27] It is one based primarily not on profit and consumerism but on the primacy of human relationships. This model is typical of African societies. "Theirs," as Green explains, "is a world where all significant interpersonal relationships, including important relationships between humans and spiritual beings, have moral content and are governed by moral considerations."[28] African activity, including economic activity rightly understood, is thoroughly shaped by relational moral concerns. These constitute the religious bent of the African person that John S. Mbiti once so famously described.[29]

Simply put, according to Mbiti, "Whatever happens to the individual happens to the whole group, and whatever happens to the whole group happens to the individual." African ethical perceptions are based

23. In Ahern, *Radical Bible*, 149.

24. See ibid.

25. See ibid.

26. John Apolinari Tenamwenye, *Solidarity and Its Evangelical Challenge for the Local Churches in Africa Today: A Theological Reflection from the Tanzanian Perspective* (Nairobi: Don Bosco, 2009) 9.

27. The *communitarian* model of African economics must not be confused with the *communist* model, as it is so easy to do. The latter is in fact much closer to the regulated model of economics and development than with communitarianism.

28. Green, *Religion and Moral Reason*, 26. Also among numerous others, Laurenti Magesa, *African Religion: The Moral Traditions of Abundant Life* (Maryknoll, NY: Orbis, 1997); Evan M. Zuesse, *African Cosmos: The Sanctification of Life in African Religions* (Athens: Ohio University Press, 1985); and John S. Mbiti, *African Religions and Philosophy* (London: Heinemann, 1969).

29. Mbiti, *African Religions and Philosophy*, 1.

on this principle. "The individual can only say: 'I am, because we are; and since we are, therefore I am,'" writes Mbiti, and the community also understands that without the individual members constituting it, it is nonexistent.[30] In other words, as John A. Tenamwenye explains, "while the individual must act in solidarity with other members, he remains himself, with personal responsibility." The dynamic of this relational principle is therefore "no longer an *'I-for-myself*, but an *I-in-the-community-for-others.*'"[31]

Pope Benedict XVI appears to argue in this communitarian manner when he emphasizes the importance of "solidarity" for the contemporary economic order:

> In the global era, economic activity cannot prescind from gratuitousness, which fosters and disseminates solidarity and responsibility for justice and the common good among the different economic players. It is clearly a specific and profound form of economic democracy. Solidarity is first and foremost a sense of responsibility on the part of everyone with regard to everyone, and it cannot therefore be merely delegated to the State.[32]

The use of the expression "solidarity" by the Pope is reminiscent of the definition of the term provided by his predecessor, Pope John Paul II, who defines solidarity not as a mere "feeling of vague compassion or shallow distress" at the suffering of other people. For him, solidarity is "a firm and persevering determination to commit oneself" to change the situation for the better.[33]

Daniel Finn explains that the pope has paid attention to the particular principle of "reciprocity."[34] This is central to the African communitarian approach to the economy. Although "reciprocity is similar

30. Ibid., 108.

31. Tenamwenye, *Solidarity and Its Evangelical Challenge*, 14.

32. Benedict XVI, *Caritas in Veritate*, §38. Tenamwenye, *Solidarity and Its Evangelical Challenge*, explores this concept usefully in relation to one African country, Tanzania.

33. John Paul II, *Sollicitudo Rei Socialis*, §38.

34. Daniel Finn, "Benedict's Third Way," *The Tablet* (13 March, 2010) 6. With reference to one African ethnic group, the Aembu of Kenya, it is what Eugene Wangiri in "*Urumwe* Spirituality and the Environment," in Mary N. Getui and Emmanuel Obeng, *Theology of Reconstruction*, 71–89 describes as *"urumwe,"* namely oneness and harmony. See also J. J. Ongong'a, "Towards an African Environmental Theology," in ibid., 50–70.

to exchange in that when I help you out, you feel an obligation to help me in return," it is more in line with "the pure gift relationship, in that you don't have to return the favour. Or you may reciprocate by helping someone else." In this approach, the reciprocity "may simply be the right thing to do; but we experience an informal social obligation as well, once we ourselves have benefited from such action by others."[35]

This approach is similar to what E. F. Schumacher describes as "Buddhist Economics," in which work has a threefold purpose: (a) work facilitates the use and development of the human faculties; (b) work encourages the reduction of self-centeredness in favor of cooperation; and (c) work emphasizes the priority of production of goods and services to satisfy a decent human life.[36] This view of economic labor "sees the essence of civilization not in a multiplication of wants but in the purification of human character," which comes about through work. Work, when "properly conducted in conditions of human dignity and freedom, blesses those who do it and equally their products."[37]

As Matthew M. Theuri argues, religion and theology must reject aspects of behavior that foster improper development for humanity.[38] Within these broader issues of economic and human development, the specific question we would like to address concerns what role African Religion or spirituality can play in the universal quest for genuine human development. What elements does African Religion bring to the project of development?

The Communitarian Approach

There can, of course, be no question that material and consumer indices must be accepted as valid and necessary assessments of human progress. Yet a new awareness seems to be dawning that bespeaks the necessity of ecological, personal, psychological, emotional, and moral or spiritual factors as equally pertinent to the process of integral hu-

35. Ibid.

36. See Schumacher, *Small Is Beautiful*, 54–55.

37. Ibid., 55.

38. See Matthew M. Theuri, "Religion and Culture as Factors in the Development of Africa," in Mary N. Getui and Matthew M. Theuri, eds., *Quests for Abundant Life in Africa* (Nairobi: Acton, 2002) 187–97.

man development.[39] For people of faith, the ideal of human development must include both material criteria and nonmaterial criteria of human dignity as essential elements encouraging or inhibiting integral human advancement.[40]

The communitarian African religious perception of the spiritual-moral dimension of development can be observed and studied. However, it is not as easy to capture and measure by pragmatic and quantitative criteria as its free market counterpart. Nevertheless, the moral dimension that forms an essential dimension of this approach must be included in any comprehensive understanding of human progress because the moral dimension is part of the innate human aspiration towards self-transcendence or spiritual satisfaction beyond material possessions. It touches the holistic, total longing of the human person that material success alone cannot satisfy.

The communitarian view of the economy gives its own order of priorities to these issues. It lays emphasis first on the satisfaction of the essential needs of every individual in society. It also underlines the moral requirements of freedom, equity, justice, participation, solidarity, sharing, and dignity of all persons. As Amartya Sen argues, "Development requires the removal of major sources of unfreedom: poverty as well as tyranny, poor economic opportunities as well as systematic social deprivation, neglect of public facilities as well as intolerance or overactivity of repressive states."[41] According to Sen, the problem is:

> Despite unprecedented increases in overall opulence, the contemporary world denies elementary freedoms to vast numbers—perhaps even the majority—of people. Sometimes the lack of substantive freedoms relates directly to economic poverty . . . In still other cases, the violation of freedom results directly from a denial of political and civil liberties by authoritarian regimes and from imposed restrictions on the freedom to participate in the social, political and economic life of the community.[42]

39. For example, see Mveng, "Impoverishment and Liberation," 154–65.

40. For instance, see the argument presented by Huston Smith, *Why Religion Matters: The Fate of the Human Spirit in an Age of Disbelief* (San Francisco: HarperSan Francisco, 2001).

41. Sen, *Development as Freedom*, 3.

42. Ibid., 3–4.

To be sure, this communitarian approach to economic order is not ideologically influential. Yet, apart from influencing African Religion's perception of the economy and development, it includes solid similarities with age-old Christian socioeconomic principles.[43] As summarized by Philip Land, John A. Coleman's "nine axioms" of Catholic Social Thought are as follows:

> 1) The economy is for people; 2) The economy is for being, not having; 3) The economic system ought to be needs-based; 4) The economy is an act of stewardship; 5) The economy must be a participatory society; 6) There must be fair sharing; 7) The system must permit self-reliance; 8) The economy must be ecologically sustainable; 9) The economy must be productive.[44]

Let us use these axioms to elaborate in a general way the African view and approach to the economy and the meaning of development. In the process we will try to indicate what contribution African spirituality can make in conversation with other economic views and approaches in the modern world.

The Economic Person and Community

No economic paradigm exists and functions independently of human intelligence, reflection, intentions and goals. Economic choices and orientations arise out of a society's perception of the world, a worldview, philosophy or spirituality (*Weltanschauung*).[45] Constructed by

43. For example, see Martin Hengel, *Property and Riches in the Early Church* (Philadelphia: Fortress, 1974); Vatican II, *Gaudium et Spes*, §§64–72; John XXIII, *Mater et Magistra* (1961); Paul VI, *Populorum Progressio* (1967); John Paul II, *Laborem Exercens* (1981), and *Sollicitudo Rei Socialis* (1987).

44. See John A. Coleman, "Neither Liberal Nor Socialist: The Originality of Catholic Social Teaching," in John A. Coleman, ed., *One Hundred Years of Catholic Social Thought: Celebration and Challenge* (Maryknoll, NY: Orbis, 1991) 39.

45. In this paper, these notions (worldview, spirituality, and to a lesser extent philosophy) are used almost interchangeably. Each is taken to mean "the actual metaphysical, epistemological, ethical, aesthetic, etc. beliefs of a people—the supreme beliefs [and values] of a people and their derivatives—all of which constitute the dominant beliefs that underpin the social institutions, policies and social practices of a people." Among preliterate peoples, and generally on the level of society as a whole, these beliefs are usually held and lived without much sustained reflective self-criticism. In literate societies they are sometimes systematically reflected on in a critical process (called philosophy proper). But in either case, a philosophy, worldview of spirituality consists of "beliefs in which an outlook on the world is

humans, the economic worldview influences images of the individual self and the community, as well as the relationship between them. In turn, notions of the self and community modify a people's economic and social worldview. This endless cyclical dynamic dictates approaches to the economy, to systems of production, structures of distribution, and tastes in consumption of goods. In other words, how we conduct our economic activity is fundamentally an outcome of *human decisions*, determined by human understanding of the world and our place in it.[46]

Accordingly, the attempt to understand the economic person and the economic community in African spirituality demands an appreciation of its perception of the universe. The procedures and purposes of production gain meaning only on the basis of what humanity and the world are seen or meant to be. It is in this sense that we can say that economics is founded on spiritual or religious principles and convictions. This remains the case even if the "religion" is exclusively "secular" in character, a doctrine consciously and explicitly disavowing any belief in, or mention of, God or any supernatural reality.

African traditional economic patterns operated from a worldview that was synchronic and harmonious in its components: the person is as much part of general nature as nature forms part of the person. In the expression of John V. Taylor, "Not only is there less separation between subject and object, between self and non-self" in the African worldview, "but fundamentally all things share the same nature and the same interaction one upon another."[47] Included in this notion of community and constant, mutual, dynamic interaction are the animate and non-animate beings, the living and the dead, the ancestors and the yet-to-be-born, and the spirits, "for all are one, all are here, all are now."[48] Everything has a spiritual component. Accordingly, Marimba

---

founded, and from which the motives of human action may be drawn." For a given community, its philosophy, worldview or spirituality is "an active director" of its life generally and that of the individuals within it. See Joseph C. A. Agbakoba, "Philosophy and Traditional African Ethics: The Problems of Economic Development," in Joao J. Vila-Cha, ed. *Revista Portuguesa de Filosofia* 65: 1–4 (Janeiro-Dezembro, 2009) 550–52.

46. Joseph Schumpeter, *Imperialism/Social Classes* (New York: Meridian, 1955) is an interesting volume to read in this connection.

47. John V. Taylor, *The Primal Vision* (London: SCM Press, 1963) 72.

48. Ibid., 72.

Ani can say that "the universe to which . . . [Africans] relate is sacred in origin, is organic, and is a true 'cosmos.' Human beings are part of the cosmos, and as such, relate ultimately with other cosmic beings."[49] There is "a basic aliveness in all things" in the African worldview. Here "the deepest recesses of the inner world interface with and interpenetrate the furthest known expanse of the external world."[50]

Thus the universe is never an *object* but always a *subject*, at one with the human person. It is not merely a space in which a person exists, but something fundamentally integrated with the person, acting as the person acts. Thus, "Knowledge of the universe comes through relationship with it and through perception of spirit in matter. The universe is one; spheres are joined because of a single unifying [spiritual] force that pervades all being. Meaningful reality issues from this force."[51] This epistemological norm determines African traditional approaches to economic activity. By taking themselves as normative, they do not leave room for ideas about constructing new economic systems. It is not possible to extrapolate the essence of the entire universe from the essence of the human being so as to manipulate it as an object "out there," since "as above, so below."[52] The universe is part of the human actor: whatever is done to it is ultimately done to the human actor. In the end, any action has the same consequences upon the actor as upon the surrounding environment.

In the process of development in Africa, this dimension of the unity of creation needs to be brought into serious consideration, updated and renewed. How can economic activity be integrated into the whole dynamics of the harmonious interaction of all existence?[53] How does this impact human attitudes towards work and investment, saving and entrepreneurship, production, revenue and distribution, self-discipline and self-control?

49. Marimba Ani, *Yurugu: An African-Centered Critique of European Thought and Behavior* (Trenton, NJ: Africa World Press, 1994) 29.

50. Edward Bruce Bynum, *The African Unconscious: Roots of Ancient Mysticism and Modern Psychology* (New York: Teachers College Press, 1999) 92.

51. Ani, *Yurugu*, 29.

52. See Bynum, *The African Unconscious*, 321.

53. However, for a critique of the African view of the universe in the context of modern economic processes, see Joseph C. A. Agbakoba, "Philosophy and Traditional African Ethics: The Problems of Economic Development," in Joao J. Vila-Cha, ed., *Revista*, 570–75.

Economy for People

Material wealth and poverty are both dimensions of human life, with physical and spiritual manifestations. Elizabeth Amoah has discussed the most important dimension of material wealth engendering psychical-spiritual satisfaction in African Religion: communion among people. Wealth is meant to serve that purpose. "Wealth in the traditional African system is not merely acquisition or piling up of material things for individual use," she explains. "Rather, it is community-centered."

> By this I mean that the emphasis on wealth is on its use to promote the welfare of the community. In this sense, the idea of sharing is an integral part of the concept of wealth. Thus wealth by itself is worth very little if it is not used to advance or promote human welfare. In other words, the essence of wealth does not lie in mere individualistic accumulation but in the requirement to use it for communal welfare.[54]

This is not to suggest, however, that conditions of poverty should be maintained in society; sharing presupposes the existence of wealth. More importantly, speaking as Christians, we must agree that there is nothing authentically human in imposed poverty. As Julius K. Nyerere lucidly points out,[55] if we believe that the human person resembles God, how can we "imagine a God who is poor, ignorant, superstitious, fearful, oppressed, wretched—which is the lot of the majority of those He created in his own image"?[56] From the point of view of Christian anthropology, poverty must be combated.

While Christian faith contradicts any glorification of imposed poverty, it does not thereby uncritically promote its opposite, the ideology that the pursuit of unlimited wealth is the ideal of human personal and social existence. This is where care is needed, especially in the contemporary world order, where "the market" rules in politics, economics and even, very often, in religion. It has been made to appear

54. Elizabeth Amoah, "African Traditional Religion and the Concept of Poverty," in Paris, ed., *Religion and Poverty*, 120.

55. The process of Nyerere's canonization in the Catholic Church is under way, having already been granted the title "Servant of God" by the relevant Vatican authorities. If the process succeeds Nyerere's case will be remarkable for a politician in a continent known for the corruption, dishonesty and arrogance of its leaders.

56. Ibid., 216. I have not tried to adjust gender-exclusive language in quoted texts throughout this article.

that in practice morality or ethics shares a very tenuous relationship, if any at all, with "the market." Takatso A. Mofokeng, however, shows that billionaire George Soros implicitly points out the connection between ethics and economics when he confesses that "if I had to deal with people instead of markets, I could not have avoided moral choices and I could not have been so successful in making money."[57] Economics is not neutral; ultimately it involves moral choices.

Economy for Well-Being

There are divergent views in Christianity about wealth and poverty. This indicates the paradox these factors present to people of faith in development discourses. One view holds that according to Scripture, legitimate wealth is in line with divine mandate to humanity to "cultivate and care for" the Earth (Gen. 2:15, *The African Bible*)—without any qualification. In fact, personal wealth is a sign of favor from God, according to this view. For the other view, there is a warning, with no less precedent in the Scriptures, that the pursuit of wealth alone cannot be counted as the *sole* or even highest good: One cannot live without bread, but "one does not live by bread alone . . ." (Matt 4:4). Or again ". . . it is easier for a camel to pass through the eye of a needle than for one who is rich to enter the kingdom of God" (Matt 19:24; Mk. 10:25). Difficult enough in its theoretical shape, this paradox is not easily resolved in real life. It implies balance between economic realism and self-transcendence.

The aspect of self-transcendence as a dimension of holistic human development is advanced to avoid the danger of reductionism or "one-dimensionalism" in the understanding of development. This runs the danger of excluding from the process of progress any consideration that facilitates solidarity, sharing and environmental conservation. But these considerations are essential, beyond the universal satisfaction of basic needs, for the goals of justice, peace, and the future of the world.

"The fundamental purpose of . . . productivity must not be the mere multiplication of products," according to the Second Vatican Council. "It must not be profit or domination. Rather, it must be the service of man"—the human person considered from all dimensions:

57. See Takatso A. Mofokeng, "The Informal Economy and the Religion of Global Capital," in Paris, ed., *Religion and Poverty*, 85–86.

"intellectual, moral, spiritual, and religious."[58] In 1967, Pope Paul VI described development in words that, almost forty years later, still have direct relevance:

> Development cannot be limited to mere economic growth. In order to be authentic, it must be complete: integral, that is, it has to promote the good of every man and the whole man . . . "We do not believe in separating the economic from the human, nor development from the civilisations in which it exists. What we hold important is man, each man and each group of men, and we even include the whole of humanity."[59]

Pope Benedict as well emphasizes that "*progress of a merely economic and technological kind is insufficient*."[60] Although in our thinking on development in Africa we must avoid the "utopia of a return to humanity's original natural state," in Pope Benedict's words, we must with equal clarity avoid exaggerating "technical progress," seeing it as the panacea of all human growth. Both temptations risk detaching human development "from its moral evaluation and hence from . . . [human] responsibility."[61]

Human responsibility in matters of development must include certain indispensable requirements: deliberate attention to the common good,[62] quest for fraternity,[63] care of the environment,[64] advancement towards human solidarity,[65] and responsible use of technology.[66] Accordingly, one of the tasks for humanity today is the effort to civilize the economy,[67] to make it ethical.[68] An ethical economy must be understood in the sense, again, that "the *primary capital to be safeguarded and valued is man, the human person in his or her integrity*: 'Man is the

58. Vatican II, *Gaudium et Spes*, §64.

59. Paul VI, *Populorum Progressio*, §14. See also Tarimo, *Applied Ethics*, 12–15.

60. Benedict XVI, *Caritas in Veritate*, §23.

61. Ibid., §14.

62. Ibid., §7.

63. Ibid., §§34–42.

64. Ibid., §§43–51.

65. Ibid., §§53–67.

66. Ibid., §§68–77.

67. Ibid., §38.

68. Ibid., §45.

source, the focus and the aim of all economic and social life.'"[69] These are different ways of saying that in order to serve the integrity of the human person and society, economic activity must be guided by these goals. This is why the state has a role to play in economic activity for the benefit of society.

If economic advancement is to be an instrument of human holistic progress, it must be "achieved on the basis of the equality and human dignity of all those involved," as Nyerere explains. True development requires "freedom, and relations of mutual respect among men. Further, it depends on responsibility, and on a conscious participation in the life of the society in which a man moves and works."[70] The purpose of true development is the whole person in every dimension, never solely as an individual, but necessarily as a member of society:

> For man lives in society. He becomes meaningful to himself and to his fellows only as a member of that society. Therefore, to talk of the development of man, and to work for the development of man, must mean the development also of that kind of society which serves man, which enhances his well being, and preserves his dignity. Thus, the development of peoples involves economic development, social development, and political development.[71]

As Nyerere sees it, "at this time in man's history . . . [development] must imply a divine discontent and a determination for change." This means concretely a spiritual outlook that goes beyond the pursuit of infinite exclusive economic progress. Development involves the rediscovery and implementation of the transcendental elements of human "being." The African spiritual perception concerning the individual person, society, and the economy can be a source that serves this rediscovery. And in as far as economic systems are a result of cultural-religious perspectives, intercultural and interreligious dialogue may enable such a contribution.

69. Ibid., §25.

70. Nyerere, *Freedom and Development*, 218.

71. Ibid., 216. See also Enyribe S. Oguh, *John Locke and Property as a Human Right Today: Towards a New Theory of Property Rights* (Koln: Lambert Academic, 2009).

Needs before Wants: Stewardship

We must always combine economic and moral considerations in development discourse because the economy has always something to do with relations—interpersonal, international, and environmental. The economy has its source and meaning in human labor: it is human labor based on land, natural resources, capital, and entrepreneurship that produces wealth and enables it to be distributed. How wealth is produced and distributed, and what consequences these processes have on human relations and the environment, are ethically fundamental and relevant questions. They bring us back to the pivotal issue of the morality of the economy. This is why Pope John Paul II can assert that "human work is . . . probably *the essential key* . . . to the whole social question, if we really try to see that question from the point of view of man's good."[72] "Thus the principle of the priority of labor over capital," he adds, "is a postulate of the order of social morality."[73]

The perspective of African spirituality is that human labor is unitive, both in procedure and in its ultimate goal at all social levels. The clan, for example, is seen as the extension of the family; the work of its members is expected to coalesce in the promotion of the life of the whole clan. To this end, traditionally, some families in a clan held special responsibilities of expertise for the sake of the whole community, including blacksmithery, divination, healing, and so on. These specializations were not understood as means for individual prosperity, but primarily for communal well-being.

This approach to the economy is not congruent with some of the principles of liberal economics which emphasize self-interest and competition as the necessary elements for economic growth and development. "It is not from the benevolence of the butcher, the brewer, or the baker that we expect our dinner," Adam Smith taught, "but from their regard to their own interest."[74] David Ricardo similarly expounded on "the principle of comparative advantage," calculating that "total output will be increased if people and nations engage in those activities for which their advantages over others are largest or their disadvantages

72. John Paul II, *Laborem Exercens*, no. 3.

73. Ibid., no. 15.

74. See http://www.brainyquote.com/quotes/authors/a/adam_smith.html/

are the smallest."[75] Here again, the emphasis is on competition rather than cooperation.

Participation, Solidarity, and Sharing

The African view, however, would resemble the general philosophical-moral idea of the Greek philosopher Democritus of Abdera (ca. 460–ca. 370 BCE).[76] Democritus advocated two basic virtues in the economic process: justice and moderation. These, for him, are the foundation for internal personal satisfaction and social harmonious existence. In terms of justice, Democritus argued against the wisdom of "material riches which resulted from transactions that aimed at the accumulation of wealth exceeding the absolutely necessary goods of life."[77] He believed that in excess, wealth corrodes moral health, insisting that personal integrity and social harmony are incompatible with any form of extreme economic inequality in society.[78] Consequently, he counseled that for the sake of personal and social well-being, the rich are obliged to help the poor, although he didn't elaborate on how this was to be done apart from pitying and lending to them.[79]

In economic organization, African spirituality in its deep structure[80] operates much out of the same root-source of person-solidarity-harmony dynamics between the individual, society and the universe. "The body of values drawn from this source," as P. F. Nursey-Bray explains, "represents what can best be categorized as a species of African natural law . . . prescriptive in relation to political and existing legal

75. See http://www.netmba.com/econ/micro/comparative-advantage/

76. See Ourania Kardassi, Panayotis Michaelides and John Milios, "On Democritus's Economic Ideas," in Vila-Cha, ed., *Revista*, 445–62.

77. Ibid., 451. He surely might have regarded such wealth as a result of unjust economic transactions.

78. Ibid., 451. See Matt 19:16–30; Mark 10:17–31; Luke 18:18–30.

79. Ibid., 452. Democritus's ideas on property and ownership are not far from those of the early Christian fathers, from the time of the death of the apostles up to the fifth century (e.g., Clement of Alexandria, Basil the Great, Ambrose, John Chrysostom, Jerome and Augustine of Hippo). Their main idea is that the world is God's gift to every human being. Almost all of them make a connection between the wealth of some and the poverty of others, and they are unfavorable to the former, attributing it mostly to greed.

80. Forming the subliminal criteria upon which the universe is understood and interpreted.

and social norms."[81] On the basis of these norms, "the most desirable goal of personal development and social interaction . . . is to attain to a condition of tranquil equilibrium of interacting forces within the self and between the self and its environment."[82]

> African cultural traditions reveal the primacy of the community as the ground and source of all religious, political, moral, and personal value. In traditional societies, personal identity necessitated a community of belonging that, in turn, implied various social obligations. In fact, the Bantu peoples . . . demonstrate the relation of the person and the community in their use of the word *ubuntu*, a . . . word for "person" as grounded in and constituted by the community . . . Ubuntu broadly speaking is the idea that other people's humanity and its claims upon one must be taken seriously. Thus . . . ubuntu . . . [is] the foundation of African personality.[83]

The well-being of the community takes center-stage as part and parcel of one's own. Without it, personal development is unthinkable. This dynamic is much more intricate and radical than the "trickle down" theory of economics, where wealth from the rich minority eventually reaches down to the majority poor. The reverse is rather the case in the African conception, in that, insofar as poverty harms solidarity, the presence of the poor destroys community and society at the core. Here wealth and poverty again form *a priori* ethical considerations.

It is incorrect to assume that in this perception of the economy, personal property does not exist. The system only warns that the social aspect of personal or "private" property cannot be ignored. Most importantly, private property should not be acquired at the extreme cost of the rest of society's basic needs, including food, shelter, clothing, health, education and security. No member of the community should go hungry or do without shelter "in order that personal property may be acquired by another member."[84] Of course, the implementation of

81. P. F. Nursey-Bray, "The Polis, the African Traditional Community, and African Natural Law," in A. A. Mazrui and H. H. Patel, eds., *Africa in World Affairs* (New York: Third Press, 1973) 32–33.

82. Evan M. Zuesse, "Perseverance and Transmutation in African Traditional Religions," in Jacob K. Olupona, *African Traditional Religions in Contemporary Society* (St. Paul: Paragon House, 1991) 177–78.

83. Peter J. Paris, "Self-initiation: A Necessary Principle in the African Struggle to Abolish Poverty," in Paris, ed., *Religion and Poverty*, 320.

84. Julius K. Nyerere, *Freedom and Unity/Uhuru na Umoja: A Selection from*

such ideals grows more complex the larger the community becomes. In complex societies, the satisfaction of essential needs cannot be achieved without some degree of regulated processes. There is a need to sort out what elements of the economic processes individuals and lower level communities can perform by and for themselves, and what must be taken over by higher level organizations such as the state or other international bodies. The crucial question is *who* should determine this division and *how*.

The principle of subsidiarity has for a long time been proposed by Catholic Social Teaching as a viable approach to this dilemma. Higher management should not usurp what can be organized, controlled and accomplished at the domestic (lower) level of society. However, the activities of multinational corporations in the modern world make this extremely difficult, even in countries with strong, well-structured systems of governance. The facelessness of these corporations often does not lend them to scrutiny and accountability, either to the authorities of their places of origin or those of the host regions. The situation becomes much more complex where governments on both sides, for different reasons, collude with the multinationals' activities. In cases like these, the profit motive is dominant, and instead of authentic development, human suffering results. In the mining and drilling sectors, Africa provides numerous examples of what can only be described as the callousness of the activities of multinational corporations in regard to people and the environment.[85] With globalization, how such corporations can or should be regulated is becoming a burning political and economic issue.

Good Governance and Economic Development in Africa

Pope John XXIII argues in some detail that there is a legitimate, even necessary, role of government in the economy, especially in the area of protecting rights and promoting duties of individuals and groups within society in the interests of justice and the common good. The

Writings and Speeches 1952–1965 (Dar es Salaam: Oxford University Press, 1966) 9–10.

85. Reportedly none of the foreign gold- and diamond-mining and oil-drilling companies in Africa operate on even minimal ethical standards. The activities of the oil-drilling giants in Nigeria's Niger Delta are a poignant illustration.

pope emphasizes that "those who wield power in the state must do this by such acts which not only have been justly carried out, but which also either have the common welfare primarily in view or which can lead to it."[86] He notes, further, that "indeed since the whole reason for the existence of civil authorities is the realization of the common good, it is clearly necessary that, in pursuing this objective, they should respect its essential elements, and at the same time conform their laws to the circumstances of the day."[87]

Yet, even judicious and occasional state involvement in regulating economic activity immediately raises questions about what kind of government is able to do this. What kind of political organization in a nation can safeguard the essential elements of the common good while at the same time conforming its laws to the essential principles of democracy? This is a primary question for development in Africa, where political and economic laws seem grossly skewed against the majority poor. While the process of finding the best expression of the common good should be ongoing, the dominant political and economic ideologies today seem to halt that process. Instead of offering liberation, these ideologies stunt African development in a number of ways, not least by severely limiting self-initiative and innovation.

"Self-Initiation: A Necessary Principle . . ."[88]

What baffles the imagination is the contradiction between Africa's immense wealth in material resources and the utter poverty of most of her people. Of course, despite protests to the contrary, this can be blamed partly on the history of exploitation of Africa and her peoples through the slave trade, colonialism, and a sort of alienating education system provided also by the churches.[89] But this is not the sole reason for Africa's economic plight. The other question we must ask is this:

86. John XXIII, *Pacem in Terris*, §53.

87. Ibid., §54. While as much as possible it should exercise neutrality, the pope writes (§56): "Considerations of justice and equity, however, can at times demand that those involved in civil government give more attention to the less fortunate members of the community, since they are less able to defend their rights and to assert their legitimate claims." See also Paul VI, *Populorum Progressio*, §54.

88. Borrowed from the title of the essay by Paris, "Self-initiation," 317.

89. For many of us, to deny the consequences of these events on the African situation is not different from denying that the Holocaust took place.

What are Africans themselves doing to stand up and counter these historical events and their effects? Peter J. Paris sees the answer in what he broadly describes as "the principle of self-initiation."

Aquiline Tarimo and Jesse N. K. Mugambi also refer to "self-initiation" respectively as the "reinvention" or "reconstruction" of Africa.[90] It is a huge task, involving not only economics, but also politics and culture. In the area of economics, for example, it means jettisoning the dependency syndrome, so much a feature of African economic life today. Politically, it demands good governance, as we have just pointed out. Although Africa's development must be based on African indigenous values, there is equal need, as Tarimo starkly states, to analyze, reinterpret and reorient those values towards the future. The values themselves are not a problem; the problem for development lies in the mistaken belief that "cultural critique is taboo."[91] African traditional cultural practices that inhibit legitimate and nonoppressive modern forms of economic growth must be questioned and changed. Nevertheless, the point is that it would be impossible to assert that African spirituality can contribute to African systems of governance and economic development when innovation founded on it is not encouraged. In today's changed circumstances, it is necessary to find new solidarities between African and other spiritualities on a grand scale.

Conclusion: A Third Way Is Possible

At the end of the 1980s, the collapse of the communist economic system was greeted with joy by dignitaries like Zbigniew Brzezinski, former U.S. Secretary of State, who triumphantly described the collapse as the victory of capitalism over socialism. But it brought sober comment from other observers. Alla G. Glinchikova writes that with such postures,

> I understood that we had all lost, simply because none of us had any ideas on alternatives for the society or social system that is now bringing us closer and closer to nowhere. This alternative is missing in Russia just as it is in America and

90. See Tarimo, *Applied Ethics*, 6–32, and J. N. K. Mugambi, *Christian Theology and Social Reconstruction* (Nairobi: Acton, 2003).

91. Tarimo, *Applied Ethics*, 15–19. See also Aquiline Tarimo and Paulin Manwelo, *African Peacemaking and Governance* (Nairobi: Acton, 2007–2008).

> in Europe. . . . [W]e are all drifting in the wreckage of a boat whose hull has already broken. One of its parts [communism] sank first and very quickly, while the other [capitalism] is taking a little longer to sink . . . that's all.[92]

Is a "Third Way" for development based on African indigenous economic ethic possible? Does it even come up for serious discussion? Considering the way the economic project has developed universally since the total collapse of strict Marxist ideologies, we cannot be unaware that the question might appear quite naïve. Moreover, the "underdevelopment" of Africa and the ostensible failure of its traditional systems[93] seem to make Africa an unlikely candidate for generating a blueprint for a "more humane" and integral economic order for the modern world. But perhaps this is a rash judgment, too easily dismissive of values in the African worldview that may positively inform the contemporary international economic situation.

Deliberating in the mid-1960s, the Second Vatican Council indicated that the "customs and traditions" of non-European peoples could provide means for the adequate exercise of the common good. Fifty years on, we are faced with increasing and scandalous contradictions of wealth and poverty throughout the world, where clearly the rights of some (the wealthiest) are an obstacle to the rights of others (the destitute). The task described by Vatican II is perhaps even more urgent now. According to the Council, "rash action should not be taken against worthy customs which, provided that they are suitably adapted to present-day circumstances, do not cease to be very useful."[94]

"We must allow ourselves to dream about what life could really be like if enough of us demanded that it were," writes Joan Chittister. "But to do that means to open for examination all the assumptions that have

92. Alla G. Glinchikova, "Russia and Europe: Two Ways to Modernity," in Vila-Cha, ed., *Revista*, 594–95.

93. There is no lack of illustrations of these "shortcomings" and "failures." For example, Aquiline Tarimo and Paulin Manwelo, eds., *Ethnicity, Conflict, and the Future of African States* (Nairobi: Paulines Publications Africa, 2009). Bill Berkeley, *The Graves are Not Yet Full: Race, Tribe and Power in the Heart of Africa* (New York: Basic, 2001); Michela Wrong, *It's Our Turn to Eat: The Story of a Kenyan Whistle-Blower* (London: Fourth Estate, 2009). Yet, one wonders whether they are unique to Africa.

94. Vatican II, *Gaudium et Spes*, no 69.

driven the world to this point. All of them."[95] Often, this might appear impossible, naïve or presumptuous; but if we are not bold enough to risk a different view, the dangers inherent in our dominant assumptions will remain and even exacerbate an unjust system. If and when we open our assumptions to examination, not only are we capable of dealing with myriad dangers, but there is more than a probable chance that we can enhance the values of justice, universal human rights and human dignity.

95. Joan Chittister, *The Gift of Years: Growing Older Gracefully* (New York: BlueBridge, 2008) 136.

10

Journey towards Faith Development Partnerships: The Challenge and the Potential

Katherine Marshall

What is the relationship between religion and economic development? Where humanitarian relief is concerned, such links tend to be fairly readily understood: religious communities are often the first on the spot to help in times of catastrophe, as was the case after horrific floods devastated a third of Pakistan in 2010 (though the alacrity with which Islamic organizations sprang into action caused some worries). Religious groups also provided immediate response when Hurricane Katrina struck New Orleans. However, particularly in international development circles, skepticism toward religious actors is common. This skepticism is compounded by significant gaps in knowledge and understanding about what religious groups think and do to further development, and about how the development world truly operates.

This paper takes stock of these challenges, focusing on where the effort to bridge the worlds of faith and development stands today. It is based on my personal twelve-year journey, marked by efforts to make the case that powerful common ground links religion and socioeconomic development. However different the language and the approach, these two worlds undoubtedly share a concern about global poverty and welfare. Where there are disconnects and discord, a probing dialogue deserves a far higher priority than it has received to date.

Caveats and Definitions

These complex and sensitive topics cannot be explored sensibly without some effort to define terms, and some essential caveats.

Religion and faith make up a huge subject, touching large and complex worlds. The most basic terminology itself is fraught: religion, faith, spirituality, secular, are all contested terms. For some, religion is a straightforward description of institutions and approaches; for others it implies formality, in keeping with the word *religion*'s Latin root, "to bind." Religion can also signify simply a broad and intangible set of beliefs. Spirituality can suggest the essence of religious belief and practice, or, alternatively, something apart from and contrasted with organized religion. Faith can imply a set of specific beliefs or convictions, a tradition or something extending well beyond organized religion, or simply a belief in something transcendent. Some comment that "everyone has faith; the question is, faith in what?" The assumption that believers are organized in formal communities (a church or congregation) sits uncomfortably for some traditions, even as other believers (some Buddhists, for example) maintain that they do not have "faith" in the commonly understood sense of the word. And while "secular" suggests clarity and virtue for some, in other settings it can imply a Godless and by implication valueless approach.

In short, definitions are difficult. This chapter uses faith more readily than religion because it conveys a broader and less formal connotation. The term "faith-inspired" institutions or organizations (as opposed to "faith-based") suggests a wider net than is commonly suggested by the term "FBO," with less assumption that there are institutional affiliations. But no definition satisfies all concerns. The definition conundrum should never obscure the intrinsic complexity of the worlds and issues that lie behind the terms.

To complicate the definitional challenges, readers would do well to appreciate how far "development" also refers to a complex world of institutions and ideas, one that is in flux, representing widely different approaches. The tendency to lump development institutions or groups of countries into simplistic baskets (secular versus faith based, north versus south) obscures both the varied actors and approaches at work. Both thinking and practice about development have changed markedly in recent decades. For example, community engagement and empowerment were barely mentioned two decades ago, but today, for most development institutions, community "ownership" is a moral and ethical imperative and a key to success in almost any venture. It is not easy to pin down what "development" really means; the concept encompasses broader and broader groups of countries and virtually any topic or sector. At one level, international development is about combating poverty, but in practice far more than abject poverty is at issue. Development work confronts basic questions about the ideal society, and thus social justice in its many forms.

The topic of interreligious dialogue and economic development can validly and usefully be approached from at least two different vantage points: one, primarily focused on theory and ideas (whether theology, economics, or sociology), starts with core features and purposes of both religion and development, seeking common ground and exploring differences. The ongoing Muslim-Christian dialogue around the Common Word project[1] is led by theologians and focuses essentially and primarily on common understandings about love of God and neighbor. A different kind of interreligious dialogue starts from a more pragmatic position, and focuses on direct efforts to encourage different groups to interact on the wide range of issues that economic development presents. Theological dialogue about development quickly comes to focus on ethical questions: what is right or wrong with current paths and how far do they reflect different ends and values? It evokes fundamental questions about the meaning and purpose of life. Any sincere reflection on the word *development* raises questions: What kind of world (or preferably worlds) are we hoping to create? Who decides which worlds are created? And how can we best accomplish both individual and collective objectives?

The more practical type of interreligious dialogue tends to move swiftly to specific problems and actions. It might, for example, grapple with questions about performance on the Millennium Development Goals (MDG), and what religious ideas, institutions, and leaders can offer in achieving and enriching this global compact to fight or end poverty. Partnership and cooperation to achieve specific results are often the objective. Such practical exploration might therefore focus concretely on why children go to bed hungry and what can and should be done about it, and by whom; or why some two thousand times more

1. http://www.acommonword.com/

women die in childbirth in Niger than in Sweden. The praxis approach draws one quickly to country and sector realities.

Both theoretical and practical paths of discussion are important, even imperative, to pursue. Paul Knitter has framed the ethical challenges brilliantly in his essay included here, emphasizing the role of dialogue in identifying what we might term jugular issues about life's purpose. However, a pragmatic interreligious engagement will involve the same set of questions and issues. My work and inclinations tend towards the practical. But we should not forget that both paths involve both profoundly ethical and profoundly practical challenges. Both paths are, in my view, groping for language and clarity on means and outcomes.

Taking the practical as a starting point, there are areas where ethics and practice point to strong common ground (common advocacy on hunger and cutting child mortality, for instance, or a strong if fairly new consensus on the vital importance of community empowerment). There is a middle territory where common ground is present but with some veiled controversies (microcredit, values and education, how to stop human trafficking). And some areas are more contentious and invite purposeful dialogue. What does equality between men and women really mean? Is greed a driver of creativity and the common interest, or a sin to be curtailed?

If interreligious dialogue (whether it starts with ideas or practical problems) is the means, the end is development, by which we should mean progress towards a fairer, more equitable world, grounded in a sustainable approach to the environment, where each individual enjoys real human rights and the chance to develop their talents and follow their dreams. This ideal of development (which is about far more than economics—social, human, and political dimensions are equally important) drives the effort to bridge the gulfs that have emerged and still separate development and religious actors, as well as different faiths. It starts with the conviction that a better way of life is possible. Remarkable, even stunning progress has been made in recent decades, showing what can be done and how far there is to go. So, instead of history's tacit acceptance that poverty is an inevitable facet of life, today's reality is that poverty is unnecessary and that, therefore, it is morally unacceptable. As Hans Rosling (the Swedish public health specialist who presents this case with great brilliance[2]) argues, "the seemingly impossible is possible." Ending poverty and avoidable suffering, achieving a society where all people have an opportunity to develop their potential and to enjoy respect, is an achievable dream and thus it becomes an ethical imperative.[3] Both theological and intellectual dialogue and pragmatic, on-the-ground efforts to address issues confronting communities can start with an inspiring vision of a development ideal. But questions about what that ideal should look like, what works and what does not, and who is responsible, will always arise.

Interfaith Praxis: Current Scenes

Tracing an accurate and complete map of interreligious development work today is a challenge. The field is dynamic and dispersed, and there is no common "clearinghouse," nor even agreement on what constitutes a valid and viable interfaith activity or approach. Various efforts underway have as an explicit aim the promotion of interfaith dialogue and action on a variety of topics linked to development. The need for better "mapping" is itself a common theme.[4] Other faith-linked initiatives do not have interfaith work as an explicit objective but often find themselves working in partnership across faith boundaries (for example, cooperative arrangements that emerged in Aceh following the tsunami and peace agreement). Several systematic interfaith efforts are long-standing. Notable examples are work on environment and religion; the work of the Alliance of Religions for Conservation led by Martin Palmer, Mary Evelyn Tucker and John Grimm stands out. Others are relatively recent and their scope is still unfolding. These include initiatives launched by the Obama administration (both the State Department/USAID and the Office of Faith-Based Initiatives

2. Several Rosling videos can be viewed at http://www.gapminder.org/videos/.

3. I explore a priority ladder of reasons for supporting development objectives in "Climbing up to the Light," *Reflections (No More Excuses—Confronting Poverty)* 97:2 (2010) 5–7.

4. The White House Office of Faith-Based and Neighborhood Partnerships and the CIFA task force were at the time of writing engaged in mapping work. The Berkley Center for Religion, Peace, and World Affairs global development work focuses on "mapping" as a means to gain a better understanding of who is doing what, where, with what resources.

and Neighborhood Partnerships in the White House). The Center for Interfaith Action on Global Poverty, linked to the Washington National Cathedral, launched an ambitious task force on Global Health and Peace, and an equally expansive "Joint Learning Initiative" began in late 2010 in London (led by Tearfund and McKinsey). The work of the Tony Blair Faith Foundation is quite deeply engaged in work on global health, and interfaith work is a central part of its vision. The World Faiths Development Dialogue, which I lead, explores the policy dimensions of development issues such as agriculture, health, gender, and peacebuilding, looking to the experience of different faith traditions, working both individually and in interfaith alliances.

The major global interfaith organizations (notably Religions for Peace [WCRP], the Parliament of the World's Religions, and the United Religions Initiative) all give increasing weight in their programs to what can be considered a broad peace, development, and social justice mission. In parallel with the recent (September, 2010) UN Summit on MDG, several faith initiatives (WCRP,[5] Micah Challenge, National Council of Churches of Christ) emphasized the moral imperatives of the MDG challenge and explored ways to increase the impact of faith advocacy and direct action.

A common theme that links these rather different efforts with interfaith dimensions is their hope that practical interfaith work offers a way to bridge discord among communities and contribute to healthy, plural societies. This takes on new importance in communities that include people practicing different religions, perhaps with histories of conflict and tension, and especially where traditional community patterns are shaken up by migration and urbanization. The idea, highly simplified, is that if people from different faith traditions work together on a practical common problem, they will come to know and understand each other. Working together on a housing project (Habitat for Humanity's concept of "the theology of the hammer") builds houses, but it also constructs relationships. Many in the public sector are also wary of any approach that favors or appears to favor one faith group over another. A striking example of possible pitfalls can be seen in the lists of officially recommended charities following a disaster like the

5. As an example see http://religionsforpeace.org/news/press/press-release-religions-for-2.html, Religions for Peace's announcement about its partnership with the United Nations on the Millennium Development Goals.

2004 tsunami, or Haiti's earthquake: it is fair to ask whether the lists include a balanced representation of different faith traditions. Or, more cogently, why are there so few Muslim groups listed? Interfaith efforts offer a greater possibility for neutrality and fairness.

Despite the host of ongoing exploratory efforts, identifying solid, positive examples of interfaith cooperation is proving more difficult than expected. One impediment is poor documentation. Many interfaith efforts emerge from specific circumstances and are not well analyzed. In other instances, the documentation that is available comes across as tinged by advocacy or self-promotion. Nonetheless, there is much to learn from the wide range of ongoing interfaith initiatives, some large and ambitious, some centered at a community or even an individual level. So the search continues.

Three quite different efforts from my own experience illustrate the diversity of interfaith possibilities, and some challenges.

An interfaith initiative to clean up the cities and environment in Ghana began largely as a response to an upcoming international sporting event. Dubbed a "crusade against filth," the effort was inspired in part by Alliance of Religions for Conservation work in Manchester, UK, and generated enthusiasm as far away as Malawi. A group of religious leaders, many of whom knew each other at least to some extent, got together and agreed on some practical measures, including community clean-up campaigns, working with youth, radio programs, advocacy on sanitation, and reflections on what was needed to anchor the effort in a more permanent program. The World Bank, which has a keen interest in sanitation as a major element in improving Ghana's public health, offered the group some logistical support.

The effort did achieve some results. But it soon hit some walls. First, the group's dream to secure funding to support a major garbage and sanitation initiative turned out to be rather impractical. The interfaith group had no real structure, no formal institutional base, and no real mandate to undertake what swiftly became a very technical project. No one "owned" the initiative full time. The interfaith garbage effort thus continues at a fairly low level, viewed in some places as an example of disappointed hopes and fizzled potential.

But some of the leaders involved in the initiative pointed to an important unintended consequence that they perceived as linked to the garbage initiative. When Ghana's close presidential elections promised to spark tensions and even violence, religious leaders from different traditions (Catholic, traditional Protestant, evangelical, Muslim, and traditional African religions) picked up their phones, calling each other and national political leaders. In their view, they helped stave off a potential threat of violence and lasting discord, in part because they knew each other and had formed a community of trust.

The team working at the Berkley Center for Religion, Peace, and World Affairs and the World Faiths Development Dialogue[6] have encountered an interesting story of interfaith cooperation touted for Aceh in the post-tsunami and post-Peace Accord era (thus from late 2004 on). The narrative describes a situation where faith-linked groups were among the first responders to the devastation of the tsunami, including (in 98 percent Muslim Aceh) stoutly Christian groups like World Vision, the Salvation Army, and Catholic Relief Services, as well as Indonesia's enormous Muslim organizations such as Muhammadiya and Nahdatul Ulama (NU). After some initial controversies over the status of orphans and proselytizing, the groups on the ground hammered out a voluntary code of conduct and worked together, overcoming both practical obstacles to program design and implementation, as well as some skepticism from their own constituencies (both World Vision and Muhammadiya stress the difficulties they faced and the significance of their cooperation). The results were tangible and led to successful program outcomes, in terms of housing and facilities, all without marked tensions.

It is worth highlighting (this is an ongoing exploration) an alternative narrative: here, the outside groups acted as a magnet for trained and moderate Muslims in the area, who thus flocked to the international organizations. In their absence, more fundamentalist elements have gained ascendance, and Aceh today may be more extremist than other parts of Indonesia, marked by cases of acid thrown at women, some brutal honor killings, and intolerance towards Muslims visiting the area. It is worth following this case to see how far tensions subside as the intensive reconstruction phase shifts to a focus on development and normal governance challenges.

A third example of interfaith action is the ambitious interfaith malaria initiative in Nigeria. Based on a review by the Berkley Center for Religion, Peace, and World Affairs and the World Faiths Development

6. NGO established to address tensions among secular and religious institutions and build common purpose around poverty; founders were James D. Wolfensohn and Lord Carey of Clifton (former archbishop of Canterbury).

Dialogue[7] showing that no real progress towards the control and eradication of malaria in Africa could be made without addressing the problem of malaria in Nigeria, the Center for Interfaith Action on Global Poverty (CIFA)[8] took up this challenge. Working with an established interreligious council in Nigeria, led by the Catholic archbishop of Abuja and the Sultan of Sokoto, an interfaith organization was set up with substantial CIFA organizational support and financing that came from an International Development Agency (IDA) grant to the Nigerian government for eradicating malaria. The resulting interfaith initiative may be the largest single interfaith initiative of its kind anywhere. The initiative is grounded in the dual roles of faith institutions in Nigeria (not dissimilar to other African countries), which include the management of a large segment of health services (hospitals, clinics) as well as those institutions' omnipresence in communities and thus their capacity to reach people and change attitudes that underlie many of the causes of malaria contraction. The training of faith leaders about malaria and the preparation of a sermon guide are among the tangible achievements of this project to date.

In Nigeria, the hope is that this interfaith initiative will have two results. The first is that it will augment and support the government's vast malaria program. There is also hope that the initiative will enhance the quality of the national program, because it invites community perspectives and supports the potential for communal mobilization, on projects such as the effective distribution of mosquito nets. The second hope is that cooperation among different religious groups on malaria eradication, at the national level and still more at a community level, will encourage a wider understanding that can address some of the interreligious tension that has sparked so much violence in Nigeria in recent years.

Interfaith Dialogue: A Tough Sell in Development Circles

Dialogue may be a positive term in religious circles, implying openness to transformation and careful joint reflection on complex theo-

7. Malaria: Scoping New Partnerships, (Jan. 2009) http://repository.berkleycenter.georgetown.edu/MalariaFinalReport.pdf.

8. See reports on work in Nigeria on CIFA's website, at http://www.centerforinterfaithaction.org/action-issues/malaria.html.

logical and practical issues. In parts of the secular world, at least—and the leading development institutions can be counted in this camp—dialogue is often equated with blah blah. It is indeed often seen as the opposite to action. When skepticism about the significance of religion for practical development work is added to the mix, it is perhaps not surprising that interfaith dialogue is often greeted with suspicion.

For those who work in development institutions, there is fear that interfaith efforts can reduce complex matters to a bland common denominator, creating expensive but not very practical institutions that sponsor warm but not very effective events lumped together under an image of groups holding hands and singing "Kumbaya." Many religious groups, for their part, are concerned with a watering down of their cherished beliefs. For many, interfaith meetings are attended by those already convinced of the value of interreligious dialogue, or perhaps by renegades who are not fully committed to the beliefs of their given faith. But these intrareligious doubts pale in comparison to secular skepticism about the achievements of interfaith meetings.

For participants in interreligious dialogue, there is also a reasonable fear that, by privileging inclusivity above practicality, the original intentions of a particular interfaith project can quickly become diluted. As an illustration, the World Faiths Development Dialogue was asked by the National Evangelical Alliance to organize, with the World Bank, a meeting with Moroccan Muslim leaders on the common challenge of climate change. When we suggested that it might be wise to include other faith traditions who shared an interest in environmental issues, the response was that it was already sufficiently demanding to bring together Muslims and evangelicals. Widening the circle would dilute and defeat the purpose.

In short, interreligious dialogue quite often meets a skeptical audience. One response is to stress interfaith action, in contrast to dialogue, though the reality is that the two are often inseparable.

Dialogue among Religious and Non-faith Inspired Organizations

The challenge takes on different and more demanding dimensions when the task is dialogue not just among religious traditions themselves, but between these traditions and the secular organizations that are most active on economic development.

Here two caveats are in order. The first is my growing doubt and disenchantment about the utility of trying to distinguish anything that might be termed the "faith sector" or a "religious sector." The terms, which are fairly widely used, are problematic on various fronts. First, the term purports to divide the world into two baskets of sheep and goats: one religious and "faithful," the other nonreligious and secular. The reality is obviously immensely complex. For a start, many if not all people have faith; the issue is what kind and how it serves as a motivating and social force. There are innumerable shades and manifestations of religiosity, and, especially in modern societies, people have multiple, complex, dynamic, and overlapping identities and motivations. The Berkley Center for Religion, Peace, and World Affairs interview series[9] probes what drives and inspires practitioners, and complexity is the main common theme. We are asking for trouble if we assume or ask that an individual or institution have a single, readily definable faith motivation. We are also plunging into deep waters when we try to ascribe characteristics and judgments to the vast galaxy and array of institutions that in one fashion or another are linked to or inspired by religious faith. My preference is to avoid lumping all faith institutions together, and to focus instead on specific groups of institutions, on countries, and on specific issues.

To illustrate, there are three important and complex questions about the relationship between faith and health that are currently under discussion. First, how large is the "faith health sector" and what share of health services does it represent? Second, is health care provided by faith institutions more effective (and how can we prove or disprove the hypothesis that it is)? And third, how far, why, and with what lessons do faith health services reach the poor more effectively and in a different way than their non-faith counterparts?

The answers point to the perils of trying to treat faith, and in this case the narrower question of health care provided by faith institutions as a group or sector. The diversity involved in these organizations and projects is simply enormous, and this diversity explains in part why

9. See http://berkleycenter.georgetown.edu/projects/practitioners-and-faith-inspired-development for a series of some 150 interviews with practitioners exploring their work and motivation.

measurement is highly problematic. Estimates of the share of health care offered by faith institutions contain enormous variability, and virtually all the estimates are based on rough assumptions and very partial evidence. There are ferocious questions of definition: what constitutes health care? Just medicine, or does it extend to spiritual health? It is an important fact that health services offered by faith institutions often fall outside public statistics. It is also true that what is considered health care is a complicated question. There are many hybrid forms that complicate the issue. Take the example of Georgetown University Hospital: it was established as and ran for years from a Jesuit university, as a medical facility rooted in a faith institution. The hospital met tough times, and was purchased by Medstar, a quite secular conglomerate. As part of the purchase arrangement, certain agreements on principles linked to the hospital's faith mission were agreed upon—on reproductive health, for example—but for all intents and purposes, the hospital runs as a hospital comparable to others in the region. Does that make the hospital a faith institution or not? What about a health clinic in Ghana that is funded by the government of Ghana, and staffed by religious orders?

A similar set of challenges bedevil the other two large questions about health services offered by faith institutions. Can we even begin to answer the question of whether such services are "better," and what would be the questions to assess? Is there indeed a common thread that links a Muslim clinic with a Catholic hospital, a Bramakumari research hospital, or a Buddhist hospice facility? My answer is, probably not. What has been true as a trend is a hesitation or lag in using rigorous evaluation methodologies in many faith institutions. This accounts for a general dearth of solid evidence on the performance of many facilities and programs. But the commonsense answer is that there are outstanding examples of care provided in faith-run facilities and other examples of shoddy service. The mounting financial challenges that a number of faith-run facilities face also complicate the picture because they squeeze key performance areas like salaries. Such challenges are part of the saga of Uganda's well-respected faith-run medical programs.

And third, as to whether faith-run facilities truly reach the poor more often and effectively than other services, the assertion is doubtful, in part because faith-run facilities normally need to charge fees.

Thus there are remarkable clinics serving the poorest communities, but also facilities that primarily benefit wealthier neighborhoods and clientele. What is particularly important, though, are the examples of health services provided by faith institutions that operate despite extraordinary obstacles in remote, often conflicted areas, for example in the Democratic Republic of the Congo.

The second caveat takes the form of a nod to those who see in the nonreligious world threads of a "secular faith." It is telling that economists are often described in non-flattering religious terms, as preaching, driven by an immutable and mysterious set of beliefs (in the market), seeking or even demanding conversion, and forming part of an exclusive, elitist community that does not welcome outsiders.

The upshot is that the faith/secular dialogue can be tougher than inter- or intra-faith discussions. The general aura of skepticism about religion that is not uncommon in universities and development institutions translates into difficulties for religious actors who seek to influence agendas or win seats at various policy tables. Perhaps the most frustrating experience is simply indifference: the tacit acceptance that religion and faith are a low priority, not relevant for the weighty issues at hand.

In some respects, the dialogue between religious and secular actors has proved particularly difficult where economists are concerned. The general problems of weak and problematic data on religion generally and specifically on religious development work limits deeper engagement with religion by an economic discipline that is profoundly data-driven. The increasing focus within the development world on measuring results, on time-bound programs with specific and quantifiable targets, and on defined goals and articulated strategies (all evident in the MDG architecture), can conflict with traditions and disciplines that stress holistic and interrelated human needs and the long-term nature of development challenges. The new focus on results, evaluation, aid harmonization and aid coordination all make for some disorientation where complex "constellations" of ideas and communities are concerned. Ambiguous understandings of public versus private responsibilities complicate governance: the "mantra" of development today is "country-focused" and "country-driven," but such orientations can contradict common and often well-founded doubts about the legitimacy and probity of public institutions.

Despite these obstacles, many development institutions today are showing greater interest in various dimensions of religion and in the potential for partnership between secular and religious institutions. The experience of September 11, 2001, has opened some eyes to the significance of religious motivation in the work of international development, as has the political mobilization led by evangelical Christians in the United States as they play significant roles in shaping U.S. development assistance approaches and programs. Among the institutions taking a new and harder look at religion and development (outside the Alliance of Civilizations which operates to date at a broad strategic level) are: the United Nations Population Fund (UNFPA), which recognized early on that working with faith communities and leaders was vital to success in advancing women's issues. Several specialized United Nations agencies, notably the United Nations Children's Fund (UNICEF), the Food and Agriculture Organisation (FAO), the World Health Organisation (WHO), and the United Nations Educational, Scientific, and Cultural Organisation (UNESCO) also have shown a specific interest in bringing faith dimensions more directly into their work. UNFPA has pioneered an effort to establish a network among development institutions to bring faith work and issues more into the light, and plans training programs in a near future. The International Monetary Fund has a long-standing history of outreach to faith institutions, as does the Interamerican Development Bank (the World Bank is discussed separately).

Several bilateral aid agencies have asserted an interest in faith led work and perspectives. The United States Agency for International Development (USAID) has a small office, and the US President's Emergency Plan for AIDS Relief (PEPFAR) focused on religion from the outset. The British development agency Department for International Development supported an ambitious five-year research program (led by the University of Birmingham and just now concluding) to research religions and development. The governments of Norway, Sweden, Switzerland, and Portugal are all actively exploring how they should take faith into account. The discussion is not always easy. Two examples of institutions which seem hesitant to engage are Japan and the Asian Development Bank. In contrast, China is showing some interest in looking more deeply at the roles of religion in development. Two meetings took place in Rome in October 2010 focused on religion, development and peace, one hosted by the U.S. Ambassador to the Holy See, the other by the Pontifical Council on Justice and Peace.

Faith and Development: The Fortuitous Case of the World Bank Debates

It is a somewhat ironic part of this history of growing interest in the links between religion and development that the World Bank began to address explicitly the links between religion and development well before most other official development agencies. The irony is that many would not associate the World Bank with openness toward religion or, more importantly, to the kinds of ethical challenges that engagement with religious institutions often implies. Against a backdrop of a glaring silence in official documentation about the role of religion in development, the World Bank's president, James D. Wolfensohn, launched an initiative in 1998, jointly with the archbishop of Canterbury, George Carey, to engage in a dialogue about common purposes in fighting poverty, and to address contentious issues which at that time focused on poor country debt, the conduct of structural adjustment programs, and environmental policies, notably the construction of large dams. Wolfensohn also cites his conviction that religious institutions were and remain the world's largest distribution system, providing vital services especially in health and education, as well as social capital within communities. He also admires the passion and drive that many religious actors bring to the fight against poverty, which he saw as strikingly similar to the World Bank's credo: "Our dream is a world free of poverty."

To tell the saga briefly, the engagement began as the very personal initiative of Wolfensohn and Carey, and thus began and largely remained at a senior, leadership level. It initially took the form of a series of meetings involving major faith traditions, the first at Lambeth Palace in 1998, the second in 1999 in Washington DC. The initiative initially built on the experience of the Alliance of Religions for Conservation, but moved to a different agenda that shifted the focus to the far broader World Development Report that the World Bank was preparing for the year 2000, which focused on poverty. Following the 1999 meeting, a decision was made to proceed with a fairly modest program, to be implemented by a small "spin off" from the World Bank, the World Faiths Development Dialogue (WFDD). Plans proceeded to create the institution, to recruit an executive director, and to launch pilot programs in Tanzania, Ethiopia, and Guatemala.

It was at this point, in late 1999/early 2000 (that is, of course, well before September 11, 2001) that the faith initiative met substantial skepticism and outright opposition from the World Bank's Board of Directors (who represented virtually all of the United Nations countries). There was minimal and tepid support for the initiative and some vociferous and direct opposition. An exploratory dialogue to understand why the controversy had erupted involved meetings with representatives of all the World Bank's member countries. It thus amounted to a rather unique exploration of uncertainties and tensions around the role of religion and development. Briefly, the outcome was a compromise whereby the World Bank withdrew from its intended governance role in WFDD and the unit within the Bank was rechristened as the Development Dialogue on Values and Ethics. The high level meetings of leaders from different world religions continued, with important meetings in Canterbury in the year 2002 and Dublin in 2005. However, when Wolfensohn left the Bank, his successors saw less strategic priority in the effort and it has continued at a lower level and with less visibility. A further meeting in the leadership series took place in Accra, Ghana, in August 2009, but future plans remain rather uncertain.

Why the controversy? The dialogue about the initiative involved a wide range of countries and views: some individuals took a rather personal view, though some countries (for example, France) took formal and official positions. To a degree the debate was a proxy for other issues that were in play; unlike other development topics that the government leaders involved were then addressing, reaching out to religious communities on development was something of an orphan issue, and it garnered very little visible support (perhaps not surprising since ministers of finance were the leading actors). But the exchanges did highlight a series of significant doubts about the wisdom of a development agency engaging, especially at a global level, with religious organizations. With dialogue and the passage of time (and not insignificantly the rethinking of religion's roles that followed 9/11), some of these doubts and issues have been resolved. However, the harsh reality is that when many World Bank leaders are asked to identify lower priority programs for budget cuts, the faith initiative, modest as it is, is frequently cited.

Such doubts are by no means confined to development institutions, and many religious institutions and leaders are dubious about the wisdom and merits of engaging formally with secular development institutions. It is thus important to stress the tough questions from the religion side. Perhaps the most vivid illustration is the complex dialogue process among the World Council of Churches (WCC), the IMF, and the World Bank, focused during the years 2002–2005, but they are also evident in other interfaith and national settings. The publication *Lead Us Not into Temptation,* prepared by the WCC as it debated whether or not to engage with the IMF and World Bank, expresses those doubts in vivid terms.[10] This dialogue process was grounded in a deep skepticism within the WCC community about what they perceived as the neoliberal, market-driven development model that, in their understanding, the World Bank and IMF advanced. They also came to the discussion with strong views about the clearly undemocratic governance structure of both the World Bank and the IMF, where weighted voting gives most power to wealthier countries. The World Bank and IMF, in turn, saw the WCC and its constituent churches as allies in fighting poverty globally and in advocating for development assistance. The dialogue process brought home how differently those who were present saw the development process and institutions but perhaps even more the challenges of vocabulary and discipline that made dialogue difficult and at times fraught with tension.

The following schematic presentation summarizes the two sets of questions and provides at least a preliminary picture:[11]

10. The dialogue process is described in the chapter "A Pathfinding Dialogue among the World Council of Churches, the IMF, and the World Bank," in Katherine Marshall and Marisa Van Saanen, *Development and Faith: When Mind, Heart, and Soul Work Together* (Washington DC: World Bank, 2007), 195–208.

11. I have written about the debates in various other settings. See Katherine Marshall, "Religion and Global Development: Intersecting Paths," in Religious Pluralism, Globalization, and World Politics, ed. Thomas Banchoff (New York: Oxford University Press, 2008).

Development actors question the wisdom of engaging with faith leaders and institutions:

Issue or Query	**Major Focus**	**Some Examples Given**	**Some Response**
Political and thus divisive nature of religious institutions Proselytizing/ conversion seen as major objective DIVISIVE	Disputes with Christianity and Islam, religion as a perceived cause of violence	How can we choose who to talk to without getting into trouble? Religious groups approach development for their own interest and to advance their power	Need to highlight the complexity of the religious world, powerful roles of religion in peace, their extraordinary work for the poor, advocacy on issues like environment and poor country debt
Religion seen as opposed to modernization and development, linked to status quo DANGEROUS	Gender relations and reproductive health dominate but hierarchical nature of many religious institutions also cited	Catholic Church position on contraception and interventions on abortion rights Siding with the powerful against the poor in countries, Africa, Philippines, Latin America	Stress diversity of views and strong support of some for gender equality. Religious voices advocating the very poor and marginalized
Importance of religion declines with development so that it is not a priority DEFUNCT	Assumption that most religious institutions are not modernized and effective and will continue to decline	Examples from North America and Europe, also urban areas	Growing evidence on continuing if not mounting strength of religion
Personal experience with religion predominated in much of dialogue EMOTIONAL	Doubts often bolstered with personal faith experience or doubts	Wide variety, including abusive priests, inspiration of Martin Luther King, Gandhi	Get facts and present them well

Faith institutions question the development actors:

Issue or Query	Major Focus	Some Examples Given	Some Response
Development institutions serve the rich and powerful, the US and multinationals EMPIRE	Perception of dominance of rich countries, limited voice for poor as well as weak voting rights	World Bank and IMF governance structure, Monsanto and other companies	Efforts to highlight voice of poor, to listen Dialogue with multinationals and Equator Principles
Development disrupts traditional communities and families People are displaced EFFECTS	Major dam projects; cultural erosion with Western music, movies, values Dangers of migration	Narmada dam and others Some question education for all	Major efforts to hold to policies to safeguard communities, bring in more voices Consult and participate Empowerment principles
Development institutions are driven by mantra of growth uber alles, lack principles of fairness and justice ETHICS	Privatization and free trade seen as villains. Widespread corruption	Water privatization Market reforms to liberalize High interest rates	Importance of growth but effort to give meaning to balanced, equitable, or sustainable growth Focus on fighting corruption
Institutions impossible to understand, full of jargon, opaque ENIGMA	World Bank and UN are very difficult to navigate, as is European Union Perception of arrogance	Pretty much the whole development community Institutions do not answer e-mail, mail, phone calls	Much better communication policies needed
Development institutions work against the true interests of the poor DANGEROUS	Genetically Modified Organisms, large farming, large-scale lending	Privatization experience, large farms, weak performance of land reform	Build on common ground, address concerns and issues with integrity

Why Does It Matter?

Less acrimony, effective dialogue about the very complex issues involved, and stronger, more balanced partnerships all offer great promise to improve the quality of development work and thus outcomes. There are many examples of areas where stronger collaboration could make a difference. Among them are the full gamut of health challenges, including but going beyond HIV/AIDS, malaria and tuberculosis, effective action against corruption, water and sanitation issues, and education. Some topics cry out for dialogue, gender issues most prominently.

This is no easy challenge. The complexity of religious worlds and ideas is remarkable, and there are few if any institutions that can truly bring anything resembling order or coherence to what they do, even at a country level. Likewise, though ostensibly more methodical and organic in their formation and respective mandates, development institutions have grown like topsy and are increasingly viewed as so complex as to be essentially unmanageable.

At the Melbourne Parliament of the World Religions in December 2009, three major themes were each the subject of rich programming: peace and the resolution of conflict (in many respects the traditional focus of interfaith work, and increasingly relevant with the contemporary focus on fragile states and the "bottom billion"), the growing imperative for action on climate change and protecting the environment, and mobilizing religious institutions more effectively to fight poverty and to support true equity. All three "streams" offered a rich menu of ideas. But they also took place largely separately from one another, and in some ways the narratives of the three themes were in tension if not in conflict. Bringing the strands together is a challenge for the future.

The interagency, interdisciplinary, inter-"worldview" dialogue about the roles of religion in both humanitarian relief and in longer term development programs matters. Sadly, too much of the current approach to the topic echoes a phrase that iconoclast Christopher Hitchens used in a different context: "The French, as it happens, once evolved an expression for this sort of prose: *la langue de bois*, the wooden tongue, in which nothing useful or enlightening can be said but in which various excuses for the arbitrary and the dishonest can be offered." What is needed is a more professional, thoughtful approach to a highly complex set of issues, that involves research and "mapping" of situations on the ground and an honest, purposeful effort to address tensions and disagreements (for example, about human rights and gender roles) that tend to be brushed to one side. The purpose and the promise is a more effective set of development interventions, ones that can speed progress in reducing poverty and that can be anchored in the positive values of different communities because they address their history, culture, and beliefs in thoughtful ways. In responding to the complex challenges of addressing religion, the "langue de bois" is far too common. The challenge—to enhance quality, avoid pitfalls, and to do real good—deserves far better.

11

The Next Horizon in Interreligious Dialogue: Engaging the Economists

James Buchanan

In the opening article in this volume Paul Knitter challenges us to embark on a variety of dialogical paths. First, there is the dialogue *among the religions* about economic development. This conversation concerns resources within and between the religions considered relevant to economic development. Second, he challenges us to engage in dialogue among the religions with *the world of the market*. This is a very different dialogue, with different participants, possibly different questions, and certainly different ways of framing and understanding the questions that have arisen among the religions. This discussion involves the economists and policy makers who both analyze and design the current techno-economic system. Finally, Knitter challenges us to engage a third path: *interreligious action* which works towards economic change. This challenge takes us beyond dialogue to engagement in social and political systems which will include other groups, as well as new ways of framing and dealing with common questions.

While drawing upon the discussion of resources from the religions (primarily from this volume), I want to demonstrate ways in which the ideas and resources found among the religions might be translated into concepts and language which come from the economists themselves. In so doing I hope to suggest that Knitter's second and third challenges add a new and critically important horizon for those of us involved in interreligious dialogue. Finally, I will suggest at least one example of how we might utilize the economist language and framework of understanding to actually change economic practice.[1]

Hermeneutical Issues

In an earlier volume in this series, *Interreligious Hermeneutics*, [2] Catherine Cornille outlined four approaches to interreligious understanding that equally apply here.. It is worthwhile returning to these approaches, adapting them to the problems of the interdisciplinary dialogue with economists.

1. The hermeneutical retrieval of resources for dialogue within one's own tradition. Are these resources the same if we focus on economic development as a discussion among the religions versus dialogue with economists?
2. The pursuit of proper understanding of the other religion. How does this change when we begin to deal with the "proper understanding" of another discipline? Are the analogical possibilities more or less challenging?
3. The appropriation and reinterpretation of the other within one's own framework. What would it mean for those of us in the religions to appropriate the framework of the economists in our understanding of key concepts such as self-transcendence, suffering, desire, justice, etc.?
4. The borrowing of hermeneutical principles from another (religion or discipline). What are the hermeneutical principles of economists? How might a deeper understanding of them be useful for our work?

1. An earlier draft of this paper explores dialogue between what I call the "interreligious engagement movement" and "global civil society." Space limitations do not allow for inclusion of that discussion here; however, I believe that the convergence between these two with the global economic system has the potential to play an important role in bringing about change to the current models of development.

2. Catherine Cornille, "Introduction: On Hermeneutics in Dialogue," in Cornille and Conway, eds., *Interreligious Hermeneutics*, Interreligious Dialogue Series 2 (Eugene, OR: Cascade Books, 2010) x.

One of the issues with which we have struggled in interreligious dialogue is that of systematically distorted communication. Jürgen Habermas reminds us that even when we are working within one tradition (a problematic concept in itself) there is always the potential that a tradition or traditions can be systematically distorted (through, for example, exclusivist or fundamentalist forms). Dialogue between disciplines presents us with similar challenges. There is a kind of economic fundamentalism which is as systematically distorted as any fundamentalist religious tradition. This raises what may be one of the most significant questions in pursuing dialogue with economists: are they interested in dialogue with the religions? And if not, what might we do to get them interested?

Conversation or dialogue, if it is to be authentic, makes many demands upon us, including the willingness to risk our presuppositions (Gadamer calls these prejudices or prejudgments) and an openness to the genuinely transformative potential of conversation. The two are directly related. Without the willingness to risk there can be no transformation, and without a commitment to the potential for transformation the willingness to risk is unlikely to manifest itself. Without both qualities, what often postures as dialogue or conversation is nothing more than presentation. Tracy describes our acceptance of the risk of transformation as "a blow to one's earlier self-understanding as well as one's initial understanding of the other person or text."[3] In interreligious dialogue, a primary question has long been: how much of our religious self-understanding are we willing to risk? If we are now to expand our conversation to engage with economists, Tracy's "blow" will be of an entirely new type, and, depending upon the degree of seriousness with which we engage, this conversation could have profound consequences for both our self-understanding as well as Knitter's challenge of engagement for change.

One thing that emerged very clearly in Boston is that while those who study and practice religion may have some disagreements on economic matters, and certainly different languages concerning economic development, there was nonetheless basic agreement on most issues. Above all, there was agreement that the current form of economic de-

3. David Tracy notes that dialogue "need not reach a full fusion of horizons or mutual understanding in order to be a successful dialogue"; "Western Hermeneutics and Interreligious Dialogue," in Cornille and Conway, eds., *Interreligious Hermeneutics*, 8.

velopment rests on foundations that are not consistent with the values found in the various religious traditions. There was agreement that the global economic system, perhaps even capitalism, is somewhere between flawed and immoral. There was deep concern about the perceived presupposition by economists that all growth is good. There were concerns about self-interest as the assumed motivation of a system that results in individualism, which in turn manifests as consumption. There was shared concern about self-interest which expresses itself as greed. There were concerns about the inequities of power and wealth created by the current system. There were concerns about the ecological impacts of the current form of economic development, now and for future generations. With regard to the current form of the market economy, the religious perspectives at the conference and in this volume are almost entirely critical. The discussions in Boston and this volume are a promising first step. There were attempts by some presenters to engage economists directly. The challenge moving forward will be finding ways to engage the economists more on their terms, in their language and within their frameworks of understanding.

The economist referenced most frequently by religious thinkers was E. F. Schumacher, whose notion of "Buddhist economics," drawn from his 1973 work *Small Is Beautiful: Economics as if People Mattered*,[4] was wonderfully prescient, but is not considered by current economists to be particularly relevant to the field of professional economics. In fact, it is doubtful that most current economists are likely to have even read Schumacher. The exception to this might be economists who teach Environmental Economics. Whether economists in general should read it and whether doing so would change the way they approach economics is a question worthy of being pursued. There are scattered references to other economists in the articles written by religious scholars. These include Adam Smith, Herman Daley, Joseph Stiglitz, Milton Friedman, Amartya Sen, Cecil Pigou, R. H. Coase, N. Gerogescu-Roegen, Vilfredo Pareto, Leon Walras, and W. S. Jevons are mentioned, but the question is whether or not we need to explore serious engagement with economists in more of their language and within their framework of understanding if we are to pursue Knitter's second challenge: dialogue with the market.

4. E. F. Schumacher, *Small Is Beautiful: Economics as if People Mattered* (London: Blond & Briggs, 1973); here I am using the reprint by Hartley & Marks, 1999.

That being said, it is important to recognize that the engagement *among* the religions in search of resources within those traditions for thinking about economic development is a critically important and necessary first step and this volume is an excellent contribution to that undertaking. After searching for resources within and between the religious traditions which are relevant to economic development, we need to commit to moving toward a constructive dialogue with economists and to an engagement with the techno-economic system[5] that works toward change.

Dialogue with Economists

There are many important areas which warrant discussion between the religions and the economists. One of these, which can seem incommensurable, is how to discuss religion's concerns with self-transcendence with the economic assumption of primacy of self-interest. Another issue is the economist's belief that economic growth *per se* is good. Ives, Knitter and all of those who dealt with ecological issues expressed deep concerns with this assumption about economic growth. The larger context within which both of these discussions arise has to do with the ultimate purpose of economic systems. Is the purpose of an economic system efficiency or should it consciously have greater social purposes in mind as part of its design? This question goes to the heart of many of the criticisms of neoliberal economic systems.

Economic growth is obviously a complicated issue and is deserving of a more nuanced discussion than it can receive in this volume. Swearer's article on Thailand's sufficiency economy raises the issue of growth in particularly interesting ways. The Thai notion of a sufficien-

5. The term techno-economic system is one which comes from the work of Joseph Schumpter and more recently Carolta Perez. See Schumpter, *The Theory of Economic Development* (New York: Oxford University Press, 1961); and C. Perez, "Technological Revolutions and Techno-economic Paradigms," *Cambridge Journal of Economics* 34 (2010). The term is important in that understanding the relationship between global economic and global technological systems is critical to change. The part of Schumacher's *Small Is Beautiful* that is missing in the various references to his work in this volume is his understanding of what he calls "appropriate technology." Understanding technology in terms of both the goals of an economic system (we might even say "appropriate economic systems") as well as in terms of redefined notions of efficiencies in the market is critical to being able to draw economists into the discussion.

cy economy is not against growth (in fact, it encourages growth), but it does so in particular ways and, one assumes, within limits.[6] But how do we measure a successful or efficient economy? One way of measuring growth is the Gross Domestic Product (GDP). The problem with the GDP as an indicator is that while it *measures* growth it does not *evaluate* growth. The GDP simply gives us raw figures of whether or not there is economic activity; it does not evaluate (or even develop criteria for evaluation) whether any particular activity is "good" or "bad."[7]

The question of whether markets should be concerned with common goods is in some ways the very heart of the discussion. While it might seem obvious to religious thinkers that moral goods should be central to any conversation about the market, we cannot assume this as a common assumption among economists. If we trace the question back to Adam Smith and his notion of the "invisible hand," it is not entirely clear whether we find an ally or not. First, his entire theory of markets is based upon the assumption that humans will pursue self-interest and that markets are about this pursuit of self-interest and nothing more.[8] He holds that if everyone pursues their own best self-interest this will result in the best products. Smith clearly believes that social goods will result from allowing a market to function freely, but he believes that these are unintended consequences (thus the hand is invisible). Finally, and perhaps most importantly, there is often an assumption made that because Smith wrote a theory of the moral sentiments that this is a philosophical background to his economic theory. This is a much debated topic. *The Wealth of Nations* is primarily about the market efficiency which results from the division of labor

6. We do not have enough evidence yet to know how such experiments will fare over time. Are there limits to growth beyond which the sufficiency model will no longer function efficiently or fairly? See, for example, The UNDP Thailand Human Development Report, http://hdr.undp.org/en/reports/nationalreports/asiathepacific/thailand/name,3418,en.html.

7. An excellent analysis of the inadequacies of the GDP as an indicator of a good economy can be found in Herman Daly and John B. Cobb Jr., *For the Common Good: Rediverting the Economy toward Community, the Environment, and a Sustainable Future* (Boston: Beacon, 1989). This book is highly recommended for anyone interested in observing a dialogue between an economist (Daly) and a theologian (Cobb).

8. There are debates as to whether this belief in self-interest is consistent with his *Theory of Moral Sentiments*, which explores our connection and concern for others and not self-interest.

and how that functions within free markets. Thus while there may be unintended socially beneficial consequences which result from this efficiency, it is not Smith's principle concern.

This concern by economists with efficiency is the key to understanding their claim of being a "science." The development of economics as a science during the twentieth century has resulted in a turn away from an analysis of social contexts and concerns, and toward a focus only on that which can be quantified. This was echoed during our conversations in Boston when Joseph Kaboski, an economist from Notre Dame, described economists as "technicians" who are unconcerned with abstract social theories. Economists are committed instead to analyzing how markets work, and to prescribing how to make markets work more *efficiently* (this is sometimes referred to as methodological instrumentalism). Understanding economists' self-understanding as technicians, and thus as value-neutral, is a key to understanding the framework and hermeneutical principles within which they claim to work. As Kaboski put it, economists "open the hood and tinker with the engine." The metaphor works because the point of the tinkering with any engine is efficiency. However, the reduction of economics to technical concerns and quantifiable analysis that no longer deals with questions concerning what kind of system that engine is being designed to run, I would suggest, is the major critical shortcoming of the field. Economists leave aside the importance of questions which deal with the ultimate purposes of an economy as they relate to larger social or even moral goals and ideals. More critically minded thinkers (some of them economists) see these very questions as foundational and would claim that they logically precede the technical questions. Technique that proceeds via unquestioned assumptions or presuppositions has limited resources to deal with the unintended consequences of the technique itself. As technicians, economists have separated themselves from these types of questions, and these are the very questions that are raised by the religious and political spheres. It is also why economists need the input of religious thinkers.

Bruce Scott, in a recent study of the concept of capitalism, notes that "over the last century and a half, the prevailing conception of capitalism has undergone a rather remarkable evolution, in terms of both its inherent structure and its impact on societal outcomes. . . ."[9]

9. Bruce Scott, *The Concept of Capitalism* (Heidelberg: Springer, 2009) 9.

This remarkable evolution is one in which economic systems gradually detached themselves from social and political concerns. In an earlier work, Karl Polanyi already begins to describe this in terms of the reduction of the notion of socially embedded economic systems to a fundamental concern with markets: "[T]he change from regulated to self-regulated markets at the end of the eighteenth century [that] represented a complete transformation in the structure of society."[10] This represented "nothing less than the institutional separation of society into an economic and political sphere."[11] Understanding "autonomous markets" in connection with "autonomous technology" will help us take Polanyi's notion of the unregulated market a step further, in that this relationship reduces markets to the quantifiable structures of mathematical models which assume rational self-interest to be universal and, most importantly, to be either context free or the only relevant context of analysis. This allows for both markets and technologies to become ends in themselves rather than means to common goods or agreed-upon social ends. Scott and other economists believe that this failure to even attempt to understand the larger questions which motivate an economy are of critical importance. The economist's claim to value-neutrality reveals a kind of fundamentalism and, as mentioned above, a systematically distorted view of the world which has ceased to even search for critical theory to break its bondage to its own ideological blindness.

My contention is, on the face of it, quite simple. I agree that we are in the midst of a global techno-economic crisis. Crisis demands change, even radical change. If the religions want to be responsive to and responsible about this crisis, they must be willing to commit to change. This presupposes engaging economists in a fundamental dialogue. As mentioned before, politics might function as the mediator in this process. While the relationship between religion and politics, as well as the relationship between economics and politics are part of the public discourse, the three-way dialogue is often lacking. Such dialogue may be able to meet both of Knitter's challenges: dialogue with the market (or economists) and the type of engagements capable of changing the current techno-economic system.

10. Karl Polanyi, *The Great Transformation: The Political and Economic Origins of Our Time* (New York: Farrar & Rinehart, 1944) 74.

11. Ibid.

For the economists we need only go back into their own tradition to find ways and language for engaging the political dimensions of the economy. I will focus on two economists, Milton Friedman and Amartya Sen. Milton Friedman published his landmark *Capitalism and Freedom* [12] in 1962, establishing him not only as a major economic voice but as the major proponent of what is now called neoliberal or neoclassical economics. In 1995, Amartya Sen published *Development as Freedom*,[13] consolidating his role as one of the leading thinkers in the field of development economics. My hope is that, by looking at some of the issues that arise in these two works, we might find some analogical leverage out of which we may begin to construct the bridges necessary for authentic conversation with economists.

There are two critical dimensions upon which I will focus: first, the relationship between the economic and political spheres in the two works; and second, both authors' emphasis on freedom. Both Friedman and Sen are concerned with the relationship between economic freedom and political freedom. Their differences on both the nature of freedom, and the path to freedom, are what interest us here. Friedman and Sen's discussions on the notion of freedom allow us to get to issues which move beyond the technical dimensions of an economy to concerns with the ultimate purposes of an economy.

Friedman begins by telling us that his book's "major theme is the role of competitive capitalism—the organization of the bulk of economic activity through private enterprise operating in a free market—as a system of economic freedom and a necessary condition for political freedom."[14] He continues by saying that its "minor theme is the role that government should play in a society dedicated to freedom and relying primarily on the market to organize economic activity."[15] It is important that we note from the outset that Friedman believes that economic freedom is a condition for political freedom, and that government should play a very limited role in regulating economic activity.

12. Milton Friedman, *Capitalism and Freedom* (Chicago: University of Chicago Press, 1962).

13. Amartya Sen, *Development as Freedom* (New York: Knopf, 1999).

14. Friedman, *Capitalism and Freedom*, 4.

15. Ibid.

Friedman is one of the seminal figures in what would be considered "conservative" economics today. However, it is worth noting that Friedman considered himself to be carrying on his interpretation of the "liberal" tradition of the Enlightenment. Friedman writes, "It is extremely convenient to have a label for the political and economic viewpoint elaborated in this book. The rightful and proper label is liberalism."[16] This rehabilitation of classical liberalism highlights the fact that debates over liberalism are also debates over freedom. Friedman draws his use of the term from his interpretation of Enlightenment thought, which, he notes, generally had human freedom as its ultimate goal, and supported a laissez-faire approach which sought to reduce the role of government in economic affairs in order to enlarge the role and importance of the individual.[17] Friedman held that it is a false appropriation of the term liberalism, to mean governmentally directed welfare and equality, thus replacing the original intent of liberalism as the extension of economic freedom as the best way to achieve welfare and equality: "In the name of welfare and equality, the twentieth-century liberal has come to favour a revival of the very policies of state intervention and paternalism against which classical liberalism fought."[18]

Friedman continues his discussion by examining the relationship between economic freedom and political freedom. He rejects the possibility of idealized political/economic configurations such as "democratic socialism," claiming that if we truly want freedom only certain combinations of economic and political arrangements are possible. A society which is socialist cannot be democratic because it does not guarantee individual freedom economically. He writes,

> Economic arrangements play a dual role in the promotion of a free society. On the one hand, freedom in economic arrangements is itself a component of freedom broadly understood, so economic freedom is an end in itself. In the second place, economic freedom is also an indispensable means toward the achievement of political freedom. . . . Viewed as a means to the end of political freedom, economic arrangements are impor-

16. Ibid., 5.

17. It is interesting that the Frankfurt School appropriates the Enlightenment project as a liberal project on similar grounds but with very different economic and social conclusions.

18. Ibid., 6.

> tant because of their effect on the concentration or dispersion of power. The kind of economic organization that provides economic freedom directly, namely, competitive capitalism, also promotes political freedom because it separates economic power from the political power and in this way enables one to offset the other.[19]

There are a number of controversial implications that flow from Friedman's position (such as the state not licensing doctors, legalizing drugs, etc.), but the heart of his position in the debate is captured by the above quotation. Economic freedom is fundamental to, and precedes, political freedom. Without economic freedom—and by this he means markets that are unregulated by the government—there can be no real political freedom. He admits that there are exceptions to this (the United States being one). As he says, "History suggests only that capitalism is a necessary condition for political freedom. Clearly it is not a sufficient condition."[20] While his position is in part a call for reformation of the US economic system, the real importance of Friedman's writing is for economic development. Following his approach, we would conclude that if what we seek is political freedom for developing countries we must first concentrate on the development of markets which allow for the exercise of economic freedom.

There are four critical issues I see emerging from our brief examination of Friedman's position.

First, even though Friedman claims otherwise, there is a degree of separation of the economic sphere from the political sphere. He sees them as related but not fully integrated. He is not interested in a full-blown political economics. Markets are not equally economic and political. This separation allows Friedman to reduce the role of government relative to the economy to one of "umpire."

Second, more than just separation, he maintains a priority of the economic realm over the political realm when it comes to the issue of freedom. Competitive capitalism or freedom in the marketplace is the necessary but not sufficient condition for political freedom, not vice versa. Freedom is based first and foremost in economic freedom and any approach to economic development must be built upon the foundation of building structures that allow for free, unregulated mar-

19. Ibid., 8.

20. Ibid., 10.

kets. This prioritization of the economic realm over the political is the source of much of the criticism of Friedman's version of neoclassical economics. There has been no shortage of such criticisms through the years, ranging from serious economic debates to popularized attacks.

Third, Friedman is a methodological instrumentalist. He is not concerned with theoretical debates concerning his notion of markets and freedom but rather with the usefulness of the conclusions drawn from general theory. His concern is outcomes, and in general he believes that the outcomes relative to freedom will be better if the economic sphere is prioritized over the political. This is not a point we need dwell on here except to point out that Sen would also see himself as a methodological instrumentalist. Neither is particularly concerned with drawn-out theoretical debates but with how to best accomplish the actuality of freedom as they each conceive it. We do not find a well-developed theory of political freedom in Friedman's work. His ideas of freedom are close to being libertarian. Some may seem extreme (such as the "freedom" of doctors to practice without a license, limits to government involvement in education, limiting fair labor practices which make discrimination illegal) but all are based upon his interpretation of the tradition stemming from Locke which sees freedom as inextricably tied to individual rights. For Friedman the ability to exercise these individual rights politically will always be preceded by the ability to exercise individual rights economically.

Fourth, and this is perhaps the most important point, in Friedman's analysis of power he sees abuses of power leading to a diminution of freedom happening only in the political sphere, not in the economic sphere. Friedman, and those economists who are the technicians of efficiency, would claim that in a genuinely free and efficient market there is no abuse of power. Such claims raise questions both about what constitutes a genuinely free market and about whether or not economic power offsets the abuses of political power or exacerbates it. The claims also raise again the question of whether political power is needed to keep excesses in the market in check, and to what degree this may be necessary. It is the power relations in systems such as the so-called Bretton Woods system or the Washington Consensus that are claimed to present the greatest threat to freedom by their critics.

Turning to Amartya Sen and his seminal work *Development as Freedom*, we find five dimensions of freedom which he feels must work together for successful development to occur. These are (in the order that he lists them): 1) political freedom, 2) economic facilities, 3) social opportunities, 4) transparency guarantees, and 5) protective security. Notably, he calls these "instrumental freedoms" and insists that they must be taken as an interrelated whole or complex system. This means that you cannot focus on one at a time, in the same way that the Millennium Development Goals must be worked on as one complex system; all of Sen's freedoms must be in play and developed at the same time. Development must focus on "public policy to foster human capabilities and substantive freedoms in general . . ." which works through the instrumental freedoms. As he says, "While development analysis must, on the one hand, be concerned with objectives and aims that make these instrumental freedoms consequentially important, it must also take note of the empirical linkages that tie the distinct types of freedom together, strengthening their joint importance. Indeed, these connections are central to the fuller understanding of the instrumental role of freedom."[21] Sen, like Friedman, believes and values markets as part of the process of development. How we develop markets and their relationship to the political (and moral) spheres will be the issue that separates Sen from Friedman. Sen is not an anticapitalist nor is he against free markets, the importance of market mechanisms, or growth. Rather, he sees economic growth, when tied to his five freedoms, to be of critical importance. As he says, "The ability of the market mechanisms to contribute to high economic growth and to overall economic progress has been widely—and rightly—acknowledged in the contemporary development literature . . . As Adam Smith noted, freedom of exchange and transaction itself is part and parcel of the basic liberties that people have reason to value . . . To be generically against markets would be almost as odd as being generically against conversations between people . . ." [22]

Because Sen's notion of economic growth is tied to "growth" of the five freedoms, his idea of a successful market will be based upon a qualitative analysis of "capabilities" rather than a quantitative analysis of income, GDP, etc. While both quantitative and qualitative growth potentially contribute to the quality of life, the focus exclusively on the analysis of increase in income can often obscure qualitative dimen-

21. Sen, *Development as Freedom*, 10.

22. Ibid., 6.

sions that are as important as income. He maintains that the origin of economics "was significantly motivated by the need to study the assessment of, and causal influence on, the opportunities that people have for good living."[23] In a move parallel to Friedman's reclamation of the term "liberalism" through recalling the Enlightenment, Sen seeks to reclaim the role of market mechanisms through reference to writers as diverse as Aristotle, William Perry, Gregory King and others. A free market, as discussed in this heritage, is one which does not "deny opportunities for transaction through arbitrary controls." Thus far Sen would seem to be in agreement with Friedman, and throughout the book he struggles with the substantive good of freedom of markets, whether they are "free," and how to make them so. Where Sen differs from Friedman is in his concern that "the discipline of economics has tended to move away from focusing on the value of freedoms to that of utilities, incomes and wealth."[24] This shift of market economics to one of utility (measured in incomes and wealth) "has been achieved at some cost: the neglect of the central value of freedom itself."[25] Sen argues that the prioritization and integration of his five freedoms are fundamental to any notion of a free market. This contrasts with Friedman's notion of economic development as detached from or being of primary importance relative to political freedom.

For Sen, a key component of freedom is democratic participation in the decision processes of economic development. This notion of democratic participation is enormously complex, spinning off into its own debates about what we mean by participation, justice, etc.[26] It also raises questions about the maintenance of tradition, social hierarchies, religious laws and structures, etc. How we balance these issues within a theory and practice of economic development are of great concern for Sen and should be for us as well. They are of much less concern for Friedman, who would agree with the overly simplistic notion, cited by Sen, that it is better to be rich and happy than to be impoverished and traditional. Sen believes, in keeping with his idea of substantive freedom, that the people should have the right and capability to make

23. Ibid., 24.

24. Ibid., 27.

25. Ibid., 28.

26. Perhaps the best example of this is the so-called Liberal/Communitarian debate, which is rich with critical issues for any consideration of economic development.

decisions about such issues themselves. When decisions are made for them by the elite or by economic command-and-control structures, economic development that fosters freedom is stymied.

Another key difference between Friedman and Sen, as they work with the idea of freedom, is that for Sen, freedom is tied directly to justice. It would not be fair to say that Friedman was unconcerned with justice; however, he never made justice an integral part of his concept of freedom. Sen draws upon the work of John Rawls whose notion of justice as fairness is perhaps the most influential notion of justice from the so-called liberal perspective. It is interesting that Rawls's use of "liberal" comes from the same tradition cited by Friedman, with its assumptions of self-interest and individual rights. Friedman, Sen and Rawls all believe that a fair and just economic or political system is built upon the assumption that individuals will pursue self-interests, and thus we are in need of both process and a system of individual rights.

Sen draws upon Rawls's notion of liberty within his theory of justice. He focuses upon Rawls's idea of "priority of liberty" which emphasizes sets of rights which trump any and all utilities. [27] These rights include things such as property rights, as well as personal and civil liberties. The question one might ask is why we should prioritize such rights when economic needs are often a matter of life and death. To phrase this in another way: should the priority of liberties apply to intensely poor countries to the same degree or in the same way that they would in more economically developed countries? Sen gives liberty a qualified priority. As he says, "The critical issue, I would submit, is not complete precedence, but whether a person's liberty should get just the same kind of importance (no more) that other types of personal advantage—incomes, utilities and so on—have."[28] For Sen the answer to the question of liberty having equal importance goes to the heart of the question of quality of life. He does not deny the importance of income to the quality of life, but would claim that income is a necessary but not sufficient condition for improvements in the quality of life.

27. See also Robert Nozick, *Anarchy, State and Utopia* (New York: Basic Books, 1974) for an even more elaborate set of rights than is found in Rawls. For a more thorough analysis of both see his recent book, *The Idea of Justice* (Cambridge: Harvard University Press, 2009).

28. Sen, *Development as Freedom*, 65.

One ways in which Sen frames his argument concerning the analysis of quality of life questions is the distinction between "income poverty" and "capability poverty." He acknowledges that the two are related, but his concern is that too much of the current analysis of poverty focuses only on the former, assuming that if one addressed income poverty, quality of life will follow. His five freedoms, which include improvement of income, are meant to address poverty as a system of interrelated capabilities. If we improve the capability of a person, we improve not only their income potential but their overall quality of life. As Sen puts it, "There is a danger in seeing poverty in the narrow sense of income poverty and then justifying investment in education, health care and so forth on the ground that they are good means to the end of reducing income poverty." [29] He holds that education, health care, etc., are ends in themselves and part of a complex that allows us to understand poverty "in terms of lives people can actually lead and the freedoms they do actually have. The expansion of human capabilities fits directly into these basic considerations."[30] Focusing only on income poverty allows us to paint statistical pictures which show that the global system of development is working, while a more detailed picture of the lives of those included in the statistics would show that the statistical jump in income does not necessarily translate into a better quality of life.

Writers such as Sen and Joseph Stiglitz believe that tying economic development to the development of democratic values is the key to transforming the system. Sen's famous observation that no democratic nation has ever suffered through a major famine is perhaps his best real and symbolic case in point. The empowerment of people through democratic participation is essential to a just and fair economic system, thus the analysis of the success or failure of any economic system should be based on qualitative criteria rather than purely quantitative ones.

Both Friedman and Sen give us glimpses of ideal types of economic and political freedom. Neither is against a free market. The difference between them is Friedman giving priority to economic freedom over political freedom while Sen is seeking the right balance between the economic and political spheres. In fact this has always

29. Ibid., 92.

30. Ibid.

been the issue with capitalism and neoclassical economics. But in the end we always come back to the combination of capitalist markets and democratic politics as the most promising way forward.[31]

It is in this nexus of markets and politics that there is both room for and need of the voice of the religions. Friedman and Sen give us the beginnings of some language with which we might engage economists. With Sen and his focus on "capabilities" we find an economic and political concept which resonates with the concern with the dignity of every human, with human flourishing, subsidiarity and with the privileged option for the poor. Understanding Friedman allows us to discuss the notion of the freedom of the market as it relates to political freedom, and to remind economists that the detachment of the market from all political, social, and moral concerns is not consistent with their own tradition. Efficiency must be balanced with fairness if markets are to acknowledge purpose beyond quantitatively rendered notions of efficiency. The unintended beneficial social consequences about which Adam Smith speaks as the invisible hand must be made intentional and become part of the design of the techno-economic system. The claim that unfettered markets are efficient does not address complex questions of other dimensions necessary for human flourishing.

I began the article with some of the hermeneutical challenges we face if we want to take up Paul Knitter's challenge to engage in dialogue with the economists. My hope for this brief analysis of certain key concepts from Friedman and Sen is to highlight examples of the two economists' language and frameworks of understanding to which the religions might relate. It gives us the beginning of some language from economists which resonates with our own religious concerns. The question of freedom is one which is of concern to religion, economics and politics. Finding the analogical connections between these will enrich the discussion for all. Sen is particularly helpful in the way in which he frames his discussion of development and the relationship between freedom and utility. The religions have resources upon which to draw which can allow us to enrich the economists' discussion of issues such as human freedom and the quality of life. Our understanding of these concepts is different, sometimes very different than

31. For an excellent history of capitalism and at least some of the other parameters of the debate see Jeffry Frieden, *Global Capitalism: Its Fall and Rise in the Twentieth Century* (New York: Norton, 2006).

what we find in even those economists with whom we find ourselves in basic agreement. The hermeneutical task of translating such terms as freedom, justice, quality of life, utilities between disciplines is the challenge. Reading the economists, even those with whom we might disagree, learning how they frame their arguments about issues with which we resonate, even when we might disagree with those arguments, sharpens our own concepts and challenges us to translate them into terms to which economists can relate. In so doing, it provides the beginning of a common language with which we might engage in conversation with them.

Sen's writing is full of good examples relating his ideas of freedom and capabilities to the issue of poverty. Let me conclude with a brief example drawn from another area that many believe relates to what should be a fundamental right, freedom from pollution. I will use the example of the pollution of a river. Pollution is an issue which we can discuss from a religious perspective, in religious language and it is an issue we can discuss from an economic perspective, in economic language. The challenge is translating from one language into the other, in hopes of finding a common language and common ground upon which to engage in dialogue.

In this volume, Elliot Dorff quotes Psalm 24, "To the Lord belong the earth and all that it holds, the world and all those who inhabit it" (24:1). He goes on to say, "Ultimately, God owns the world. We enjoy the right to use it and make our living on it only at God's behest, and only when we abide by the rules God has set for such activity." He continues by saying that, in Judaism, "we begin not as individuals with rights, but as members of a community with duties." He contrasts this with the American emphasis upon rights of the individual.[32] Christopher Ives notes that Thich Nhat Hanh has laid out fourteen "mindfulness trainings," the eleventh of which reads, "Aware that great violence and injustice have been done to our environment and society, we are committed not to live with a vocation that is harmful to humans and to nature."[33] Laurenti Magesa draws from Pope John Paul II's 1990 *Message to the World* in which he says, "The commitment of believers to a healthy environment for everyone stems directly from their belief in God the Creator . . . Respect for life and for the dignity of the human

32. Elliot Dorff, in this volume.

33. Christopher Ives, in this volume.

person extends also to the rest of creation."[34] The religions have been among the leaders in advocating for stewardship of the environment. They have provided resources from within their traditions that have had an impact on changing lifestyles and public policy. From Lynn White's seminal article "The Historical Roots of Our Ecological Crisis" in 1966 to the *Religions of the World and Ecology* book series, a rich and powerful body of writing has been produced from within the religious traditions and through dialogue among the religions. This work has helped us understand that the environmental crisis is "also a moral and spiritual crisis which, in order to be addressed, will require broader philosophical and religious understandings of ourselves as creatures of nature, embedded in life cycles and dependent on ecosystems."[35]

Paralleling this is an equally rich literature produced by philosophers, political scientists and activists who draw upon different resources but share many of the same values found in the religious traditions. One concept that has been developed by these writers is that of "the commons." In the simplest terms possible, the commons refers to resources that are collectively shared (or "owned") by a people or by all people. Forests, rivers, oceans, air, fisheries, cultural resources, even the human genome, are all examples of resources that are spoken of as commons. There is a growing body of literature which is attempting to address a range of issues such as: rights as they relate to the commons, the privatization of the commons, governing the commons, etc.[36]

While the language of the commons is generally legal, political or philosophical, there is great resonance with the language of religions, as they speak about the environment as something in which we all share through our relationship to the divine or of nature being sacred. It also provides a language we might use to engage the economists on their own terms because we can translate the political concept of "the commons" into what economists call "public goods."[37]

34. Laurenti Magesa, in this volume.

35. Mary Evelyn Tucker and John Grim, "The Nature of the Environmental Crisis," http://www.hds.harvard.edu/cswr/resources/print/ecology_foreword.html.

36. There are many books on the problem of the commons. Two I have found helpful are: Elinor Ostrom, *Governing the Commons: The Evolution of Institutions for Collective Action* (Cambridge: Cambridge University Press, 1990); and Michael Goldman, ed., *Privatizing Nature: Political Struggles for the Global Commons* (New Brunswick, NJ: Rutgers University Press, 1998).

37. There are many good discussions of environmental resources as public goods

Typically economists describe public goods as having two aspects: "nonexcludability" and "nonrivalrous consumption." Nonexcludability means that the cost of prohibiting someone from a good or service is prohibitively high or impossible. Nonrivalrous consumption means that a good or service for which some pay is not diminished by non-payers or what are called "free riders." I will focus only on the latter.

Staying with our example of the river, we first recall that in the United States, rivers cannot be privately owned. Rivers belong to everyone. In political terms, rivers are part of the commons. In economic terms, rivers are public goods. Rivers, as public goods, are nonrivalrous because my use of the river should not impact your ability to also use and enjoy the river. Even though it is a public good, people will look for ways to commodify the river and to charge for goods or services connected to using the river. For example, one might charge for access to the river for recreation or for equipment that is used for fishing. This does not privatize the river because public access is legally required for all rivers, thus these activities, within limits, are still nonrivalrous.

The economic and political issues arise when we consider the use of the water for economic purposes.[38] One of these issues is property rights. A basic premise of any efficiently functioning economic system is clearly defined property rights. The use of the water for economic gain blurs the line between private and public goods. Economists such as Ronald Coase have admitted the inefficiencies of public goods and want to deal with them by defining clearly the property rights involved (the Coase Theorem). But if we take the case of the industrial use of the water from the river, the question of who "owns" the water arises. As a public good, the water in the river is theoretically available to all people for all reasonable uses. However, if an upstream company uses that water for industrial purposes and in the process pollutes the water before returning it back into the river, the river has been partially "privatized" because it no longer functions as a public good for those who would use it recreationally or for any other use impacted by the

(less that tie these into the political notion of the commons) in Natural Resource Economics texts. See for example, James R. Kahn, *The Economic Approach to Environmental Natural Resources* (Mason, OH: Thompson/Southwestern, 2005).

38. Whether water is sacred or a commons and whether and how it should be privatized is being hotly debated worldwide. There is not only a growing body of literature on the topic but increasingly the political and legal systems are taking up this question of privatization.

pollution. The public good is no longer a public good because there is no longer nonrivalrous consumption. Likewise the river as a commons has been compromised because privatization compromises common ownership.

In economic terms, this would be a case of a bad "externality." Externalities are the costs (financial, social, environmental) incurred by people who are external to the industry that has polluted the river and who do not gain from the "free rider" advantage the company gains from the water's industrial use. The company is a free rider because the cost of the loss of use-value of the river and the cost of cleaning it is not born directly and exclusively by the company but by everyone. One way to deal with this privatization of the public good is to attach a price to it, to internalize the externality through a fee structure, taxes, fines, etc., so that the polluter has to pay for their act of privatization. This can only be done through the political process of regulation. This internalization of the externalities will result in a higher price for the product which will be passed along to the consumer. In turn, this will impact utility at the margins or whether the consumer is willing to pay for more units of the product at that higher price. The preference of the polluter as a consumer of the water for production will be determined by the preferences of the consumer of their product at that higher price point. The internalized externality has to be high enough that it changes the market behavior (or both producer and consumer) which is polluting the river. While the motivation here, in market terms, is driven by preference and price structure, and not by sacred duty, we can at least take solace in the practical (instrumental) outcome of having been good stewards to God's creation.

In the brief example, our relationship to the river is seen from three different perspectives, within three different frameworks of understanding and in three different languages. For the religions, the relationship to the river is through the divine or is one of ontological interrelation (such as codependent origination). This relationship demands of each of us, as individuals and as communities, a sacred responsibility of stewardship. From the political or activist perspective, the river is a commons. It is a resource which is owned by all and which is a shared responsibility which should be legally mandated. For the economist, the river is a commodity which is also a public good which places limits on our individual right to use it for profit.

Tying this back into our discussion of Friedman and Sen and their disagreement concerning relationship between economic freedom and political freedom, it is clear that those attempting to protect the commons from privatization prioritize the political over the economic or engage the political process to establish parameters for the economic use of the river. Regulations, fines, and taxes which internalize the bad externalities of the river's pollution are means of keeping the commons secure from privatization. This is a political choice which has moral foundations. It raises the metaeconomic question of the ultimate purpose of a good economy by contextualizing the economic process within a set of higher values which have to do with the quality of life. This example can also be viewed from the perspective of Sen's idea of the five instrumental freedoms as they relate to quality of life issues. The river as sacred trust or political commons fits into his concerns with political freedom, social opportunities, transparency guarantees and protective security. As noted these are central to how he understands poverty. Poverty is not purely quantifiable. This is also at the heart of the concept of sustainable development, since the time of the Brundtland Report and United Nations Conference on Environment and Development. Sustainable development understands environmental quality and poverty as integrally related. Long-term poverty, and the modes of development employed to address it, pose the greatest threats to the environment. Tying poverty to conservation of the commons as public goods allows for models of development which address more than just income poverty and include quality of life issues which for Sen are best understood in terms of capabilities and freedoms.

The hermeneutical and dialogical point is, while the religions are unlikely to be able to convince the economists that they should not commodify the river because it is part of God's creation or that we have a sacred duty to respect and protect it, we might be able to engage the political and legal language of the commons and the economic language of public goods to open a dialogical space. Within that space, we might then be able to draw the economists into conversations which raise questions concerning the ultimate purpose of any economy (metaquestions beyond efficiency and utility) and perhaps even into questions of the common (or even universal) good which help us answer those questions of ultimate purpose. In addition, by using legal and regulatory strategies which seek to internalize the bad externalities, we are able to engage in the stewardship our faith tradition demands.

This is but one very brief example of how we might attempt to translate between religious, political and economic language and frameworks of understanding. To some degree, like Friedman and Sen, the approach is, at least initially, methodologically instrumental. We begin the conversation with discussions of theory or theology but by attempting to use languages and concepts from the political and economic spheres with which we find instrumental compatibility.[39] By doing so, we open the possibility of engaging both the political and economic thinkers in conversation wherein we can begin to interject our own religious values and concerns in our language and within our frameworks of understanding.

The question is whether we feel dialogue with the economists or as Knitter puts it "with the market" is of sufficient critical importance to invest the time and energy necessary to meet the hermeneutical challenges. I believe that it does rise to this level of critical importance. The religions, the economists, the policy makers, and those in civil society need to find ways to cross the hermeneutical divides and together begin to search for new paths forward. It is only together that we will find these new paths, and there is too much at stake for us not to rise to meet the challenges of this new horizon.

39. This is analogous to Paul Knitter's argument that interreligious dialogue should put aside or delay their theological and theoretical debates and begin their conversation by focusing upon relieving human and nonhuman suffering. His approach is one of methodological instrumentalism.

Part II

Economists' Responses

12

Charity and the Technical Economist: A Response to Paul Knitter

Joseph Kaboski

The Need for Dialogue

No one field of knowledge can be our sole guiding light when it comes to the economy, society, and political decisions. These are important questions that involve all of society, and they require a variety of expertise and input. Indeed, religion plays a foundational role in helping us understand who we are. Without religion we cannot answer two questions that echo in all ages: what is the good life, and what is the good society? Authentic religion helps answer these questions by revealing man to himself: our nature, our purpose, and our ultimate destination. If we are to have a system of principles and values that ultimately enable what economists call normative analysis, it should stem from a fundamental anthropology.

As a theist, a Catholic, I look to my religion for this foundation. Recent Popes (Paul VI, John Paul II, and Benedict XVI) have emphasized an understanding of development that addresses these two great questions, at least in part. True development, they say, is not merely technical progress or growth in average income, nor even economic development more broadly, but rather "integral" development. By integral, they answer that the good life involves the whole person (body, mind, and soul), and the good society involves the whole of society (all people and all aspects of society and culture.) In Christianity, it is Christ himself, a visible example of the good life, that introduces man to himself, and it is the Trinity that gives us an example of the good society.

But religion cannot answer moral questions alone, especially if our ethic has any teleological element. When the morality of decisions depends on their effects, we need to have some sense of what the effects of our decisions might be in order to properly evaluate those decisions. In today's economy, which has become increasingly complex, these effects are not obvious. Indeed, they are quite difficult to measure even after the fact, let alone predict.

I'm no expert in interreligious dialogue, but I imagine that there are two essentials that are necessary for true dialogue. The first, I presume, is that it is important for a person to have a clear understanding of who they are and whom they represent. In this case, I feel that I am well qualified, as I am unabashedly Catholic and unabashedly an economist. I study growth, development, and international economics. I am a mainstream research economist. I studied under two Nobel laureate economists, one macroeconomist and one microeconomist, at the University of Chicago, have consulted for multiple Federal Reserve Banks and the World Bank, and have conducted research, including field research, in Asia, Africa, and Latin America. I am also a cradle Catholic whose main impetus for studying economics was a concern for the poor. I teach a course on economics and Catholic social thought, and I organize an annual interdisciplinary conference on the topic.

I imagine the second essential for true dialogue is some basic knowledge of the other. Some effort at learning the basics of the other field and having a mutual respect, knowledge, and understanding of the other person is essential. This is the difference between true dialogue and polemics. Here, I don't claim to be particularly qualified. While I do know my own faith, I am no theologian, and I am admittedly ignorant regarding many aspects of religious thought.

Paul Knitter falls well short on this front as well. His essay conveys very little understanding of economics and economic language. Indeed, it confuses many ideas and terms. For example, he uses "Free Market Economy," which describes an economic system, as a blanket term covering a list of different phrases with much more precise meanings, such as "Casino Capitalism," a term used to describe financial instability, and "general equilibrium theory," a methodology that tries to model the economy as a whole, including the feedback between different sectors and markets within that whole. More importantly, Knitter's essay shows little understanding of what economists actually do or what we're about. This is where I hope to add some insight.

Economics Is *Not* a Religion

Knitter's second argument is that modern economics is a religion. I use the term "modern economics," whereas he uses "Free Market Economy," because I find it a more appropriate moniker for what he describes as "the understanding of the market that has been taught in American universities and followed in the global market since the late '70s."

I strongly disagree with the assertion, advanced not only by Knitter but also by others in this volume, that modern economics is a religion. Indeed, I think it reflects a prejudice of discipline that can harm true dialogue. Knitter references the mystical qualities of Adam Smith's "invisible hand" analogy. Smith mentioned the analogy in his *Inquiry into the Nature and Causes of the Wealth of Nations*, a fundamental contribution in the history of economic ideas written in 1776, but the idea was first and more fully developed in *The Theory of Moral Sentiments* (1759). I would venture that most economists and theologians have heard of this analogy.

But economists today don't spend our time reading *The Wealth of Nations*. Most economists, especially those trained since 1970, the period Professor Knitter singles out, have never read it. It is probably not surprising to note that the field of economics has changed a great deal over the past 235 years. I often think that critics in the humanities focus on the work of Adam Smith because it is one of the few influential economic works that is broadly accessible. They also focus on the popular discourse of economics for the same reason. Unfortunately, even Nobel laureate pundits such as Milton Friedman, Paul Krugman, or Joseph Stiglitz, despite long resumes of influential past academic research, are not representative of the field. They are the brash few, endowed with a sort of über-confidence in their own knowledge of the truth, who have left the fields of humble research in search of truth for the perilous oceans of political advocacy. Such brazen advocacy may or may not be warranted; my point is that it is certainly not representative.

So let us put some caricatures to rest. Most economists are not ideologues. We don't believe markets cure every evil, nor do we sit in our basement trying to derive systems to make the rich richer and the poor poorer. We are not grand social philosophers. We don't spend our time inventing new economic "systems."

Our focus is on the technical aspects of the economy, rather than the philosophical aspects. We are much more like technicians, which is an assessment of both our personalities (technically oriented) and the nature of our work. Our field is highly mathematical. It needs to be mathematical in order to answer technical questions. This does make interdisciplinary discourse difficult, and perhaps economists should spend more time translating our work for the general public. I do think a deeper dialogue is important, so I would also encourage people interested in fostering dialogue to invest the time into learning both theology and economics on a deeper level.

Economics does have its philosophical presuppositions, as does any discipline, but to call it a religion is to miss the essence of the profession. Again, we are technicians, and, like auto technicians, we spend most of our time under the hood, trying to figure out what makes things work, and what seems to be broken. We collect and analyze data, write down and test models, and measure and predict the impacts of policies.[1]

Such work is slow and tedious, and it requires a great deal of care and effort. For example, one project of mine evaluated the impacts of a microfinance program in Thailand. My coauthor and I used data that we collected from nearly one thousand households over seven years in rural villages in Northern and Central Thailand. The research involved several steps. In Thailand, we made trips to interview real people, but we also employed a survey staff of nearly seventy young Thai adults. Back home, we developed a theory, wrote computer programs, and used these programs to simulate the theoretical behavior of households. Then we analyzed the actual impacts suggested by the data,

1. Clear use of language is important for dialogue. Economists and theologians use the word *model* to mean very different things. To my understanding, theologians use "models" to describe either a type of economic system or alternative visions of the economy. In economic use, the word *model* refers to *a system of mathematical equations used to predict some aspect of economic behavior*.

looking both at the aggregate impacts and the distribution of impacts across households. We compared the results of our theory to the actual data, and finally used the theory to try to predict the possible impacts of some alternative policies. This example is not extraordinary. In my career, the average time from the beginning of a research paper to its publication is about five years.

Why do economists focus primarily on the technical side of economic problems? One reason is that technical questions are precisely the expertise of economists, or what economists call our "comparative advantage" and it is the comparative disadvantage of religion. I know that the Catholic Church does claim to be an "expert on man," if by this we mean that our faith provides answers to the principle characteristics of a good life and a good society. As a Church, we understand that each field has its sphere, and in principle the Church respects the role of the social sciences. What a crazy world it would be if we asked economists to spell out our moral principles, and asked theologians for policy advice on how to implement them.

And yet we must acknowledge that such an idealized division becomes blurred from both sides. Economists have values, and theologians have opinions on how economic policies might play out. To my ears, hearing a theologian call for or propose new economic "models," however, is comparable to hearing an economist commenting on the Israeli-Palestinian conflict by proclaiming a vague idea that what we really need is a new Judeo-Islam hybrid religion. In each case, the ideas involved would be naïve and offensive to genuine dialogue. To paint economics as a religion is as absurd as saying that theologians are really practicing economics, but the latter is closer to the truth.

A technical approach has great merit, especially in the frequent cases when the technical issues are more puzzling than the ethical goals. For example, we can talk and write about the right to a living wage and the right to work, but the virtues of these things are relatively clear. There isn't an economist or a politician in the world who would ever propose low wages and high unemployment as goals.

How to achieve these goals is the real question. Much of the difference in opinion among people doesn't stem from a difference in fundamental values, but rather from different predictions about the effects of different policies. In either case, difficult decisions require understanding what is at stake. And we can't answer questions about goals without understanding the technical aspects of achieving those goals. The road to economic hell is paved with good intentions.

A World of Crises

Knitter raises three concerns in particular: the economic crisis, the environmental crisis, and global poverty and disparity. I should mention that, much like the living wage and right to work, simply stating these concerns requires little research or new insight. They are well known. Again, I studied at the University of Chicago, and I don't know a single person who is pro-financial crisis, pro-global warming, and pro-poverty.

Consider the recent economic crisis in relation to other large crises. In Figure 1, I have plotted average income per capita for the recent recession (United States) through the middle of 2010, as well as for the two biggest financial crises of the last century, the Great Depression (United States) and the East Asian crisis of the late 1990s (Thailand). The vertical dashed line indicates the beginning of the crisis for each episode.

Several things are immediately apparent.

- First, growth leading up to crises differs across the three countries, with recent growth in the United States, and especially Thailand, far outpacing the relatively flat and volatile growth of the "roaring" 1920s United States
- Second, the drop in income in the Thai crisis and in the Great Depression was quite similar during the first two years. After two years, Thailand returned to its high growth projector, while the Great Depression sank deeper into a prolonged recession.
- Third, in comparison, the recent recession is negligible, hardly visible relative to the other two recessions.

I don't want to minimize the crisis in any way, or ignore the suffering of people who are out of work or who have lost their retirement savings, but I want to keep things in perspective. The current crisis is nothing compared to the other episodes, especially in human terms. There are several reasons. Of course, the biggest difference is simply the level of income. While I have scaled the three lines to be equal at the start of the recession, real incomes in the United States before the recession of 2008 were roughly five times as high as they were in 1929 or in 1997 Thailand. In the earlier episodes, a severe drop in income made meeting basic subsistent needs difficult for large segments of the populations. In 2008, even hypothetically, if income had dropped as severely as it did in the Great Depression (one-third), we would be back at 1993 incomes. I'm not old enough to remember 1932, but I was a student in 1993. Poor as I was, it didn't feel like the Great Depression. Of course, average income doesn't tell the whole story; it doesn't capture the unemployment and lost wealth of this recession. Unemployment has risen much more than average income has fallen. Still, the 10 percent unemployment we have pales in comparison to the 25–30 percent unemployment of the earlier episodes. Moreover, the United States of 1929 and Thailand in 1997 had neither social security nor unemployment insurance; losing one's life savings or job hurt because, except for friends, family and private charity, there was nothing to catch the fall.

Of course, problems do exist in financial markets—I don't think anyone denies that—though there are differences in opinion on how to shore things up. But we can't focus on the crisis alone and ignore the existence of tremendous growth. This crisis is not a reason to start rethinking the foundations of our economy. Indeed, one might even look across the three episodes in Figure 1 and consider the possibility that economists may have learned something over the past eighty years.

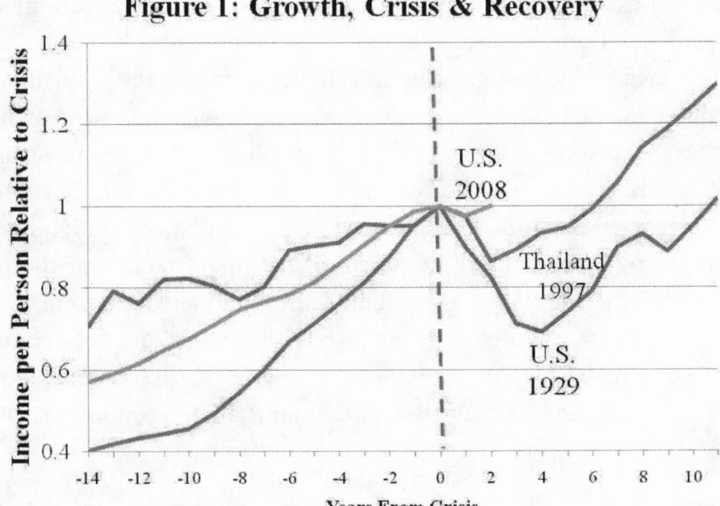

Economists' Approach to the Environment

Let me address the environment as well. Pollution is a clear example of the technical rather than ideological approach of economics. Pollution has long been a clear example of laissez-faire market failure, even from an efficiency standpoint. Clearly, some level of pollution must be allowable, since we wouldn't be able to function or live without producing some pollution. From an economic efficiency standpoint, the primary problem is that people tend to pollute excessively because the private costs of polluting are much lower than the true social costs.

Nearly every economist would agree about this market failure. Most economists would agree that government intervention can improve the situation. Some economic answers include: (1) regulating polluters through direct quotas, or (2) taxing polluters to increase the private cost of pollution so that it better reflects the social costs. Both answers presume an important role for government.

But just as the limits to markets are real, so are the limits of governments. It is difficult to know what the optimal level of pollution is, and this optimal level of pollution surely varies by the circumstances. A neonatal care unit should have less pollution than a coal mine; a power plant in a less populated area should be allowed to produce more pollution than a downtown restaurant. The potential variety of circumstances is nearly infinite.

Given these limitations, economists have suggested assigning legal property rights and using markets in conjunction with regulations. For example, to prevent overfishing of ponds, local governments typically sell licenses to catch a maximum number of fish. That is, the license owner has the legal right to fish. Alternatively, the government might allow the pond to be privately owned, in which case the owner protects against overfishing. In the case of pollution, the cap-and-trade policies are an example. Power plants would have the rights to produce specified amounts of CO_2. Economists suggest combining these property rights with markets, where plants might come together to buy or sell their legal right to pollute. Since polluters have to buy the rights to pollute, polluters face the costs of their decisions, but markets put decisions back into hands of people with the best information. Understanding the facts is also quite important to economists. One fact is that pollution tends to fall as countries grow beyond a certain level of income. Emissions for nearly every major contaminant have fallen over the past thirty years not only in the United States and other advanced economies, but also in China, the emerging industrial giant. The reduction in emissions has been accomplished through three interrelated sources: new technologies, government intervention, and an increased desire for clean air, which accompanies higher incomes. Poor people typically have low willingness to pay for cleaner air and water.[2] Of course, CO_2 is the important exception—emissions have risen rather than fallen. A second fact is that the U.S. is no longer the world's biggest producer of CO_2. This underscores the limitations of national governments, since the U.S. government limited power to control the world's biggest polluter without international negotiation.

In my opinion, it is clear that any action must be international, and the bulk of the burden to reduce pollution must fall on the advanced economies. But the point is that this cannot be accomplished without understanding the technical issues, economic and scientific, involved.

Global Poverty and Disparity

Development economists know a great deal about poverty; that is our business. The level of poverty in the world is hard to imagine for most Americans. Most people in the world live on less than $3/day or $1000/year. I think Knitter did a good job emphasizing the other issues involved: low life expectancy, high infant mortality, a lack of education, etc.

How did people get this poor? We know a fair amount about this as well, and the answer is that before the industrial revolution, outside of a few elite in each society, all of humanity was poor. Today the poor areas of the world are overwhelmingly simply those that have remained poor. Their incomes simply haven't grown.

Knitter's figures show that inequality within societies lowers many measures of aggregate social well-being. Although the true picture is

2. The water in poor countries is typically already contaminated from natural sources, e.g., bacteria.

much more nuanced, the statement is generally accurate.[3] But even here, average income is very important: in rich countries, the health, education and income levels of even the poor segments of society far exceed average levels in the poorest countries. Surviving on a dollar a day means eating a bowl of rice and some vegetables, wearing the same clothes every day, no shoes, no health care, no education, drinking water from a local stream, and living in some makeshift shanty quarters, but this is how the "bottom billion" that Knitter references typically live. Almost no one in the United States lives on a dollar a day. In the rich countries, high inequality is more likely to cause social exclusion than extreme material deprivation.

As dire a problem as poverty remains, poverty rates are thankfully declining, due in large part to the recent growth of China and India. Growth is absolutely critical for the poor. Indeed, if we look at changes in global poverty and inequality, these are driven by some countries growing and others not, or some regions within countries growing and others not.

Economists have learned some things about growth over the failures and successes of the past fifty years. We've witnessed disastrous economies and miraculous economies. Most of the disastrous economies fall under two categories: economies that are centrally planned (e.g., North Korea, China under Mao), or economies suffering from civil war or revolutionary unrest (e.g., sub-Saharan Africa and Latin America).

At the same time, we've seen high growth economies that have transformed whole countries. Examples include South Korea, Taiwan, Thailand, and post-Mao China. More people have been lifted out of poverty over the past thirty years than at any time in history. In China alone, home to one in five people, poverty rates fell from 86 percent to 16 percent from 1981–2005. These miracles have also had common

3. There are entire literatures studying and debating each of these patterns. I am inclined to believe Knitter's interpretation, but it is very difficult to establish causal relationships. I point out one example of a nuance. Life expectancy in the United States is lower than other advanced countries, but this has little to do with our physical health or health care. Americans have an odd passion for guns and automobiles, and both result in a great deal of deaths at young ages. After correctly adjusting for this disparity, the United States has the highest life expectancy in the world.

elements—namely, that they are market economies, and that they are globally integrated, particularly in trade.

There are stark, even grave, examples showing that markets and openness matter. I want to emphasize these because there have been religious sub-groups—liberation theologians in Latin America, for example—who have argued against global integration and who have even pushed for centralized economies, devoid of private property. Using Marxist social analyses, these theologians have been confident that they knew what changes were needed. The only question was igniting the fire of change.

But as I mentioned before, the road to economic hell can sometimes be paved with good intentions. Consider the fateful divergent paths of North and South Korea. At the time of the cease-fire, both were poor, but North Korea was the more economically advanced. Today, it is one of the poorest countries in the world, where 2–3 million people died of famine in the 1990s. In contrast, South Korea is now a prosperous country with incomes fifteen times higher than its northern neighbor. Consider the example of China, where under the central planning of Mao, incomes failed to even double over the twenty-eight years of 1950–78, and an estimated 25–60 million people died of famine during the Great Leap Forward of 1958–62. Contrast these realities with the quadrupling of incomes in the twenty-eight years of economic decentralization after Mao. There is no way to sugarcoat this. These disasters have been man-made. They put our current economic crisis into perspective, and they clearly underscore the need for dialogue.

The Limits to Growth

Does growth solve everything? Of course not. I have already mentioned the important problem with carbon emissions. The lack of political freedom in China is a second example. Figure 2 underscores another concern.

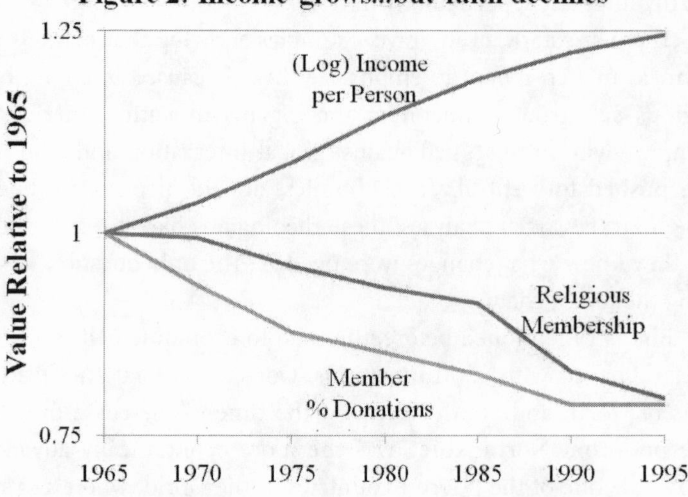

Over the past forty years, incomes in the United States have grown, but at the same time, we see a troubling decline in religiosity. The measures shown are the fraction of people who affiliate with any religion (Catholic, Protestant, Buddhist, Hindu, Muslim, Jew, and others) and also religious giving, and both show a steep decline. Some of this may be the tendency to claim to be "spiritual," but not "religious," but other measures of religious values in the Socioeconomic Survey show a decline as well. Indeed, the most striking trend is the twofold increase over the 1990s in those with no religion at all. Is this the type of integral development that the pope had in mind, when he talked about development of the "whole person"?

This "poverty of the soul" is, I believe, an equally grave concern. There is certainly much debate and a large literature in the social sciences on the decline of religion, some of which I have read, and much of which I have not. These trends weren't always so. As late as the 1950s, the data show a large upswing in religiosity and religious donations. Like the other crises, combating the decline in religiosity is a real challenge for the current generations: theologians, economists, religions, and societies in general.

I would make two empirical points. First, the decline in religiosity mirrors the decline in the family. Over the past thirty years, the size of families has decreased. Divorce rates have spiked. Roughly one of four pregnancies ends in abortion. Second, the decline in religiosity has also coincided with a boom in college education, and indeed, across individuals, a lack of religion is more strongly correlated with education than with income.

I conjecture that these trends have some bearing on the decline in religion. In Catholic thought, the family is both the fundamental cell of society and the "domestic church." It is the family that most closely mimics the Christian model of the good society, the Trinity. It is in the example of parents where children best learn their faith, and it is in families where we learn fundamental social principles like solidarity, subsidiarity, concern for others. The question is whether people of faith can live up to this model. The relationship with education also should be a challenge to us people of faith in higher education. The experiences in current and former Communist countries highlight the importance of the history of ideas when it comes to religion. Again, the onus is on us educators to provide an intelligent, well-articulated presentation of religion as a compelling alternative to atheism, materialism, and skepticism.

For all the growth we've experienced, we are left with the key questions: What is the good life? What is the good society? Are we gaining the world but losing our souls? Is the good life a life of gluttony? We have lost the virtues of moderation, self-control, and prudence, and we pay the price. We suffer from gluttony in many ways: obesity, shop-aholism, sex addiction, environmental degradation, and even the gluttony of our own autonomy, which leads to abortion, divorce, never committing to marriage. We are even gluttons when we are not gluttons. We all diet, but no one fasts. One is done for vanity, the other for humility. Does more always lead to true happiness?

Is the good society a society lacking charity, justice, and solidarity? Again, we, as individuals and as a society, are certainly guilty. I do research in developing countries, where I know one in ten infants die. Yet I live in relative comfort. I give my own children medicine, but there are children elsewhere who go without. It's not that we do nothing, but if I ask the old question—What would Jesus do?—I look at the cross, and the certain answer is, "More." But charity, an essential part of the good life and the good society, doesn't negate technical questions.

13

Theology, Economics, and Economic Development

Peter N. Ireland*

Nothing to me the life of Gyges and his glut of gold. I neither envy nor admire him, as I watch his life and what he does. I want no pride of tyranny; it lies far off from where I look.

—ARCHILOCHUS OF PAROS[1]

In my work as an economist, I rarely consider what anyone might call the "big picture." Instead, my research focuses on very specific aspects of very specific problems, most having to do with the details of Federal Reserve policy and how it has affected the U.S. economy during the post-World War II period. It deals, that is, with the activities of one particular government agency within one particular country during one particular historical episode. And since economists are social scientists who, for the most part, lack the ability to conduct controlled experiments, I spend most of my time collecting and analyzing statistical data to find support for *ceteris paribus* theoretical arguments based on actual events in which the *ceteris* are definitely not *paribus*.[2]

* I would like to thank participants in Boston College's Seminar on Catholic Intellectual Traditions for numerous conversations that helped clarify my thoughts on these and many related issues.

1. *Greek Lyrics*, trans. Richmond Lattimore, 2nd ed. (Chicago: University of Chicago Press, 1960) 2.

2. One might guess that the first part of these exercises, involving data collection, would be easier these days, thanks to the large volume of information available freely through the World Wide Web. But this often turns out not to be the case. For

Implications, conclusions, and recommendations must therefore be stated tentatively, with all of the necessary qualifications, always leaving a host of unresolved issues to be dealt with in future research. Progress is slow but steady.

So I really wouldn't say—as Paul Knitter suggests earlier in this volume—that economics is a religion for me. A craftsman builds a nice, sturdy table that is first and foremost functional, but perhaps pleasing to look at as well. I'll be honest enough to say, at the risk of sounding presumptuous, that I hope my best research articles offer up something of the same, in the form of useful, although narrowly focused, insights into the workings of the U.S. economy, drawn from careful and detailed mathematical and statistical analyses that at least a few readers might find aesthetically pleasing. But there's absolutely nothing in any of my work that even remotely approaches the divine.[3]

And so it was simultaneously a pleasure, privilege, and welcome change of pace to participate in the Boston College Symposium on Interreligious Dialogue and Economic Development—a chance to take a big step back from my day-to-day work and consider, for once, bigger issues concerning the effects of economic growth on the spiritual and material well-being of developing countries and their inhabitants. It was also a chance to reflect on the ways in which the efforts of economists, or at least those who call themselves economists, get interpreted by scholars outside of my own field. In these reflections, I'll argue mainly that theologians and economists agree on far more and

instance, the Federal Reserve, which as our nation's central bank is responsible for regulating the quantity of money in circulation, no longer supplies the public with accurate and coherent data on the money supply, a fact discussed further in some of my recent work: Michael T. Belongia and Peter N. Ireland, "The Barnett Critique after Three Decades: A New Keynesian Analysis," Working Paper 736 (Chestnut Hill, MA: Boston College, Department of Economics, April 2010). For a related analysis that links the lack of accurate monetary data to policy mistakes, public and private, that may have contributed to the onset and severity of the recent financial crisis, see William A. Barnett and Marcelle Chauvet, "How Better Monetary Statistics Could Have Signaled the Financial Crisis," Manuscript (Lawrence: University of Kansas, Department of Economics, April 2010). For developing countries, reliable economic statistics are even harder to come by, but that is more understandable, when their governments face far more pressing concerns than getting all of the data up on the World Wide Web.

3. For the craftsman, though, things might be quite different in this last regard, as suggested by Richard Sennett, *The Craftsman* (New Haven: Yale University Press, 2008).

to a much greater extent than, probably, the papers collected here suggest. But how can we really agree when we seem so much to disagree? Answering this question requires first going back to my day-to-day work, to explain how economists see their job and how economic results are sometimes misapplied or misinterpreted by economists and non-economists alike.

Positive and Normative Economics

An example helps illustrate my first point, regarding the nature of economists' work. Consider two economic actors. One is a late-evening commuter, the other is a robber. The robber approaches the commuter on an otherwise abandoned subway platform and pulls a knife. A threat—"your money or your life"—makes clear the terms of trade. The commuter hands over the money and escapes with his life. One might use the language of economics to call this an "efficient" outcome: both agents are better off with the exchange of money for life than they would have been without.

This example is a joke that no one—economist or otherwise—would take seriously. Yet it also provides an illustration of how a theory that relies on the assumption that each individual acts rationally in his or her own self-interest can have predictive power, since the most likely outcome is probably the one that the example describes, in which the commuter escapes death and the robber runs off with the money. This is an outcome that, however likely, would not be considered just—both agents may not, in fact, be better off.

The example highlights a distinction that economists see themselves making all the time, the distinction between positive and normative analysis. Most economists use the assumption that consumers, workers, and business owners are rational and self-interested to predict how those economic actors will respond to changes in their environment, such as changes in technologies, government policies, or the availability of natural resources. By using logic in this way, to trace out the predictions or testable implications of our explicitly stated assumptions, economists as social scientists emulate our colleagues in the physical sciences, seeing the world as it is rather than as we wish it might be.

Of course, the conclusions of their positive analyses are going to be influenced by the choices that economists themselves make about what factors to consider in detail, and what aspects of reality to deemphasize when developing theories and tracing out their implications. At the same time, however, data provide an unforgiving check against prejudices and biases. If an economic theory has testable implications that are systematically contradicted by observations of actual economic behavior—perhaps because the economist has made assumptions that reflect how he or she would like the world to be in place of assumptions that reflect how the world actually is—then that theory gets rejected and a new one must be found to take its place. That is how the scientific method works.

None of this is to say that economists don't have strong feelings about how the world should be, compared to how it actually is. I myself certainly do. It is simply to say that when, for example, an economist writes that certain provisions of the U.S. tax code or certain aspects of the way in which technological changes have affected American workers appear to have led to an increase in income inequality, he or she is doing scientific work in economics, making positive statements about the sources of this growth in inequality. And if the same economist later decries that same growth in income inequality, perhaps even using arguments that echo those of theologians, he or she is making normative statements about how the world should be. There is no inherent contradiction, by which doing the first line of scientific work requires one to abandon the moral sentiments that underlie the second line of normative reasoning.

When discussing a robbery, the distinction between positive and normative analysis is easy to make. But there is also a very famous set of economic studies—having to do with Adam Smith's "invisible hand" and the theorems of welfare economics presented by Kenneth Arrow and Gerard Debreu—which demonstrate that, under certain circumstances, the rational and self-interested actions of individual consumers, workers, and business owners generate equilibrium resource allocations that are Pareto optimal, giving rise through free and voluntary exchange to outcomes in which it is impossible to make anyone better off without making at least someone else worse off.[4] Here is

4. See Adam Smith, *An Inquiry into the Nature and Causes of the Wealth of Nations*, ed. Edwin Cannan (New York: Modern Library, 1937) 423. See also Kenneth

where the lines between positive and normative economics begin to blur, because these theorems do connect what is, and what in a very particular sense should be.

Although all economists recognize stringent requirements for testing these welfare theorems, I concede that many of us display a tendency to forget these stringencies and too quickly make the claim that free markets deliver optimal outcomes. Many economists too frequently forget that what might appear at first glance to involve free and voluntary exchange often involves elements of coercion that are disturbingly similar to those described in my joke example from above. So let's consider this a first point of agreement between economists and theologians: all too often, a very large gap persists between what is and what should be.

The Invisible Hand and the Environment

Although economists probably do overestimate the extent to which free markets give rise to desirable outcomes as predicted by the welfare theorems of Arrow and Debreu, here is a second point on which theologians and economists can agree: unregulated free markets generally lead to excessively rapid natural resource depletion and undesirable if not disastrous environmental degradation. Statements like the following, taken from a leading undergraduate economics textbook, can in fact be found quite easily: "Economists use the term market failure to refer to a situation in which the market on its own fails to produce an efficient allocation of resources. As we will see, one possible cause of market failure is an externality, which is the impact of one person's actions on the well-being of a bystander. The classic example of an externality is pollution."[5] More advanced textbooks in economics go

---

J. Arrow, "An Extension of the Basic Theorems of Classical Welfare Economics," in *Proceedings of the Second Berkeley Symposium on Mathematical Statistics and Probability* (Berkeley: University of California Press, 1951) 507–32; and Gerard Debreu, *Theory of Value: An Axiomatic Analysis of Economic Equilibrium* (New Haven: Yale University Press, 1959). Finally, for a very forthright expression of the unease with which a Nobel-prize-winning economist views popular applications and interpretations of these ideas and results, see Joseph E. Stiglitz, "The Invisible Hand and Modern Welfare Economics," in *Information, Strategy and Public Policy*, ed. David Vines and Andrew A. Stevenson (Oxford: Blackwell, 1991) 12–50.

5. N. Gregory Mankiw, *Principles of Economics* 5th ed. (Mason, OH: South-Western Cengage Learning, 2009) 11.

much further, adapting narrower but more conventional measures of national income (such as gross domestic product) in order to account appropriately for changes in environmental quality, and thereby introducing the notion of sustainability into theories of long-run economic growth.[6]

Among economists, even skeptics about the topic of sustainability agree that the Clean Air Act of 1970 and its various amendments have been crucial to improving environmental quality in the United States.[7] And even those who criticize harshly the design of the Kyoto Protocol assert that the United States and other high-income countries must take the lead in the fight against global climate change by unilaterally adopting government policies that curtail greenhouse gas emissions.[8] Indeed, something of a consensus—a rarity among economists and, I assume, among theologians as well—has emerged from the many economic studies of global climate change, calling for governmental policies that take effect immediately and gradually impose tighter and tighter restrictions on emissions.[9]

Economists and Economic Policymakers

"Beware of false prophets . . ." This is something that theologians have said all along, but which economists are now learning the hard way. Hence, it is another point on which we all can agree.

The most popular account of the economic history of the past three decades runs as follows. The election of Margaret Thatcher as Prime Minister of the United Kingdom in 1979, followed by the election of Ronald Reagan as President of the United States in 1980, marked a fundamental shift in two of the world's biggest and richest economies, away from a system dependent on government intervention and towards the unfettered workings of the free market. These

6. See, for instance, Martin L. Weitzman, *Income, Wealth, and the Maximum Principle* (Cambridge: Harvard University Press, 2003).

7. See A. Myrick Freeman III, "Environmental Policy Since Earth Day I: What Have We Gained?" *Journal of Economic Perspectives* 16 (2002) 125–46.

8. Warwick J. McKibbin and Peter J. Wilcoxen, "The Role of Economics in Climate Change Policy," *Journal of Economic Perspectives* 16 (2002) 107–29.

9. See William D. Nordhaus, "A Review of the *Stern Review on the Economics of Climate Change*," *Journal of Economic Literature* 45 (September 2007) 686–702, esp. 687 n3.

changes accelerated and spread further and further throughout the world following the collapse of the Soviet Union in 1991. At first the gains seemed impressive, with high rates of growth recorded in income and wealth, albeit distributed unequally both within and across countries. Yet even for the relatively fortunate, the apparent prosperity turned out to be an illusion, based largely on speculative activity financed with borrowed money. Eventually, the bills came due, and in 2007 and 2008 the world economy plunged into its deepest contraction since the 1930s, where it remains mired today, with little sign of meaningful recovery.

My purpose here is not to take issue with this popular account of recent history, to point out ways in which it may be oversimplified, incomplete, or inaccurate. Instead, my focus is on the story itself, particularly the fact that within this story, many of the biggest apparent heroes-turned-villains are economists—or at least people popularly viewed as economists. Chief among them stands Alan Greenspan, Chairman of the Federal Reserve System from 1987 through 2006.

But, truth be told, few of my colleagues would recognize Alan Greenspan as a serious economist. He holds a doctorate in economics, but one received under somewhat dubious circumstances many years after he left New York University, the institution granting the degree.[10] On those grounds alone, Alan Greenspan should be considered unqualified to teach even introductory-level college classes in economics, let alone hold a regular faculty position at an American university. And my own sense is that the feeling is mutual: as Federal Reserve Chairman, Alan Greenspan appeared at best uninterested in, and often openly hostile to, the research agendas pursued even by his own staff of PhD economists at the Federal Reserve Board.

Alan Greenspan did hold government positions—all unelected—throughout most of his career, culminating in his lengthy term as Federal Reserve Chairman, for which he is most famous. I therefore suggest that it would be both fairer and more accurate to call Alan Greenspan an "economic policymaker" rather than an "economist." And, as an economic policymaker, the popular account of history probably gets it right: Greenspan's biggest legacy stems from the many years during which he overlooked his institution's public duties as

10. Robert D. Auerbach, *Deception and Abuse at the Fed: Henry B. Gonzales Battles Alan Greenspan's Bank* (Austin: University of Texas Press, 2008) 36–38.

a bank regulator, responsible for ensuring the safety and soundness of the American financial system. Indeed, Greenspan's expression of "shocked disbelief" during his October 23, 2008, testimony before the Congressional Committee on Oversight and Government Reform might remind theologians, economists, and many others of the sorts of statements about clergy sexual abuse that used to come from Boston Archbishop Bernard Francis Law's office. Hearing these things leaves one wondering, reasonably, whether either man, even after being confronted with evidence, will ever fully appreciate the depth of the tragedy that happened under his watch.

Of course, there is no governing body—local, national, or international—that certifies or licenses those who wish to call themselves "economists" the way, for example, there is for medical doctors, barbers, and other trained professionals. Still, it needs to be emphasized that other major figures involved in economic policymaking just before, during, and after the U.S. financial crisis of 2007 and 2008 also lacked formal training that would qualify them as economists. Henry Paulson, Secretary of the United States Treasury under President George W. Bush when the crisis began to unfold, holds an MBA from Harvard and worked for Goldman Sachs from 1974, serving as the investment bank's Chairman and Chief Executive Officer beginning in 1999, up until his nomination to public office in 2006. As Treasury Secretary, therefore, Paulson was a former investment banker with long-standing and rather strong professional ties to one of the firms that he was charged with overseeing and which, ultimately, benefited enormously from the U.S. government's unprecedented involvement in the financial markets during October 2008.

Perhaps deeper investigations, conducted after everyone's memoirs get published, will reveal that Henry Paulson was as tough on his former firm as he would have been on any other individual or institution that asked the Bush Administration for federal assistance and was turned away. Perhaps those investigations will show that Goldman Sachs and other large financial institutions were simply much more deserving as welfare recipients than, for instance, many of the families that felt slighted by the government's feeble response to Hurricane Katrina just a few years earlier. It could be. But, based on information that is available now, there would appear to be at least the possibility of troublesome conflicts of interest behind the very generous treatment given by the U.S. Treasury to the big investment and commercial banks in 2008, following a quarter century of deregulation, fiscal austerity, welfare reform, and reliance on the blind justice of the free market.

Finally, Timothy Geithner, President of the Federal Reserve Bank of New York during the early stages of the crisis and, later, Henry Paulson's successor as Secretary of the United States Treasury, does hold a master's degree in international economics from the Johns Hopkins University. And, to be sure, it stands as a truly remarkable accomplishment, reflecting enormous talent of some kind or another, that Timothy Geithner, who just before his Senate confirmation hearings in January 2009 revealed himself to be someone incapable of correctly filling out his own federal income tax forms, now heads up the U.S. Treasury, which includes the Internal Revenue Service as one of its major divisions. Yet however admirable his personal success in overcoming this handicap and rising to power, Timothy Geithner, like Alan Greenspan, lacks strong academic credentials and has no record of scientific or scholarly achievement. Instead, like Greenspan, Geithner has spent most of his career in unelected government positions. He is an economic policymaker, not an economist.

Ironically, it was a true economist—a University of Chicago economist, in fact—who sounded the loudest and clearest alarm in the years leading up to the crisis. In a paper presented—even more ironically—at a 2005 Federal Reserve conference honoring Alan Greenspan, Raghuram G. Rajan warned that developments in the U.S. financial system, including the strong trend towards deregulation, had given rise to an environment in which fund managers had greater incentives than ever before to take on risk, to conceal that extra risk, and to engage in herd-like behavior that amplifies both upward and downward swings in asset prices.[11] Rajan went on to describe how "tail risks"—extreme events that occur with low probability— could trigger a "catastrophic meltdown" quite closely resembling the crisis that did indeed occur just a few years later.

The fact that when the crisis did occur, it was interpreted by many as decisive evidence against the efficient markets hypothesis, which

11. Even the title of the conference volume in which Rajan's paper appears takes on a new, and almost laughable, significance when viewed against the backdrop of the events that soon followed: see Raghuram G. Rajan, "Has Financial Development Made the World Riskier?" in *The Greenspan Era: Lessons for the Future* (Kansas City: Federal Reserve Bank of Kansas City, 2005) 313–69.

posits that prices in financial markets accurately and rationally reflect all information available to traders in those financial markets, strikes me as the biggest irony of all.[12] To the contrary, in September 2008, the financial markets priced commercial paper issued by Lehman Brothers and AIG perfectly, identifying quite exactly what that paper was worth: zero. Those were insolvent institutions that should have been placed into receivership and liquidated in the same way that, for instance, bankrupt savings and loan institutions were disposed of during the previous U.S. financial crisis in the 1990s.[13] Scarce taxpayer funds would then have been available to help the truly needy, instead of going to help pay the extraordinary salaries and bonuses awarded to executives at those and other financial institutions that were driven to the brink of failure and beyond by managers and regulators who were unwilling to control the risks outlined so clearly by Rajan.

But economic policymakers chose to ignore Rajan's warnings in 2005. And even today, six years later, no one from the Federal Reserve or the U.S. Treasury—nor for that matter any economist from any institution—has offered up any sort of convincing explanation as to why it was necessary for the U.S. government to intervene in the economy so heavily in 2007 and 2008, on behalf of what had been some of the biggest and most profitable financial institutions in the history of the world. Some still assert, without supporting evidence, that if the government had not intervened to save the big banks, the broader economic downturn that followed would have been far worse. But John Taylor's extensive analysis shows, to the contrary, that the worst of the financial crisis actually *followed* testimony given by Treasury Secretary Henry Paulson and Federal Reserve Chairman Ben Bernanke to the U.S. Senate Banking Committee on September 23, 2008, asking for $700 billion in aid to rescue what would otherwise have been bank-

12. For a brief introduction to the efficient markets hypothesis, see Mankiw, *Principles of Economics*, 606–7.

13. Indeed, since neither Lehman Brothers as an investment bank nor AIG as a life insurance company qualifies as a depository institution—that is, a bank that primarily issues deposits and makes loans—the creditors of these institutions were not, strictly speaking, entitled to any of the special treatment given to the holders of small, federally insured deposits issued by failed savings and loan associations. With this distinction in mind, one could argue, more strongly, that both Lehman Brothers and AIG should simply have been liquidated through standard channels, like any other bankrupt business, without the need for any special government intervention whatsoever.

rupt financial institutions.[14] Taylor's observations suggest that the government bailout worsened, rather than ameliorated, the financial crisis and its aftereffects. Again, all signs now visible point to the large financial institutions themselves as the biggest, and perhaps even the sole, beneficiaries of the U.S. government's renewed involvement in the economy in 2008.

In mentioning all of this, I suppose that I am calling for an elaboration on the popular account of recent history after all. A more complete and comprehensive account of that history, it seems to me, would have to observe that both the financial crisis and the subsequent policy responses reflect the workings, not of markets that are truly free, supervised by trained economists and competent regulators who would have recognized that when free markets work efficiently, they do so partly because they deem no business "too big to fail," but rather the successful efforts of the rich, the greedy, and the politically well connected to use government coercion for their own further enrichment.[15] As common as it is, this sort of perverse redistribution of wealth, away from the most needy and towards the most affluent, remains something to be abhorred, regardless of whether it occurs under a socialist dictatorship, an oppressive theocratic regime, or a representative democracy. And that point, too, is one upon which theologians and economists can agree.

Conclusion

The Notorious B.I.G.—who was quick to point out that he himself held no doctorate in theology, economics, or any other field—famously lamented that, all too often, more money simply leads to more problems.[16] True enough. And, likewise, economic development is usually

14. John B. Taylor, *Getting Off Track: How Government Actions and Interventions Caused, Prolonged, and Worsened the Financial Crisis* (Stanford: Hoover Institution Press, 2009).

15. For a more thorough account of the financial crisis along exactly these lines, as well as a more nuanced and compelling account of recent U.S. history that identifies the myriad social, cultural, and political as well as economic forces that set the stage for the crisis, see Etay Zwick, "Predatory Habits: How Wall Street Transformed Work in America," *The Point* (Winter 2010) 33–46.

16. The Notorious B.I.G., "Mo Money, Mo Problems," *Life After Death* (New York: Bad Boy Records, 1997).

accompanied by the emergence of new problems, to which many of the papers in this volume usefully point. Certainly, it is quite easy to find in the United States, the world's richest economy, vulgar displays of conspicuous consumption. And globalization seems to bring with it a spread of that same kind of vulgarity, which becomes all the more tragic when it erodes noble habits, displaces worthy traditions, and disturbs more peaceful ways of life.

But while, thus far, I've emphasized that there are quite a few points of agreement between theologians and economists, before finishing I will suggest that it might be a mistake to conclude, just yet, that economic growth is on balance a bad thing. To defend this claim, I would cite the obvious case studies, comparing living standards in North Korea to those in South Korea and in the stagnant economies of Africa to those in the rapidly expanding economies of Asia. I would refer to the evidence showing strong correlations between gross domestic product as a measure of national income and other, more important issues that theologians and economists should really care about, like life expectancies and literacy rates.[17] I would also point to recent work casting doubt on the so-called Easterlin Paradox, which suggests that an economy's level of development bears no relation to the average level of happiness expressed by those who populate that economy.[18] Finally, I would mention evidence associating rising income within a country at first with a decrease, but later with an increase, in environmental quality.[19] Apparently, wealthier people do choose to spend more of their income in order to enjoy the benefits of a cleaner environment. More money, by itself, won't save the world. But perhaps more money might at least be of some help.

Still, genuine progress on the significant problems that remain requires more than just hope or wishful thinking. And so, I'd like to conclude by seconding James Buchanan's call, made earlier in this

17. See the table of statistics presented by Mankiw, *Principles of Economics*, 523.

18. For a comparison, see Richard A. Easterlin, "Does Economic Growth Improve the Human Lot? Some Empirical Evidence," in *Nations and Households in Economic Growth: Essays in Honor of Moses Abramovitz*, ed. Paul A. David and Melvin W. Reder (New York: Academic Press, 1974) 89–125; and Betsey Stevenson and Justin Wolfers, "Economic Growth and Subjective Well-Being: Reassessing the Easterlin Paradox," *Brookings Papers on Economic Activity* (Spring 2009) 1–87.

19. See Gene M. Grossman and Alan B. Krueger, "Economic Growth and the Environment," *Quarterly Journal of Economics* 110 (1995) 353–77.

volume, for serious dialogue or, better yet, "engagement"—Buchanan's own word, implying the need for actions as well as words—not just between the world's religions but between theologians, economists, economic policymakers, and religious and political leaders as well, aimed at tackling head-on the problems associated with economic development. Indeed, at the risk of further complicating the logistics of dialogue, I would invite scholars across all academic disciplines, in the humanities, social sciences, and physical sciences, to join us in these conversations and endeavors. For, as Buchanan rightly notes, the problems of economic development loom larger than any others faced by humanity today. Consider this one final point of agreement. The time certainly *has* come for us all to stop cowering in the face of these problems and to demonstrate, clearly and forcefully, what we have to contribute in working towards solutions, which surely must exist.

14

Different Views of the World: Economists and Theologians

Walter Nonneman

Genuine dialogue between theologians or religious thinkers and economists proves to be notoriously difficult. While the reasons for this difficulty may be many, I suggest that, at bottom, it may be grounded in fundamentally different views of the world. This leads to different reading lists. What theologians read on economics and consider important economic literature, is likely to be dismissed by most economist as "heterodox economics" or not even within the domain of economics. It would seem that economic development for economists is a far more complex issue than for theologians, as made evident by recent work in the area of development economics. However, I do believe in a possible common agenda for economists, social scientists and theologians which might lead to a better understanding of real world problems.

Different Visions

Theologians and economists clearly have different visions of the world. Thomas Sowell has sketched what these differences of vision imply quite well in several books.[1] Most economists hold what Sowell calls "a tragic vision of the world." Their view of the world is tragic in the sense of ancient Greek tragedies. Fate is inescapable and man's capabilities are limited by the nature of things. The tragic vision holds that resources are universally scarce and that it is simply impossible to fulfill all needs or wants. Eventually, many needs and wants are left unmet. Discrimination between which needs and wants are fulfilled and which are not is unavoidable. The economist's vision of man's nature is still close to Adam Smith's view proclaimed in his *Theory of Moral Sentiments*. The human being is self-interested, but not immoral, and evaluates "the propriety of action, as well as to reputation, the regard to the applause of his own breast, as well as to that of others."[2] The tragic vision also holds that social causation does not result from the deliberate plans of the few. Social causation comes not from a limited group of the *politei*, from multinational corporations, from the Bretton Woods institutions, or from whatever clan supposedly rules the world. On the contrary, social causation is embedded in slowly evolving and difficult-to-change systemic processes that are the result of the experiences, preferences and strife of the billions who inhabit this planet. In the tragic view, the practical unarticulated knowledge and experiences of the many are far more important for the business of daily life than the articulated intelligence of the educated few. The tragic view holds that justice lies in just and fair rules, rather than in equalized results. Economists put more trust in decentralized mechanisms of resource allocation than in centralized control by intellectuals or other elites, because decentralized mechanisms fully exploit the unarticulated but practical knowledge within the population at large.[3]

This tragic view of the world contrasts sharply with the vision held by many intellectuals. Theologians are intellectuals *par excellence*, insofar as intellectuals—academics, historians, writers, etc.—produce "ideas" or "mental schemes formed by thinking; mental impressions

1. Thomas Sowell, *Intellectuals and Society* (New York: Basic, 2010); Sowell, *The Vision of the Anointed: Self-Congratulation as a Basis for Social Policy* (New York: Basic, 1996); and Sowell, *A Conflict of Visions: Ideological Origins of Political Struggles* (New York: Morrow, 1987).

2. Adam Smith, *The Theory of Moral Sentiments* (Cambridge: Cambridge University Press, 2002 [1759]) 198.

3. An classical argument well developed by Friedrich von Hayek, "The Use of Knowledge in Society," *American Economic Review* 4 (1945) 519–30.

or conceptions; opinions or beliefs."[4] Ideas are different from practical knowledge. The latter can be proven correct or false, useful or worthless. Ideas are not falsifiable but are accepted if they sound right to fellow intellectuals, resonate with the public, or usefully inform political debate. Intellectuals often exert a powerful influence on policymakers and public opinion. An idea catching on with the public or with policymakers may dominate political thinking and action for many years. This may be for better or worse. Based on the historical track record, the influence of ideas (and ideology) in the last century or so has not been very positive. The monstrous regimes of the twentieth century—Nazism and communism, having claimed the lives of millions—based their legitimacy on the ideas of some "anointed" claiming to have found the key to heaven on earth.

Intellectuals—being highly educated and rhetorically strong—think they are as if "anointed" to guide the powerful and public opinion. Not without disdain, Sowell calls the world outlook of intellectuals "the vision of the anointed." The "vision of the anointed" contrasts sharply with "the tragic vision." Human capability, for the anointed intellectual, is seen as vast and basically unlimited. Universal scarcity is rejected. Wants and needs are seen either as "created" by marketing or as suppressible by reforming human nature. The position is that there is enough for all, but that it simply is not justly distributed. The intellectual believes in definite solutions for social problems—usually to be implemented by a third party, not by themselves. For the realist, social problems can only be managed but never solved. The intellectual defines justice in terms of equalized results rather than in terms of equality of opportunity. Also, he is skeptical of specialization, which creates strong interdependency, and he distrusts decentralized processes. Finally, social causation is considered to be driven by deliberate actions of a few actors who to a large extent control the behavior of the many, who in turn are seen as rather gullible and easily guided (or misled) by those in control.

It is no wonder that dialogue and conversation between economists and theologians is difficult. It is a confrontation between two different visions: "the tragic vision" and "the vision of the anointed." Economists are not really loved by theologians. Especially neoclassical economists—the mainstream of the profession—are branded as real

4. As defined by the *Oxford Dictionary of Current English*.

"dismal scientists." For a professional economist—devoted to thinking through practical problems that matter to people and society—it is discomforting to hear theologians express views on what economists are—not *homo sapiens* but rather *homo rapiens*—what they are doing—helping to spread *moneytheism* or consumerism—and how they go about doing this—using dehumanizing models and concepts of human beings.

Demonizing people with a different vision is not very helpful for dialogue and conversation. Most economists are not cynical "raptors" but quite normal people. They are concerned human beings, honestly trying to understand how the world *de facto* solves the universal problem of scarcity. They dislike designing untested utopian schemes but love looking at descriptive data, formulating hypotheses and models about causal relations and checking out their practical predictive performance. They study the features and consequences of different mechanisms used to handle the scarcity problem—ranging from markets, political or collective choice, cooperative arrangements such as families, hierarchical structures such as businesses, and many other institutions. As lecturers, they are not teaching or preaching the market and only the market. Any standard economic textbook[5] has more material on non-market mechanisms than on markets. Most textbooks cover how allocation mechanisms—from markets to collective choice—may be modified to avoid waste, to enhance efficiency, and to meet equity standards produced through societal negotiation. A reasonably well-trained economist is not ignorant of the presuppositions in the scientific approaches, the critiques of methodologies, the possible normative implications of what she is doing, and the limitations of her discipline.[6]

Most economists—when minding their business rather than joining the world of "the anointed"—would refrain from making sweeping statements on deeply researched subjects of theology or religion. They would not dream of demonizing theologians explaining certain theological thought through positions or displaying specific religious beliefs. But this restraint seems to be lacking when members of other

5. For example David Begg, Stanley Fisher and Rudiger Dornbush, *Economics*, 9th ed. (London: McGraw-Hill, 2008); or Michael Parkin, Melanie Powell, and Kent Matthew, *Economics*, 7th ed. (Harlow: Pearson Education, 2008).

6. See Roger E. Backhouse, *The Puzzle of Modern Economics: Science or Ideology?* (Cambridge: Cambridge University Press, 2010).

disciplines discuss economics. This is not new. In the late sixties and early seventies Milton Friedman wrote columns for *Newsweek*. He used to send a 1891 quotation of John Neville Keynes—the father of more famous John Maynard Keynes—to correspondents who, with the best of intentions but economically illiterate, offered their own economic panaceas. The quote went as follows:

> People think themselves competent to reason about economic problems, however complex, without any such preparatory scientific training as would be universally considered essential in other departments of enquiry. This temptation to discuss economic questions without adequate scientific preparation is all the greater because economic conditions exert so powerful an influence upon men's material interests. 'Few men,' says General Walker [a famous American economist of the nineteenth century], 'are presumptuous enough to dispute with the chemist or the mechanician upon points connected with the studies and labours of his life; but almost any man who can read and write feels himself at liberty to form and maintain opinions of his own upon trade and money.' The economic literature of every succeeding year embraces works conceived in the true scientific spirit, and works exhibiting the most vulgar ignorance of economic history, and the most flagrant contempt for the conditions of economic investigation. It is much as if astrology were being pursued side by side with astronomy, or alchemy with chemistry.[7]

By quoting this, I am not demonizing theologians or dismissing their genuine criticisms on the state of economics as a science, but to warn against uninformed judgment. Mutual demonization is a MAD strategy—mutually assured destruction of all further dialogue.

Different Reading Lists

Dialogue needs common ground and a common language. That is lacking. It is commendable and applauded that theologians who want "a place at the table" of the *politei* make the effort to read and study economics. But reading thirty books on theology would not make this economist a proficient theologian. By analogy, studying thirty books

7. Milton Friedman, *There's No Such Thing as a Free Lunch* (LaSalle, IL: Open Court, 1975).

on economics does not make someone an economist, especially when there is a real morass of publications to choose from, ranging from nonsense best sellers to good scholarly work, rooted in years of serious research. Discernment of what is worthless and what is valuable takes years of reading, scholarly study and practice.

It must be confusing for a theologian to wade through the spate of books on globalization, economic development and planetary challenges. Writings on these subjects are a real minefield, dangerous if you thread around without the map. There are plenty of popular economics books[8] that promise a drink from the fountain of wisdom. There is an equal set that offer a nightmarish view in the abyss, warning you that the study of economics is the ultimate peril for your soul.[9] All such books are no doubt entertaining to read and profitable for the authors and the publishers, but most of the time they will not offer a nuanced view on the science of economics.

Globalization also sells well. For some[10] it is full of immoral mechanisms to be corrected (by the authors or their followers); for others[11] it is the ultimate source of wealth and welfare. Even a well-

8. The titles of a few references tell it all: J. Kay, *Everlasting Light Bulbs: How Economics Illuminates the World* (London: Erasmus, 2004); S. Levitt and S. Dubner, *Freakonomics: A Rogue Economist Explains the Hidden Side of Everything* (London: Penguin, 2006) and its sequel, S. Levitt and S. Dubner, *Superfreakonomics: Global Cooling, Patriotic Prostitutes, and Why Suicide Bombers Should Buy Life Insurance* (London: Allen Lane, 2009); S. Landsberg, *More Sex is Safer Sex: The Unconventional Wisdom of Economics* (New York: Free Press, 2007) and its sequel, S. Landsberg, *The Big Questions* (New York: Free Press, 2009); T. Harford, *The Logic of Life: The New Economics of Everything* (London: Abacus, 2008); T. Harford, *The Undercover Economist* (London: Little, Brown 2006); R. Frank, *The Economic Naturalist: Why Economics Explains Almost Everything* (London: Virgin Books, 2008) and its sequel, R. Frank, The *Return of the Economic Naturalist: How Economics Helps to Make Sense of Your World* (London: Virgin, 2009).

9. For example E. Fulbrook, ed., *A Guide to What's Wrong with Economics* (London: Anthem, 2004); N. Klein, *Economics Confronts the Economy* (Cheltenham, UK: Elgar, 2006) or S. Marglin, *The Dismal Science: How Thinking Like an Economist Undermines Community* (Cambridge: Harvard University Press, 2008).

10. R. Reich, *Supercapitalism: The Battle for Democracy in an Age of Big Business* (London: Icon, 2009); J. Stiglitz, *Globalization and Its Discontents* (New York: Penguin, 2002) or J. Stiglitz, *Freefall: Free Markets and the Sinking of the Global Economy* (London: Allen Lane, 2010).

11. See for example M. Wolf, *Why Globalization Works* (New Haven: Yale University Press, 2005); or J. Baghwati, *In Defense of Globalization* (Oxford: Oxford University Press, 2004).

trained economist is bound to lose his footing in this morass of best sellers, blogs or websites.

The reputation of the author and the recommendations at the back of the book offer little guidance. Some authors are Nobel laureates—Becker, Stiglitz, Krugman—and academics of high standing who have done serious scholarly work. Others are former politicians of good standing—Reich, Gore—or well-known columnists or popular TV commentators. Even good-looking starlets or famous pop stars feel called to proclaim their great ideas for how to better the world.

Nearly all of these popular books are rhetorically convincing and strongly opinioned. The authors joined the club of "the anointed" offering their "ideas" for how things should be changed. Most of these books are political. Sometimes this is plainly stated, but most of the time it is not. People reading or studying these books by great names in the gallery of famous economists may get the impression that this political writing is what economics is about. Friedman on capitalism, Sachs on development, Stiglitz on globalization, Reich on capitalism, and so on—they all have an ax to grind. They offer a one-sided view of the world, but are not reflecting complexity or "the tragic vision." Because these authors take a stand and have prominent political ideas, their books sell well. A vast part of the reading public is in the market for strong, straightforward views on the world. Books that painstakingly present the full complexity of the world's problems are difficult, boring, and no fun to read. They leave the reader puzzled or confused. He is left facing practical dilemmas of real-world policy choices. He is forced to make up his own mind and to weigh pros and cons of policy alternatives. Such complex and challenging books do not sell well. Best sellers require clear defense of a particular position and preferably a radical and principled outlook. To support their position, the evidence, if offered, is usually selective and supporting the chosen outlook. Whatever does not fit within the "right" frame is ignored.

Unfortunately, books on economics and economic development cited in the theological papers are of the "positional kind." Much of this literature ignores empirical evidence and lacks objective analysis. The prime objective is to defend a stance, usually about the terrible effects of capitalism, trade and globalization. The incredible standard of living of the top billion, enabled by the market, is flatly ignored.

Some authors cited and almost idolized by the theologians—such as E. F. Schumacher[12]—are on the margin of economics as a scholarly field of study. "Buddhist economics"—one of Schumacher's ideas—is on the fringe of what is called "heterodox economics." Other works cited are mostly by economists who at the end of the scientifically productive phase of their lives turned "from astronomy to astrology" by writing political bestsellers or newspaper columns, or dumping "ideas" on websites, blogs or Twitter. Taking such work on the fringe seriously and flatly ignoring what is considered scholarly by the profession is not the way to engage economists in conversation.

On Economic Development: The Tragic Vision

Not all "popular science" books on economics are of a polarizing nature, proclaiming yet another vision of the anointed. For example, the groundbreaking work of Paul Collier and his team of researchers at Oxford University explains the complex problems of practical development policy. This work, rooted in painstaking empirical research, typically reflects the "tragic vision" which emerges from an in-depth understanding of development economics.

In Collier's 2008 book[13] *The Bottom Billion*, he reports on years of experience at the World Bank and in Africa, and research with teams of bright and dedicated researchers. Because of fast growth in India and China, poverty has declined over the last two decades or so. But the outlook for a billion people living in sixty or so countries of the world is bleak and ever growing worse. The bottom billion are caught in a development trap. The bottom billion live in "Africa+" as seventy percent are on the African continent, but also in such places as Haiti, Bolivia, the Central Asian countries, Laos, Cambodia, Yemen, Burma, and North Korea. Life expectancy in those countries is about fifty years compared to sixty-seven in other developing countries and about seventy five years or more in the rich world. One in seven children die before their first birthday among the bottom billion (one in twenty-five in other developing countries). One-third of all children

12. E. F. Schumacher, *Small Is Beautiful: A Study of Economics as if People Mattered* (London: Blond & Briggs, 1973).

13. Paul Collier, *The Bottom Billion: Why the Poorest Countries Are Failing and What Can Be Done About It* (New York: Oxford University Press, 2008).

have symptoms of long-term malnutrition compared with one in five in other developing countries and almost none in the rich world.

It is all very well to lambast economic growth (and it is right not to equate development with mere economic growth), but the central problem of the bottom billion is that they have had no growth at all. Economic growth in these countries has been negative over the last four decades or so and the divergence in growth rates between the bottom billion and the middle four billion has increased steadily. The simple mathematics of compound growth rates predicts that absolute differences in living conditions between the bottom billion and the rest of the world will become ever larger. Evidently one should not only be concerned with growth *per se* but also with how countries grow, making sure that growth is sustainable and pro-poor. Collier's stand on the necessity of growth to get the bottom billion out of the poverty trap is very explicit:

> We cannot make poverty history unless the countries of the bottom billion start to grow, and they will not grow by turning them into Cuba. Cuba is a stagnant, low-income, egalitarian country with good social services. If the bottom billion emulated Cuba, would this solve the problem? I think that the vast majority of people living in the bottom billion—and indeed in Cuba—would see it as continued failure. To my mind, development is about giving hope to ordinary people that their children will live in a society that has caught up with the rest of the world. Take that hope away and the smart people will use their energies not to develop their societies but to escape from it—as have a million Cubans. Catching up is about radically raising growth in the countries now at the bottom. The fact that stagnation has persisted over such a long period tells us that it is going to be difficult.[14]

Collier and his team of researchers found that all fifty-eight countries of the bottom billion are caught in one or more of four traps: a conflict trap, a natural resources trap, being landlocked with bad neighbors, or bad governance in a small country.

About three-quarters of the countries of the bottom billion recently had some form of civil war or are still in one. Empirical research examining hundreds of conflicts shows that economic stagnation or decline, taking away from young men and women all hope for a better

14. Ibid., 12.

life, is the most important cause of civil strife and civil war. The prime causes of civil war do not seem to be political repression, inequality, ethnic tension or former colonialism but mainly the lack of economic progress. Civil war in the bottom billion typically lasts for many years. It is very costly with long-lasting consequences such as displacement of populations, crippling diseases, and repressive regimes prone to repeated coups and further strife. Civil war and conflict is a trap. The root cause of civil strife is lack of growth and lack of prospects for a better future. Civil war is development in reverse. Breaking out of the conflict trap is not something these countries can do by themselves. Possible ways out of a conflict trap were studied by Collier and his Oxford group in greater detail.[15] Breaking out of the conflict trap usually requires outside help from the international community less in the form of surface indicators of democracy such as supervised elections, and more in the form of military action, such as peacekeeping or "over the horizon" guarantees of military intervention.

Another frequent problem trapping the bottom billion is the so-called resource curse. In a poor country, ample natural resources are often a cause not of wealth and progress but of poverty. There are several explanations for this paradox. Some are based on economic reasoning but the more convincing arguments come from political theory. A well-researched phenomenon is the so-called Dutch disease referring to the effects on the Dutch economy of the discovery of gas reserves in the 1970s. The sudden increase of natural resource exports lead to a revaluation of the Dutch guilder. That made other exporting industries uncompetitive and triggered industrial decline and job losses. This crowding out of exporting industries has serious consequences when natural resource availability declines. Another explanation of the resource curse is partly economic and partly political. Reliance on natural resource exports leads to boom-bust cycles, as resource prices tend to be volatile. Such boom-and-bust cycles entail an unstable and difficult-to-manage economy. Instability undermines the political credibility of even the best governments. It becomes impossible for the voting public to discern between effects of government policy, and external effects beyond government control, leading to a general mistrust of the voting public in government and the state. Good governance

15. Paul Collier, *Wars, Guns & Votes: Democracy in Dangerous Places* (London: Vintage, 2010).

becomes indistinguishable from bad governance and is not rewarded by voters. In the end, politics tends to attract the wrong people. In yet another book,[16] Collier develops these arguments based on political theory. Ample natural resources in a poor country create huge resource rents, such that competition for these rents is often contained within a kleptomaniac political autocracy. Replacing autocracy by forcing such countries to hold elections is no guaranteed solution. Even after elections and democratic reforms, resource-rich countries tend to get trapped in some dysfunctional form of democracy. Autocrats succeed in hanging on to power by suppressing or manipulating elections. Here again, prolonged external intervention seems required to help these countries escape from a resource trap. The way out is very complicated and there are no guarantees for success.

A third trap is being landlocked with bad neighbors. Adam Smith already argued in 1776 in his *Wealth of Nations* that being landlocked inhibits commerce and development. Jeffrey Sachs estimated that being landlocked reduced the potential for economic growth by approximately ½ percent in annual growth.[17] There are landlocked countries—like Switzerland, Austria or Luxemburg—that do well, but being landlocked with nasty neighbors is devastating for a country's growth potential. Bad neighbors may limit access to seaways and hence international markets. But more importantly, a bad neighbor itself does not offer markets for goods and services for the landlocked country. Starved of markets in neighboring countries, and denied access beyond, landlocked countries with bad neighbors are forced into self-reliance and autarky, and miss out on the economic gains of specialization.

Finally, there is the curse of bad governance in small countries. Bad governance is not a trap *per se*. Some countries suffered from terrible regimes—e.g., the Soviet Union under Stalin, China under Mao (applauded by the "anointed" in the West, making Mao's *Red Book* a real cult item), but eventually, due to the pressure of public opinion or to the rise of a new ruling elite, both systems took a turn for the better. Many factors contribute to a turnaround. The size of the country

16. Paul Collier, *The Plundered Planet: How to Reconcile Prosperity with Nature* (London: Allen Lane, 2010).

17. Jeffrey Sachs, *Common Wealth: Economics for a Crowded Planet* (New York: Penguin, 2008) 212–18.

and its international importance matter. Bad governance lasts longer in small countries than in large ones, because they are ignored by the international community.

Some poor countries have stayed clear of traps or even escaped from them. The problems of the bottom billion seem fixable, but the fixes are extremely complicated. Under a subtitle "Beyond the headless heart: accepting complexity"[18]—reflecting the typical "tragic vision" of a practical economist—Collier sketches the complexity of the tasks at hand. Change is going to come from within these countries. The rich world can use a range of policy instruments to encourage the countries of the bottom billion to initiate and sustain change for the better. There is no silver bullet. Collier's most fundamental recommendation is that development policy should be more coherent, requiring a "whole-of-government" approach rather than piecemeal efforts which are often counterproductive. Putting the issue of the bottom billion on the agenda on meetings of heads of state such as the G8 meetings is of crucial importance. The task remains daunting, complex, messy, involving long time frames, unavoidable setbacks, and occasional failures—a true "tragedy."

A Common Agenda for Economists and Theologians?

Can there be a common agenda for economists and theologians with such differences in vision and understanding of reality? If so, what themes or topics could be explored where joint efforts would lead to synergy and better understanding of issues than when pursued separately?

For social scientists, it is no news that religion matters for economic behavior. It matters for behavior "in the small" and "in the large." In the mid-eighteenth century, the godfather of economics, Adam Smith, perceptively argued that belief in God—but not so much religious practice—adds an extra dimension to people's behavior:

> The regard to the propriety of action, as well as to reputation, the regard to the applause of his own breast, as well as to that of others, are motives which they suppose have the same influence over the religious man, as over the man of the world. But the former lies under another restraint, and never acts deliber-

18. Paul Collier, *Bottom Billion*, 12.

> ately but as in the presence of that Great Superior who is finally to recompense him according to his deeds. A greater trust is reposed, upon this account, in the regularity and the exactness of his conduct. And wherever the natural principles of religion are not corrupted by the factious and party zeal of some worthless cabal; wherever the first duty it requires, is to fulfill all the obligations of morality; wherever men are not taught to regard frivolous observances, as more immediate duties of religion, than acts of justice and benevolence; and to imaging, that by sacrifices, and ceremonies, and vain supplications, they can bargain with the Deity for fraud, and perfidy, and violence, the world undoubtedly judges right in this respect, and justly places a double confidence in the rectitude of the religious man's behavior.[19]

In the early twentieth century, Max Weber argued that the ethical attitudes associated with Calvinism—frugality and hard work—set the stage for capitalism.[20] Weber's position was contested, especially by Marxists convinced that all superstructure followed from economic structures rather than the other way around, or who considered religion as an "opium for the people." Later work on economics and religion showed religions do affect economies. By the 1950s it was a standard textbook theory of development[21] that some religions are more conducive to economic growth than others.

Now all ingredients—good quality data, sophisticated statistical methods to check for reverse causalities, and cheap and fast computing power—are available to test the hypothesis that religion affects economic development and growth. Careful empirical research, for example by Harvard economists Barro and McCleary, shows that religions have important autonomous effects on the economic performance of states.[22] Just as Adam Smith contended, they find that religious belief is more important than attendance of religious services and engagement in religious activities.

19. Adam Smith, *Theory of Moral Sentiments*, 198.

20. Max Weber, *The Protestant Ethic and the Spirit of Capitalism*, trans. Talcott Parsons (New York: Routledge, 1992 [1930]).

21. For example Arthur Lewis, *The Theory of Economic Growth* (London: Allen & Unwin, 1955) 105.

22. Robert J. Barro, "Spirit of Capitalism: Religion and Economic Development," *Harvard International Review* 25 (2004); R. M. McCleary, "Religion and Economic Development," *Policy Review* 148 (2008).

This is corroborated by empirical research on the effect of religion on economics "in the small." Rodney Stark[23] and others[24] have used individual data from the World Values Surveys to explore the importance of religious belief for moral attitudes on economic issues such as declaring taxes or using government benefits unjustified, etc. This empirical research shows two things. First, religions with a "high God" concept—a unique, personalized, all-seeing and -judging God such as the God of Judaism, Christianity and Islam—do affect moral attitudes. This is not the case for religions with many gods or with a diffuse or remote god concept. Second, it is belief that matters for moral attitudes—the extent to which people believe in God and find God important—rather than attendance, participation or religious practices. Not all religions have an equal impact on economic behavior and development. It takes theological probing to explain such differential effects of belief in empirical studies.

These and other issues concerning the relation between religion and economics have been taken up by economists and sociologists of religion, especially since the 1970s. A new and thriving subfield—"economics of religion"—has developed since.[25] This field could benefit greatly from theologians willing to engage this literature and develop theological understandings of empirical findings. This is not only important because of the sheer joy derived from knowledge and understanding, but also to probe into the future of our societies, especially European society but possibly also the Americas and beyond.

23. Rodney Stark, "Gods, Rituals and the Moral Order," *Journal for the Scientific Study of Religion* 40 (2001) 619–36.

24. See for example D. Johnson, "God's Punishment and Public Goods," *Human Nature* 16 (2005) 410–46; A. L. Owen and J. R. Videras, "Culture and Public Goods: The Case of Religion and the Voluntary Provision of Environmental Quality," *Journal of Environmental Economics and Management* 54 (2007) 162–80; L. Guiso, P. Sapienza, and L. Zingales, "People's Opium? Religion and Economic Attitudes," *Journal of Monetary Economics* 50 (2003) 225–82; B. Torgler, "The Importance of Faith: Tax Morale and Religiosity," *Journal of Economic Behavior and Organization* 61 (2006) 81–109.

25. For a nontechnical but excellent overview see Larry Witham, *Marketplace and the Gods: How Economics Explains Religion* (Oxford: Oxford University Press, 2010).

Particularly in Europe, secularization is an unmistakable trend with many causes.[26] Sociological research[27] shows that reducing "life insecurity" plays a key role in secularization. Religious competition and pluralism are likely to slow down the secularization process.[28] It is also well documented that children, even when they are not as religious as their parents, tend to take over the values of their parents. But what happens if belief in a "high God" disappears? Will the disappearance of a "high God" ultimately affect morality and ethics? To what extent will the vital classical virtues of "bourgeois ethics" (prudence, justice, valor and temperance) still govern daily life if most or all belief in a "Great Superior" has gone? What other "social cement" will govern daily life? These questions are not only intellectually challenging but of great importance for the future of our postindustrial societies. They require insights from many disciplines, from theologians knowledgeable about the intricacies of religions, from sociologists offering deep understanding of social change, and from economists focusing on the necessity of choices under conditions of scarcity.

26. See for example Steve Bruce, *Religion in the Modern World: From Cathedrals to Cults* (Oxford: Oxford University Press, 1996).

27. See P. Norris and R. Inglehart, *Sacred and Secular: Religion and World Politics* (Cambridge: Cambridge University Press, 2004).

28. R. Stark and R. Finke, *Acts of Faith: Explaining the Human Side of Religion* (Berkeley: University of California Press, 2000).

15

Economics and Religion: A Theoretical Problem

Francis McLaughlin

Prior to the eighteenth century, economic matters were subordinated to moral philosophy and moral theology. Philosophers and theologians regarded the object of economic activity as the common good of a human community sharing a common end, and economics was the art concerned with the provision and the fair distribution of the material goods needed by that community. Economics served the common good.

There is a marked similarity in this view of the relation between economics and the common good, and that of modern Catholic social thinkers. But modern economics is an autonomous social science, and its theoretical relationship with the common good is problematic. And although it is not difficult to show a relation between practical economics and the concept of the common good, the assumptions underlying important parts of theoretical economics are not so easily related to the common good.

At the center of modern neoclassical theoretical economics lies a highly abstract notion of the perfectly competitive market economy. Economic theorists have shown that under certain quite restrictive conditions, such an economy has a large number of efficient potential outcomes, each outcome implying a different distribution of the economy's output, and depending upon the prior distribution of income and resource ownership. Theoretical welfare economics seeks to discover a basis for choosing among these various possible distributional outcomes. One conclusion of this immense theoretical effort is that it is impossible to specify a method for making social choices based upon assumptions that modern economists, *qua* economists, would find broadly acceptable.[1] Economic theorists now accept the proposition that a social choice about the appropriate income distribution requires an ethical judgment, and they regard ethical judgments as outside their competence as economists. The role that remains for the economist—pointing out the potential costs necessary to achieve a particular distributional outcome—is technocratic.

Despite this purely technocratic role, economists frequently recommend specific policies and programs on the basis of their predicted distributional effects. As a group, economists are not shy in making their opinions known. Occasionally some economists refer to the common good as the norm guiding their economic policy judgments, but more frequently they speak of the public interest or social welfare. The concrete meaning economists give to such terms as the common good, public interest, or social welfare will be influenced by the social and political views of the economists using the terms. But in the United States there is a broad consensus among economists in favor of policies and programs they believe will improve productive efficiency, measured in terms of favorable benefit-cost ratios, particularly when coupled with actions that compensate for the expected adverse distributional effects. Many economists also support policies and programs they believe will bring about less unequal income and wealth distributions, even at the price of lost productive efficiency, although the losses regarded as acceptable vary widely. This broad policy consensus is usually a mix of conclusions drawn from both economic theory and political and moral judgments. In their policy recommendations, economists may not always distinguish sharply or explicitly between those aspects of their policy positions based in economic theory, on the one hand, and

1. Kenneth Arrow, *Social Choice and Individual Values* (New York: Wiley, 1951). Arrow was concerned with the ability of democratic societies to make social decisions. He showed that, in general, these societies cannot make social decisions under assumptions about voting procedures that are consistent with the individualist presuppositions underlying neoclassical economic theory. Individuals' desires for social outcomes on any matter, including distribution, may not aggregate into a consistent set of social decisions on these outcomes under assumptions that economists would find broadly acceptable.

those aspects dependent on their political and moral judgments, on the other. But despite the fact that the policy prescriptions of practical economists cannot be grounded rigorously in theoretical welfare economics, and despite the fact that economists may mix economic theory and political or moral judgments in ways that are not always clear, normative positions have a solid place in the history of economic thought.

Adam Smith's *Wealth of Nations* foreshadows the beginning of modern economics as an autonomous social science separated from moral and political philosophy. Smith, who sought to articulate the best way of ensuring that society had the material prerequisites for well-being, described a world in which self-interest as it operates through competitive markets ensures society's material provisioning. Smith measured a nation's wealth by the size of its stock of vendible commodities, and he believed that an environment of liberty was most conducive to the growth of this stock. And Smith's concern with the material provisioning of society remains a primary focus of the work of practical economists. The fundamental truth underlying Smith's theoretical work was that human beings have material needs, and the efficient supplying of these needs is a necessary element in improving well-being. But the fact that both production and distribution in Smith's economic thought are governed by market forces responding to self-interest meant that the link between justice and the operation of the economy was sundered. There is no guarantee that markets and self-interest will lead to a result that can be considered just, and there is no requirement that individual actors be just people—a requirement stipulated by classical and medieval philosophers and theologians for just relationships among human beings.

Modern theoretical economics, as contrasted with the classical economics that began with Smith, is often described as a general science of choice. This view can be derived clearly from the work of Gary Becker for whom "[T]he combined assumptions of maximizing behavior, market equilibrium, and stable preferences, used relentlessly and unflinchingly, form the heart of the economic approach . . ."[2] The economist Jack Hirshleifer has argued that Becker's approach

2. Gary S. Becker, *The Economic Approach to Human Behavior* (Chicago: University of Chicago Press, 1976) 4, cited in Jack Hirshleifer, "The Expanding Domain of Economics," *American Economic Review* 75:6 (1985) 53.

> has powered the imperialist expansion of economics into the traditional domains of sociology, political science, anthropology, law, and social biology . . . [and he concludes that] . . . it is ultimately impossible to carve off a distinct territory for economics, bordering upon but separated from other social disciplines. Economics interpenetrates them all, and is reciprocally penetrated by them. *There is only one social science.* What gives economics its imperial invasive power is that . . . [its] analytical categories, scarcity, cost, preferences, opportunities, etc., are truly universal in applicability. Even more important is . . . [the] structured organization of these concepts into the distinct yet intertwined processes of optimization on the individual level and equilibrium on the level of social analysis. Thus economics really does constitute the universal grammar of social science. But there is a flip side to this . . . [E]conomists . . . have to become aware of how constraining has been their tunnel vision about the nature of man and social interactions. Ultimately good economics will also have to be good anthropology and sociology and political science and psychology.[3]

The roots of this imperialist thrust identified by Hirshleifer are found in what has been for over a century, in the English neoclassical tradition, the quintessential economic problem of constrained maximization,[4] or the best way to allocate a fixed quantity of resources in order to maximize utility or satisfaction.[5] From this perspective, the human agent is an individual interested in maximizing the value of his subjective

3. Ibid.

4. The allocation of a fixed volume of resources among alternative uses to achieve an output that is optimal, in the sense that no incentive remains for a different allocation, became the focus of economic science in the last quarter of the nineteenth century. This followed the work of W. Stanley Jevons, Carl Menger, and Leon Walras, all of whom explained exchange value in terms of utility rather than in terms of cost of production as classical economists had done since Adam Smith. The notion of utility was present in economic thought long before the work of Jevons et al., but Jevons, Menger, and Walras showed how utility affected exchange value and their ideas became widely accepted and entered mainstream economic thought.

5. There is a certain looseness in equating maximum satisfaction with maximum utility, but the looseness is unimportant for the purposes of this essay. On this point see I. M. D. Little, *A Critique of Welfare Economics* (London: Oxford University Press, 1960). Little explains that maximizing utility means simply that an outcome is chosen from among alternatives, and the choice conforms to the transitivity principle. That is, choices are consistent. If outcome A is chosen in preference to outcome B, and if B would have been chosen in preference to outcome C, then A would also be chosen in preference to C.

satisfaction, subject to constraints of time, money, or resources. The price or cost of anything to an individual is what he must give up when he chooses it. This reasoning can be applied to social choices that are made collectively as well. But the presuppositions about human beings that underlie this reasoning are highly problematic from the perspective of classical and religious notions of the common good.

Every economist admits that the abstract model of a perfectly competitive economy is, at best, an approximation to reality. Although economists differ widely among themselves about how close to reality this approximation actually is, virtually all of them regard the model as a useful analytical construct, helpful in varying degrees when analyzing real-world economies. The model has a powerful conclusion, i.e., that under conditions of perfect competition the outcome of the economy will be efficient, in the sense that all resources will be fully employed in ways that make the best use of them, given the desires of consumers who are sovereign when considered collectively. The economy is efficient in the sense that there is no way to make one person better off without making another person worse off.[6] This theoretical conclusion is the basis for the normativity of a competitive market system. It is what disposes economists to regard policies that interfere with competition as undesirable. It is also an important reason why economists are inclined to be confident that they are on solid scientific ground in recommending more competitive markets as a way of improving productive efficiency.

This theory has roots in Smith's argument that in the particular historical and institutional context of eighteenth-century Europe, self-interest operating through a market system in an environment of liberty was most conducive to the expansion of a nation's material wealth. But modern theory, unlike Smith's writing, is highly formal and abstracted from any particular historical and institutional context.[7]

6. A state of an economy where the subjective utility of one person cannot be increased without reducing the subjective utility of another is called Pareto optimal. The reference is to Vilfredo Pareto (1848–1923) an Italian economist and sociologist. Pareto actually used the word *ophelimity* to refer to economic satisfaction, but he established the principle that an action "that improves the economic situations of some while it injures those of others . . . [cannot] be justified on economic grounds that are also scientific . . . and [he thus] assumes the incomparability of wants as between individuals." See *International Encyclopedia of the Social Sciences* (New York: Macmillan) 11:414.

7. The description and exposition of competitive market theory contained in

The key assumptions about human nature that underlie modern economic theory are found in the work of early modern philosophers as Thomas Hobbes. He described human beings as solitary by nature, rather than social, and ruled by their passions, rather than their reason.[8] This contrasted with the premodern view of human beings as naturally social beings who, if properly habituated, will keep their passions under the control of their reason. Hobbes regarded organized civil society as a contrivance for enabling human beings to gain their individual objectives of comfortable living and safety from violent death. Hobbes argued that happiness for an individual is just the satisfaction of a succession of desires that cease only with death. Reason for Hobbes was simply the ability to calculate how best to achieve the object of one's passions. Hobbes's thought bears a strong relationship to the core presuppositions of modern economics, where reason is the ability to calculate, preferences are subjective, and each individual seeks to maximize the value of those subjective preferences, whatever they may happen to be.

The anthropology underlying modern economic theory is thus sharply at variance with the anthropology underlying the classical and religious notions of the common good. This anthropology leads to the proposition, central to competitive market theory, that if any individual will not approve a policy aimed at changing the distribution of income, because it makes him worse off according to his subjective preferences, then an economist cannot judge whether the policy is desirable or undesirable. Considerations of the classical and religious notions of the common good have no place within a theoretical framework in which social welfare is defined in terms of the maximization of subjective preferences.

This is not the whole story. It is not as frequently acknowledged, or perhaps even recognized, that the normative proposition, *perfect competition is productively efficient*, also presents a problem from the perspective of classical and religious notions of the common good. The

---

this paper is highly simplified. There is a large literature in economics concerned with the limitations and inadequacies of the static theory of perfect competition, but discussion of this literature has been omitted in order not to complicate the principal argument of the paper, which is to show the individualist presuppositions of modern economic theory, and the implications these presuppositions have for the relation between economic theory and the notion of the common good.

8. Thomas Hobbes, *Leviathan* (New York: Collier, 1962), esp. chap. 13.

actual goods and services produced in a competitive market system will reflect the subjective preferences of market participants. There is no particular reason why this mix of goods and services would correspond to what would be judged optimal from the perspective of the common good. Goods and services may be produced by and for people whose self-interest reflects the vice of greed, or a more general lack of virtue. These individuals may be selfish hedonists. Thus insufficient resources may have been put into the production of good education for children, or good courts to ensure a proper administration of justice. And substantial resources may have been devoted to pornographic films and books, or luxury housing and playthings for the very rich. Thus, the common good requires a different mix of goods and services as well as different distribution. Questions of production and distribution cannot be easily separated when discussing something like standard of living, as is implied by economists' inclinations to confine any moral question to the realm of distribution. In fact, the common good has a production dimension, and the best composition of production, as well as the best distribution, depends upon virtuous people. The separation of production and distribution, and the belief that improved distribution has an efficiency cost, does not give consideration to the fact that an optimal solution of the production problem from a Hobbesian point of view will not be optimal in terms of the common good.[99]

Thus, even at the level of practical economics, where the focus is on material provisioning, economic actions that will contribute to the common good are not confined to distributing more fairly the income maximized in a system of free competition. The common good *also* depends on what goods are produced. This is a fundamental point. Since

9. An extensive discussion of the question of the compatibility between the normative criterion of modern welfare economics derived from the concept of Pareto optimality, and the requirements of justice as developed by Scholastic moralists in the Thomistic philosophical tradition, is contained in the *Review of Social Economy.* The protagonists were Stephen Worland and Edward Kane. See Worland, "Justice and Welfare Economics," 17:2 (1959) 97–111, and "Welfare Economics: Some Observations," 22:1 (1964) 25–29; and Kane, "Justice and Welfare Economics: A Slightly Mathematical Approach," 21:2 (1963) 103–15, and "Voluntarism versus Rationalism: A Reconciliation," 22:1 (1964) 21–24. In Kane's argument about a lack of compatibility between modern welfare economics and scholastic ideas about justice, he expressed the view that scholastic moralists "never accepted individual preferences as the ultimate arbiter of individual welfare," 22:1 (1963) 111.

a mix of goods and services produced in response to hedonist motives cannot be assumed to be truly good, measuring the reduced efficiency of better income distribution is inadequate. The economic aspect of the common good is not simply a question of a fairer distribution of an existing volume of goods in which the price, or the cost of greater fairness, is having to be content with a smaller volume of the same kind of goods. *Both* production and distribution impact the common good. Thus, a theoretical assumption that it is possible to make efficiency statements that are independent of ethical and moral judgments—i.e., that are morally and ethically neutral—is misleading.[10] There is a deep gulf at a theoretical level between the common good and the concept of economic efficiency. Thus, the conflict between the focus of economics and the common good shows up chiefly at the theoretical level, and not at the practical level.

From a theoretical perspective, it is important to recognize that subjective utility, not material wealth, is the maximand in the theory of the competitive market economy. Adam Smith believed that an environment of liberty would allow people to follow their self-interest, resulting in greater material wealth, and leaving people better off materially on average than any alternative economic policy. But the focus of contemporary theory, although related to material wealth, is something different from what Smith had in mind. For example, Smith regarded labor devoted to providing personal service as unproductive, and as not contributing to the expansion of a nation's wealth. He was wrong from our modern perspective, but for Smith, an improvement in aggregate economic welfare required, and always accompanied, an increase in the amount of tangible physical goods available. The distinction between physical output and utility is significant. Economists now justify competition because it leads to Pareto optimality, an economic outcome in which the subjective utility of one person cannot be increased without reducing the subjective utility of one or more

10. Strictly speaking, it is not correct to say that economists believe that efficiency statements are independent of ethical and moral judgments. Reflective economists recognize clearly that the concept of Pareto optimality is based on a moral judgment that individual preferences should be honored. They know that there is a moral judgment contained in the view that consumer preferences should be sovereign. Nevertheless, the moral debate does not for the most part involve a questioning of this ideal, but rather a concern about how much consumer sovereignty should be given up in the interests of a fairer distribution.

others. In practical discussion economists refer to the value of marketed output as if it were an unambiguous measure of utility, although at a theoretical level they do not identify greater total utility in society unambiguously with more measured income.

If economic science were narrowly focused on tangible goods and services, as it was in Smith's time, questions about what enhances economic welfare would be easier to answer than they are presently. Smith was confident that an improvement in the capacity of an economy to house, feed, and clothe its population would improve economic welfare, although he recognized that it might not increase the sum total of happiness. He did not work within the confines of a theory which based judgments about productive efficiency on Pareto optimality, and his thought was grounded in a particular historical and institutional context.

Would it be better for economists to abandon the belief in an autonomous economics, and decide forthrightly to embed economics in moral philosophy as it was up to the time of Smith? Would it be an improvement? Would subordinating economic analysis to moral and political philosophy put an end to economic science and objectivity? Would it confuse analysis and advocacy? Perhaps it would, but analysis and advocacy are already interwoven in the writings of economists who support particular economic policies on the basis of political and moral judgments about distributional equity and productive efficiency. Isn't it possible to keep analysis and advocacy distinct even if they must always be present necessarily in practical economics? The work of many contemporary economists demonstrates that commitment to a moral perspective and careful analytical work are not incompatible. The belief in value-free economics is mistaken. Economics is embedded necessarily in moral philosophy, although some economists may not be as forthright and reflective as they should be about the presuppositions that underlie their theorizing and policy recommendations. Would it be better to confine economics to the study of material wealth, and use reason explicitly to decide what economic activities should be constrained by law and custom in the interest of human welfare? Would it be better to ground the concept of human welfare in careful practical reasoning and hard thinking about what justice requires? Such an approach might be better than the tendency to treat questions of justice as if they were beyond the reach of rational processes rooted in subjective preferences formed by our passions and interests, rather than in reasoned thinking about what it means to be a human being. For virtually every thinker in the Western tradition, up to and including Smith, economic questions were discussed as part of practical science, and thought about in terms of what Aristotle called practical reason. Economics was not discussed as part of theoretical science, and thought about by means of speculative reason, which Aristotle reserved to the study of such matters as metaphysics, physics, and mathematics. Adopting such an Aristotelian approach would be an explicit recognition that economics is necessarily a moral science.

It should be pointed out that many economists might argue that the problem focused on in this paper is of limited relevance to the way in which they see their work. They would argue with considerable justification that modern economics is a set of tools for thinking systematically about the best way to achieve whatever it is that the political community decides upon. Thus if the body politic can specify the content of its notion of the common good in a way that makes measurement possible, then economists are the people to consult to find out how the objectively defined common good can best be realized. Or, economists can at least suggest how the measurable elements in the common good can best be realized.

There is much to be said for this purely technocratic perspective of the economist's role, and many working economists view their role in exactly this way. In fact, no less an economist than John Maynard Keynes expressed this view as an ideal to be hoped for when he wrote: "If economists could manage to get themselves thought of as humble, competent people on a level with dentists, that would be splendid."[11] But this perspective does not confront directly the philosophical difficulty embedded deeply in the emphasis given to subjective utility maximization in the structure of economic theory.

These questions bring us to the heart of the ethical dilemma posed by the Enlightenment rejection of the notion of the *telos*. What is the good for human beings if the opinion that there is no *summum bonum* or *finis ultimus* is accepted? The answer implicit in modern economics is Hobbes' answer. Each person decides for himself what is the good for him on the basis of his own subjective preferences. Thus there may

11. John Meynard Keynes, "The Future," in *Essays in Persuasion* (London: Macmillan, 1933).

be as many goods or ends as there are people, and this notion is at the heart of modern liberal political thought.[12] Hobbes described human beings as driven by their passions, and therefore as rational only in the sense that they are good calculators of what must be done to achieve the objects of their passions. A rational human being in the Aristotelian sense is the person who subjugates his passions to his reason. For an Aristotelian there is a common good for human beings which derives from their nature as rational beings. Would it make sense for us to go back and consider once again the views of the premoderns and build our economics on a different, more hopeful view of human beings?

12. Michael Sandel has used the term *political economy* to describe the consideration of economic matters within a framework which pays explicit attention to civic virtue. He argues that in the early part of the twentieth century in the United States the debate about the implications of a modern industrial economy took place in a context in which the participants focused on the implications of economic developments for democratic self-governance. He refers to Louis Brandeis and Theodore Roosevelt, neither of whom would be identified as economists, as major figures in the debate over the direction of the United States' political economy. Although their positions about how industrialization could be made compatible with democratic self-governance and the preservation of a common understanding of civic virtue differed, they shared the same conviction that economic matters should be subject to political concerns. Sandel argues that after World War II and the rise to ascendancy of Keynesian economics the questions of production and distribution moved to center stage, and the belief that economic prosperity would make it possible for each person to seek his own good triumphed. The recognition of the need to foster a common civic virtue and a wider and common vision of the good dropped out of the discourse of politics in the United States. Sandel's story is not incompatible with the story of this paper. Despite Sandel's description of the economic and political thinking of men like Brandeis and Roosevelt, economists from the time of Smith focused narrowly on understanding matters of production and distribution. The loss of the notion of a common or shared civic good, and its replacement by the notion that the best political society is one in which each person seeks his own good in his own way, may be traceable more directly to John Stuart Mill's essay *On Liberty*. The ideas expressed in Mill's essay may help explain the shift in post-World War II United States that shook economics questions loose from their older moorings in politics. Sandel mentions John F. Kennedy's 1962 address at Yale as a significant marker in this transition, Michael Sandel, "America's Search for a New Public Philosophy," *The Atlantic Monthly* (Mar 1996) 57–74.

Contributors

James Buchanan is the Besl Family Chair in Ethics/Religion and Society at Xavier University in Cincinnati. From 2003–present he has been University Professor and Director of The Edward B. Brueggeman Center for Dialogue at Xavier. He has been involved in NGO work worldwide, including being an advisor to negotiations at the United Nation Conference on Environment and Development (in biotechnology), a board member of Friends of the Earth, The Council for Responsible Genetics, The Prince of Wales Business Leaders Forum and a variety of other organizations. He has published articles and books on topics ranging from comparative ethics to the social and environmental impacts of technological change including *Changing Nature's Course*, and the forthcoming books *Confronting Mortality: An Interdisciplinary Dialogue*, and *Wagers into the Abyss: Ethics in an Age of Globalization*.

Caner K. Dagli is Assistant Professor in the Department of Religious Studies at College of the Holy Cross. He received a PhD from Princeton's Department of Near Eastern Studies, and an MA from the Department of Religion at George Washington University. In 2006–2007 he served as Interfaith Affairs Consultant in the Royal Hashemite Court of Jordan, where he participated in such projects as An Open Letter to the Pope (in response to the Regensburg lecture) and the recent and ongoing A Common Word Between Us and You (addressed to the world's Christians). He is the author of *The Ringstones of Wisdom* (2004), and has published in the fields of Islamic philosophy and Sufism. He is an associate editor for the forthcoming *Study Quran* from HarperCollins, under chief editor Seyyed Hossein.

Elliot N. Dorff, Rabbi, PhD, is Distinguished Service Professor of Philosophy at the American Jewish University in Los Angeles and Visiting Professor at the UCLA School of Law. A Conservative rabbi, he chairs that movement's Committee on Jewish Law and Standards. He also co-chairs the Priest-Rabbi Dialogue of the Los Angeles Archdiocese and the Board of Rabbis of Southern California, and is Immediate Past President of the Academy of Judaic, Christian, and Islamic Studies. He was awarded the *Journal of Law and Religion*'s Lifetime Achievement Award, and he holds three honorary doctoral degrees. His most recent publications include *The Jewish Approach to Repairing the World (Tikkun Olam): A Brief Introduction for Christians* (with Cory Willson) (2008) and *Jewish Choices, Jewish Voices: Social Justice* (edited with Danya Rutenberg, 2010).

Waleed El-Ansary is Assistant Professor of Islamic Studies at the University of South Carolina. He received his PhD in the Human Sciences with a concentration in Islamic Studies from George Washington University and an MA in economics from the University of Maryland. He is a consultant to the Royal Court of Jordan as well as the Grand Mufti of Egypt, and involved in interfaith dialogue. He is author of *Not by Bread Alone: Lectures of E. F. Schumacher* (forthcoming) and "Economics and the Clash of Civilizations: Reexamining Religion and Violence" in Qamar al-Huda, *Crescent and Dove: Peace and Conflict Resolution in Islam* (2010).

Peter Ireland is the Murray and Monti Professor of Economics at Boston College and an Editor at the Berkeley Electronic Journal of Macroeconomics. His research and teaching focus on Federal Reserve policies and their effects on the economy. Professor Ireland received his PhD in Economics from the University of Chicago in 1991. His recent publications include "Stochastic Growth in the United States and Euro Area" in *Journal of the European Economic Association* (forthcoming), "A New Keynesian Perspective on the Great Recession" in *Journal of Money, Credit and Banking* (2011) and "On the Welfore Cost of Inflation and the Recent Behavior of Money Demand" in *American Economic Review* (2009).

Christopher Ives is Professor of Religious Studies at Stonehill College. In his scholarship he focuses on modern Zen and ethics, and currently he is working on Buddhist approaches to nature and environmental issues. His publications include *Imperial-Way Zen: Ichikawa Hakugen's Critique and Lingering Questions for Buddhist Ethics* (2009); *Zen Awakening and Society* (1992); *The Emptying God* (co-edited with John B. Cobb Jr., 1990); *Divine Emptiness and Historical Fullness* (edited volume, 1995); a translation of Nishida Kitarō's *An Inquiry into the Good* (co-translated with Abe Masao, 1990); a translation of Hisamatsu Shin'ichi's *Critical Sermons of the Zen Tradition* (co-translated with Tokiwa Gishin, 2002).

Joseph Kaboski is the David F. and Erin M. Seng Foundation Associate Professor of Economics in the Department of Economics at the University of Notre Dame. His research focuses on growth, development and international economics, with an emphasis on structural change, finance and development, schooling and growth, microfinance, explaining international relative price patterns, and the role of inventories in international trade. He has published in the American Economic Review, the American Economic Journal: Macroeconomics, Econometrica, the Journal of the European Economic Association, IMF Review, the Journal of Economic Dynamics and Control, the Journal of Economic Theory, and the Review of Economic Dynamics. He has consulted for the Federal Reserve Banks of Chicago, Minneapolis, and St. Louis, as well as the World Bank, and is a Faculty Research Fellow of the National Bureau of Economic Research.

Paul F. Knitter is the Paul Tillich Professor of Theology, World Religions, and Culture at Union Theological Seminary, New York. Previously, for some thirty years, he taught theology at Xavier University in Cincinnati, OH. He received a Licentiate in theology from the Pontifical Gregorian University in Rome (1966) and a doctorate from the University of Marburg, Germany (1972). Most of his research and publications have dealt with religious pluralism and interreligious dialogue. Since his groundbreaking 1985 book, *No Other*

Name?, he has been exploring how the religious communities of the world can cooperate in promoting human and ecological well-being. This is the topic of *One Earth Many Religions: Multifaith Dialogue and Global Responsibility* (1995). In 2002, he published a critical survey of Christian approaches to other religions, *Introducing Theologies of Religions,* and most recently *Without Buddha I Could Not Be a Christian* (2009).

David Loy was the Besl Family Chair Professor of ethics/religion and society at Xavier University from 2006 to 2010. He has been practicing Zen since 1971 and is an authorized teacher in the Sanbo Kyodan tradition of Japanese Zen Buddhism. His books include *Nonduality: A Study in Comparative Philosophy* (1997); *The Great Awakening: A Buddhist Social Theory* (1997); *Lack and Transcendence: The Problem of Death and Life in Psychotherapy, Existentialism and Buddhism* (2001); *A Buddhist History of the West: Studies in Lack* (2002); *Money, Sex, War, Karma: Notes for a Buddhist Revolution* (2008); *Awareness Bound and Unbound: Buddhist Essays* (2009); and *The World Is Made of Stories* (2010). He also co-edited *A Buddhist Response to the Climate Emergency* (2009).

Laurenti Magesa is a Catholic priest of the Diocese of Musoma in Tanzania. At present he is teaching at Hekima College Jesuit School of Theology and at Tangaza College, both constituent colleges of the Catholic University of Eastern Africa, Nairobi, Kenya. He also teaches at the Maryknoll Institute of African Studies of Saint Mary's University, Minnesota, Nairobi campus. He specializes in African culture and theology and interreligious studies. His books include *African Religion: The Moral Traditions of Abundant Life* (1997), *Anatomy of Inculturation: Transforming the Church in Africa* (2004) and *African Religion in the Dialogue Debate: From Intolerance to Coexistence* (2011).

Katherine Marshall is a senior fellow at Georgetown's Berkley Center for Religion, Peace and World Affairs and Visiting Professor in the Government Department. She is also a senior advisor for the World Bank. She was closely engaged in the creation and the development of the World Faiths Development Dialogue and is its Executive Director. She serves on the boards of several NGO's and advisory groups. She is a member of the Council on Foreign Relations and served as a core group member of the Council of 100, an initiative of the World Economic Forum to advance understanding between the Islamic world and the West. She is author of *Development and Faith: Where Mind, Heart and Soul Work Together* (2007), and *The World Bank: From Reconstruction to Development to Equity* (2008).

Francis McLaughlin is Associate Professor of Economics at Boston College where he has been a member of the faculty since 1961. He is currently teaching courses in Labor Economics and The History of Economic Thought. He received BS and MA degrees from Boston College and the PhD from the Massachusetts Institute of Technology. From 1972 to 1981 he was a member of the faculty of the Harvard University Institute of Employment and Training Administration, and from 1985 to 1999 he was a member of the faculty of the Harvard Trade Union Fellows Program.

Walter Nonneman is Professor of Economics and Econometrics at the University of Antwerp, Belgium, and managing director of the University Center Saint-Ignatius Antwerp (UCSIA). He published internationally on a wide variety of topics such growth theory, health economics, economics of education, labor economics and economics of religion. He was previously dean of the University of Antwerp Management School, president of University Faculties of Saint-Ignatius Antwerp and Chief of Staff of the Belgian Prime Minister.

Siddhartha is a writer, journalist and social activist. He writes regularly on ecological, cultural and social issues in leading Indian and international newspapers and journals. He is the founder of the interreligious Fireflies ashram, outside the city of Bangalore. He is the director of Pipal Tree, an NGO working with indigenous communities in South India on forest rights, education and the National Rural Employment Guarantee program. For the past twenty years, he has organized ecological and cultural workshops as well as international conferences on the topic of sustainable development. His is author of two books: *Lettres du Gange* (2009), and *The Birdwoman* (2010).

Donald K. Swearer is Distinguished Visiting Fellow at the Center for the Study of World Religions, Harvard Divinity School and the Charles and Harriett Cox McDowell Professor of Religion Emeritus, Swarthmore College. He has published widely in the fields of Buddhist Studies and comparative religions. His recent books include *Becoming the Buddha: The Ritual of Image Consecration in Thailand* (2004), *The Sacred Mountains of Northern Thailand and Their Legends* (2004), and *The Buddhist World of Southeast Asia*, 2nd ed. (2009). As a Fulbright Senior Research Scholar at Payap University, Chiang Mai, Thailand, 2010–11, his research has focused on Buddhist Economics and Thailand's Sufficiency Economy.